G. H. Mead

A Contemporary Re-examination
of his Thought

HANS JOAS
Translated by Raymond Meyer

D1376654

The MIT Press
Cambridge, Massachusetts

First MIT Press edition, 1985

Originally published in German under the title *Praktische Intersubjektivität. Die Entwicklung des Werkes von George Herbert Mead.*

© Suhrkamp-Verlag, Frankfurt, 1980.

Library of Congress Cataloging in Publication Data

Joas, Hans.
    G. H. Mead, a contemporary re-examination of his thought.

    (Studies in contemporary German social thought)
    Translation of: Praktische Intersubjektivität.
    Bibliography: p.
    Includes index.
    1. Mead, George Herbert, 1863–1931. 2. Inter-
subjectivity. 3. Interaction (Philosophy) I. Title
II. Series.

B945.M464J613 1985   191   85-5181
ISBN 0-262-10033-9

Typeset by Freeman Graphic, Tonbridge, Kent
Printed in Great Britain by T. J. Press Ltd, Padstow, Cornwall

Contents

For Heidrun

1

Introduction

This book is the result of a critical study of the work of George Herbert Mead that lasted for years, a study that, although interrupted from time to time, was always taken up again. This undertaking began in a period of intense sociolinguistic debate. In this context, Mead's work seemed to me, after a first brief encounter, to hold the key to the desired convergence of two very different philosophical and scientific traditions: the dialogical approaches of linguistic theory in the German tradition of the hermeneutic humanities, and the approaches to a 'generative' theory of grammar that followed upon the great strides made by Noam Chomsky toward an investigation of human language which is both universal in orientation and empirically fruitful.[1] Quickly it became clear that the fecundity of Mead's thought, as well as of the question of the meaning of language and of communication itself, could not be contained within the narrow bounds of the disciplines of linguistics and sociolinguistics. A scientifically adequate understanding of the fundamental characteristics of human intersubjectivity promised to have far-reaching consequences for both the logic of the social sciences and for a contemporary reformulation of historical materialism.[2] This insight made it possible to bring into my study the whole range of motives that had originally directed my interest towards sociolinguistics. It seemed possible to formulate more clearly and on a firmer basis the criticism, in part abstract and in part superficial, of the established forms of empirical social research. Along this path, so it appeared, the discussion of issues in historical materialism which have been widely raised but never satisfactorily resolved could be advanced: the relations between individual and society, language and work, economic bases and social movements.

It hardly needs to be mentioned that these interests would

1

inevitably lead me to the writings of Jürgen Habermas, who has undertaken to develop further the Critical Theory of the Frankfurt School with the help of linguistic and communication theory. However, the originality and brilliance of Habermas's writings had not only a stimulating, but often an intimidating and oppressive effect on me. In addition, my complete agreement with large sections of Habermas's work collided with complete dissent from him in other parts, particularly with regard to the fundamentals of his analysis of advanced capitalism, his position with regard to the critique of political economy, the shape of his programme for reconstructing historical materialism, and the consequences of all this in the field of socialization theory. My own need for independence and the search for the exact location of what, to my eyes, seemed to be a 'rupture' in Habermas's thought combined in my desire to find a sort of Archimedean point that would allow the independent formulation of a theory of intersubjectivity in the midst of a discussion dominated by Habermas. This Archimedean point I hoped to find by acquiring a thorough and precise understanding of the thought of George Herbert Mead, whom I would now call the most important theorist of intersubjectivity between Feuerbach and Habermas.

The question whether or not Mead's work would in fact provide this Archimedean point could not be decided on the basis of the single work that is truly widely known, *Mind, Self, and Society*. This book, fascinating and rich in ideas as it is, bears all the defects one would expect from its origin in posthumously published transcripts of Mead's lectures: unreliability, insufficient precision in the recording of Mead's words, and obfuscation of the coherence of Mead's thought. Thus the question was whether Mead's other books, which came into being in a similar manner, and in particular the essays and reviews that he had written and prepared for publication himself, could make up for these shortcomings. Thus began my journey towards a comprehensive philological study of Mead's work, an effort which extended further and further to include writings whose existence I had to discover for myself and the thorough examination of Mead's literary archive. The further I advanced along this path, the stronger became the feeling that I was unearthing long-buried treasures.

During this journey there seemed to be no danger that I was following circuitous routes to goals that could be reached more easily some other way. Rather the reverse seemed to be true. The thematic breadth of Mead's work requires for interpretation equally broad background knowledge and this fact in turn made it tempting to add more and more new motives to my original undertaking. An organic whole cannot easily emerge from such a process. Indeed, at the end of my philological investigations I found myself with a maze of notes I had taken to clarify my own thinking. These notes pointed in different directions and were extremely unsuitable for the purposes of achieving an intersubjective understanding. The only way out of this dilemma was a radical 'trimming' of my copious notes. The guiding thread of my presentation had to be Mead's works in the context of their development; everything else could only serve as background, entering into and giving structure to the interpretation. This strategy has led to thematic limitations, inasmuch as alluring fields of inquiry not explicitly dealt with by Mead – such as the methodology of empirical social research based on the interpretation of meaningful structures – and the scientific developments of the last decades, which extend far beyond the limits of Mead's knowledge, had to be excluded. Consequently, it must be left to future studies to draw conclusions for those areas from his systematic reflections. However, the usefulness of the present work as secondary literature about Mead is certainly increased by its concentrated focus on his works.

But is not a monograph about an eminent thinker, the form of presentation chosen here, a methodological anachronism – one that is, to be sure, not uncommon in academic scholarship? Is it not a sign of theoretical naivety, not only to introduce a work with auto-biographical remarks, but also to conceive it as the biography of a thinker and thus to mingle the issues of the theoretical validity of a system of thought with those of the system's historical genesis? Even if this mingling were admissible, is it then not at least naive, from the standpoint of the sociology of science, to limit the historical genesis of that system to the life and career of a single individual, instead of taking as the object of one's investigation the conditions in which the scientific enterprise was carried out, the complex of relationships within which the results of scientific research were utilized, and the groups formed within those conditions and relationships?

In reply to these questions it is necessary, first of all, to point out that a theoretical study which undertakes the critical interpretation of a seminal figure offers the opportunity to begin formulating a theoretical position which cannot yet be presented in full systematic clarity. This might be called the autodidactic purpose of a biographical study. It is characteristic of such a study that in it a freely chosen obligation – the nature of which, however, is by no means accidental – is incurred by the researcher, an obligation that must be fulfilled completely. Hence a preliminary answer to the question about the relationship between the genesis and the validity of a system of thought: precisely because the theoretical system and the circumstances of its origin are not yet torn asunder in the biographical form, this kind of study counters the assumption that theories can be judged according to criteria of merely internal coherence or in a way that remains external to the theory as a whole, namely by examining the validity of individual propositions. Rather, theories are to be understood as attempts to solve the particular problems arising in a particular period; they can only be properly judged when they are treated as historical phenomena and brought into contact as such with the present-day, historically changed situation of science and society. It is, then, only the biographical study that makes it possible to grasp comprehensive theoretical approaches. At the same time it allows the biographer to distance himself to a certain extent from the historical situation in which the spontaneous attractiveness of the chosen thinker has its roots.

This 'high office' of the biographical study can lead to the belief that it represents the fundamentally most appropriate approach to historical reconstruction in the sphere of cultural objects, of the 'objective spirit' in general. This view was developed especially by Dilthey, one of Mead's academic teachers, in his reflection on his own and others' historical research.[3] If one agrees with this point of view, then it is, of course, of decisive importance whether the biographical form of presentation should be used only for outstanding individuals even when – as in the realm of science – the production of theories takes place collectively. This is to say that the question whether individual theoreticians, schools of thought, or still larger complexes of social relations are to be made the object of analysis cannot be dogmatically decided *a priori*, but rather only in accordance with the actual circumstances.

Mead, for example, for the greater part of his life was immersed in the intense discussion taking place in Chicago at the time. His principal innovative ideas cannot, however, be traced back to those discussions alone. Mead passed freely between philosophy, psycho-

logy, sociology, and the natural sciences at a time when the specialization and professionalization of these disciplines was just beginning
and was still slight. The corresponding scholarly associations,
journals, and courses of study in the USA arose between 1890 and
1910, in the very decades during which Mead's theories took shape.[4]
The broad range and variety of topics dealt with by his theories was
therefore something he took much more as a matter of course than
would later be the case in the increasingly specialized organization of
scientific enterprise. But even if this were not true, and Mead's ideas
ought to be attributed to him as an individual in lesser measure, I
would still consider it wrong to prescribe for the sociology of
knowledge or the critique of ideology the analytical ideal of deducing
a given theory from the conditions in which it originated, instead of
an analysis based on a systematic understanding of the theory itself.[5]
This, it seems to me, is a demand that by the very nature of things
cannot be fulfilled, since a theory, as a creative attempt to formulate a
solution to a complex of problems, does not simply ensue from those
problems. Were such a derivation of a theory possible, then the
achievement of subjectivity which is the content of a theory would be
reducible to its objective conditions. If, however, such a deduction is
impossible, then, despite the fact that the issues of genesis and
validity of a theory are finally inseparable subjects of inquiry, the
question of the theory's truth or validity always has a claim to priority
over the inquiries of the sociology of knowledge or science about the
theory's origin.

Previous research on Mead and the reception of his work have taken
a number of different directions. The first direction is a result of
Mead's own assignment of his theories to *behaviourism*. This has
been the source of countless misunderstandings and confusing
criticisms of his work. By distinguishing his 'true' behaviourism
from false 'Watsonism', Mead attempted to formulate a non-
reductionist orientation in psychology that nevertheless drew on the
natural sciences and was concerned with the theory of action. The
result of his efforts, however, was rather that his own theory was
understood as only an inconsequent variation of rigorous behaviourism. This turn of events was not to Mead's advantage in behaviourist
circles, while outside these circles it served to compromise him. The
description of Mead's theory as a social behaviourism, put forward
by his student and editor, Charles Morris, merely led to the

assumption that this theory was a behaviourism interested in reciprocal processes – such as, for example, Homans's theory of exchange – rather than to the understanding of it as an independent conception radically different from Watson's behaviourism.[6] Morris's efforts generally to enhance pragmatism's reputation by bringing it closer to the nascent neopositivist theory of science were for the most part unsuccessful and in the longer run harmful.[7] The interpretation of Mead's work by Israel Scheffler,[8] a present-day representative of this approach, demonstrates that preconceived conceptual dichotomies – for instance, the dichotomy between mentalist concepts and those of physics – completely obstruct understanding of Mead's thought. Within empirical psychology, dominated by the varieties of behaviourism, Mead played hardly any role. Only the so-called Iowa School borrowed concepts and hypotheses from Mead,[9] principally those having to do with role-taking and, guided by a neopositivist conception of scientific method that took no notice at all of the metatheoretical claims of Mead's approach, subjected these concepts and hypotheses to experimental testing procedures. In recent years, in the discussions of fundamental principles aimed at liberating social-psychological research from the constraints of behaviourism in its many modifications, Mead's name could become a symbol for a re-orientation of such research.[10] This use of his name did not, however, lead to a very profound study of Mead's work by those calling for a new orientation of social psychology.

Another direction taken in the reception of Mead's thought was also begun by one of his students: *symbolic interactionism*, founded by Herbert Blumer at the end of the 1930s with a programmatic essay on sociological social psychology.[11] Today symbolic interactionism is one of the most important currents in Western academic sociology. The proponents of this theory bestow on Mead the honour of being its ancestral progenitor, and can adduce many good arguments for their claim. Blumer's critique of all 'factorial theories', which understand the individual as a mere shuttlecock buffeted about by external or internal forces, and the conception that he opposed to such theories – a conception centered about the collective, problem-solving activity of human individuals having a socially constituted self – are indeed in the spirit of Mead. It is also true that symbolic interactionism has brought forth a highly fruitful tradition of empirical research. Nevertheless, it cannot be regarded as the authoritative interpretation of Mead's thought. For this theory's understanding both of social organization and of human needs, its reduction of the concept of action to that of interaction, its linguistic attenuation of the concept of meaning, and its lack of any consideration of evolution and history are enormous deviations from Mead's positions and, furthermore, achieved by means of an extremely fragmentary appropriation of Mead's work.[12] Only those aspects of Mead's thought that are completely ignored by symbolic interactionism make it possible to correct this tradition's 'subjectivist' features.

A comprehensive interpretation of Mead has been offered by yet a third direction of his work's reception: *phenomenology*.[13] Alfred Schutz who, while differing from him on many points, had repeatedly called attention to Mead's importance,[14] gave the direct impetus to Maurice Natanson, whose book *The Social Dynamics of G. H. Mead* was to influence decisively many sociologists' and philosophers' image of Mead. This book has two critical weaknesses however. First, it assumes a development in Mead's work 'from a problematic empiricism toward an idealistic and subjectivistic account of the nature of social reality',[15] for which the book's author can give no evidence. His reference to the publication dates of Mead's books is, from a philological standpoint, absurd, since they all appeared after Mead's death, and their publication was guided by principles formulated by others. However, Natanson requires such a fabrication in order to make plausible his interpretation of *Philosophy of the Present* and *Philosophy of the Act*, which attributes to these works a subjectivist character. This construct however conceals the unity as well as the real development of Mead's thought.[16] The other weakness of Natanson's book is that he measures Mead's theories only against the orthodox view of a Husserlian or Schutzian phenomenology, and does not generally set forth and document the difference between Mead and these philosophers or between pragmatism and phenomenology. Accordingly, Mead's freedom from the constraints of transcendental phenomenology appears in Natanson's book as 'naturalist' naivety.[17] In consequence of these two weaknesses, the book is in large measure unreliable and unusable. Nevertheless, the awareness of differences between Mead and Schutz contained in Natanson's critique of the former is much preferable to their complete effacement in a pseudo-unitary 'interpretative approach', such as has become common in sociology in recent years.[18]

The fourth direction taken by the reception of Mead's work is *theological.* Here it appears that the challenge to examine Mead's non-religious theory of intersubjectivity with its connections to the natural sciences came primarily from the framework of Martin Buber's existentialist personalism. The fruit of these attempts at confronting Mead's work is, to be sure, quite varied. At the time of its publication the book by Pfuetze offered a very fruitful presentation of Mead's thought,[19] although it did go on to criticize him for not taking into account the possibility of mind prior to evolution, the existence of God, and the pre-existence of the human soul. This criticism obviously undoes Mead's intellectual evolution, which consisted, in part, in the secularization of Christian themes. Gillin argues essentially the same way, but in a less differentiated form.[20] In contrast, Konrad Raiser's theological work attains a much higher intellectual level. By regarding Buber's writings from Mead's point of view, Raiser clearly perceives their deficiencies:

> But the radical reduction of the personal dimension to the immediate linguistic encounter of 'I' and 'you' led, beyond the neglect of the communicative function of language, to a devaluation of all relations aimed at social cooperation and mediated by material objects. Personalism thereby deprived its fundamental insight into the social dimension of human existence of fruitfulness and led to a still more radical turning away from the question of the importance of society for the individual human existence.[21]

This important insight leads Raiser to relate Mead's social psychology to his fundamental philosophical approach and to recognize the significance of Mead's theory of the constitution of the permanent object and of time. In Raiser's book the theological critique of Mead is not a framework that falsifies the presentation of the latter's thought; Raiser's concept of God is rationalized to such a degree that, if I understand it correctly, it means nothing else than the ethical principle of universal sociality.

I would call the fifth direction of the interpretation of Mead's work the '*metaphysical*' one. Some authors, in particular Andrew Reck and Harold Lee,[22] have based their interpretations on Mead's later works and have construed these as a rudimentary metaphysics. Those parts of Mead's work which were completely neglected in its sociological reception because they were considered 'obscure' were thus subjected to serious examination and elucidated here and there. However, it is problematical not only to interpret these writings as metaphysical,[23] but also to attempt to discover the unity of Mead's work in a metaphysics of sociality. Similarly oriented to Mead's later writings is the book by his student David Miller,[24] which without doubt offers the most substantial detailed overview of Mead's life and work to date. Especially meritorious is Miller's attempt to relate Mead's theories, if only in a rudimentary fashion, to present-day concerns, those of analytical philosophy, for example, or of the psychology of cognitive development. To be sure, Miller's effort in these directions is only a beginning.

The most important shortcomings of this book have in part already been indicated in some reviews.[25] It has been pointed out that Miller does not present Mead's work in its evolution as a system, but instead eliminates all movement and development from it through the simple division of it into subject areas. A further criticism has been that Miller establishes only Mead's relationship to American traditions, passing over in silence the European, and especially the German complex of intellectual relations that were so important for Mead. Both criticisms became important for my own undertaking. They need to be supplemented, though, with the observation that Miller touches upon Mead's political development only in the framework of a sketch of the latter's life and studies neither this development nor Mead's political publications in their own right. The access that these give to the social-historical context of Mead's thought is thus left unexplored. In his study Miller exploits neither Mead's numerous articles nor his literary archive to any appreciable extent, with the result that in many respects he advances Mead scholarship only insignificantly; his book can by no means be considered a definitive monograph on that thinker.

Finally, I would place together, as representing a sixth direction, all those studies by scholars – young, for the most part – who, against the background of the renaissance of pragmatism, have turned their attention to Mead with *new understanding* of him. The best are Gary Allan Cook's writings on Mead's ethics and his functionalist psychology.[26] In his studies of Mead, Cook seeks out the real core of Mead's thought, from which all else can be made understandable. He does this with a clarity previously demonstrated only by a few of Mead's contemporaries.[27] The scattered, and controversial, articles by Tibbetts and Rosenthal give evidence of the increased awareness in the USA of the problems posed by Mead's work,[28] but none of them does more than treat isolated aspects of it.

Familiarity with the way Mead's work has been received and with the present state of scholarship on it is necessary for an understanding of the structure of and the procedure used in my own interpretation. First of all, I have tried to examine the entire corpus of Mead's work, including his literary writings, the available correspondence, and writings that I found myself and that are interpreted here for the first time. The inclusive nature of the material studied broadens the basis on which the interpretation of Mead's thought can be built. Further, I have tried not to impose a static system on Mead's work, but rather to proceed genetically. Admittedly, this holds true in the main only for the period up to the end of the development of the concept of symbolic interaction. From my study I have concluded that the development of Mead's thought after about 1912 is to be understood more as the unfolding of his conception of symbolic interaction, so that from Chapter 6 onwards the form of presentation becomes less genetic and more systematic.

The chapter immediately following this introduction deals with Mead's biography. Its purpose is expressly not to present an account of the vicissitudes of his life that is in any measure complete.[29] Rather it tends toward political biography. It is my intent to present, on the foundation provided by Mead's political writings and letters, the path followed by this radically democratic intellectual in his political development and thereby simultaneously to shed light on the social-historical background of his theories. In my presentation of Mead's political evolution I attach great importance to the political interpretation of the First World War by him and other members of his generation, since consideration of this historical point shows the limits of the pragmatist intellectuals' radical reformism, as well as the alternative paths for a continuation of pragmatism in the theory of society under changed historical conditions.

The third chapter proceeds beyond the political and social-historical situation during the period of Mead's development to consideration of that period from the standpoint of intellectual history and treats Mead from the point of view of the history of ideas. The latter task requires clarification of what it meant for him to classify his work as pragmatism, and what the differences between pragmatism and irrationalist European 'Lebensphilosophie' were. I emphasize here Mead's significance for the complex of problems that are central in the German philosophical tradition (especially as represented by Dilthey, Husserl, Heidegger, and Philosophical

Anthropology) and the importance of German traditions for Mead. Discussion of the last point draws particularly on little known early writings of Mead on philosophy. The most important thesis of this discussion is that Mead's approach to a theory of intersubjectivity is incomprehensible without an understanding of his relationship to German idealism, and that on the other hand some problems of the German philosophical tradition can be solved precisely with the help of Mead's approach.

The fourth chapter traces Mead's development from the formation of his early philosophical position to the formulation of his standpoint in the controversy over the fundamental principles of psychology. This chapter is devoted entirely to a single lengthy text by Mead, never before interpreted, entitled 'The Definition of the Psychical', which it places both in its contemporary context of intellectual discourse and in the context in which it could be discussed today. The central thesis of this chapter is that Mead was striving to introduce, in the most penetrating manner, a fully developed concept of subjectivity into psychology. The relevance of this can only be understood in the light of the then recently resumed controversy over the fundamental principles of psychology. At the end of this chapter I point out inconsistencies in the theory of intersubjectivity implicit in Mead's paper on the 'psychical'.

In chapter 5 I undertake to document the origination – for the first time – of a concept of symbolic interaction based on investigation of human beings' fundamental and intrinsic features. I do this by following the development of Mead's thought in a series of articles published by him from 1909–13. The outstanding features of this concept developed in those articles are then formulated again in the systematic inter-relationship that Mead established among them in his lectures on social psychology. With this step my study of Mead turns to a systematic presentation of the implications of his concepts of action and intersubjectivity for various problem areas. Chapter 6 deals with Mead's ethics and in a rudimentary way situates the approach of pragmatist ethics within current discussions of ethics. My theses are that pragmatist ethics is a meta-ethics that is itself practically oriented, arises from social problems, and is therefore not neutral, and that pragmatist ethics demonstrates the ethical implications of experimental, intersubjective action. The assessment of the relationship between ethics and politics provides the basis for discussion of the limitations of pragmatist ethics.

The seventh, eighth, and ninth chapters contain my interpretation of Mead's later works as well as of the thematically relevant earlier writings. Chapter 7 is devoted to Mead's theory of perception. There I stress that Mead, reflecting on a basic point in perceptual development, the so-called constitution of physical objects, elaborated the germ of a new theory, the significance of which has remained unrecognized to the present day. Mead maintains that the development of elementary communicative capabilities is a constitutive prerequisite for the advancement in cognitive development to the constitution of physical objects. Mead's claim has to be examined in the light of competing theories. The eighth chapter is devoted to the problem of a theory of 'time', with which Mead principally concerned himself towards the end of his life. Here I attempt to counteract the belief that in this phase Mead became a speculative metaphysician. I show, rather, how Mead, spurred on by his theory of history and his conception of the self, and challenged by the discussions among natural scientists of the theory of relativity, formulated an approach to a theory of the intersubjective constitution of the consciousness of time. Hitherto no attempt has ever been made to carry forward Mead's reflections on the constitution of the physical object or of time by relating them to questions of developmental psychology or of the theory of socialization, although Mead's work considered in its entirety suggests that such an attempt would be profitable. Finally, the ninth chapter considers Mead's theory of science from two perspectives: first with regard to the constitution of science in the everyday world of action and perception; and, second, with respect to the significance of the fact that Mead takes scientific progress as the model for his conceptualization of history. The latter question bears upon the scope and the limits of the concept of rationality Mead employed in his philosophy of history.

This survey of the present work shows that an attempt to do justice to Mead requires treating a broad range of topics. Since my study, in spite of its breadth, could not be exhaustive, I will indicate those areas that have not been included. The discussion of Mead's later works could have been connected more closely with the theoretical discussions of the foundations of physics, and in particular of the theory of relativity, than was possible for me as a social scientist. Mead's writings on the history of philosophy cover a wealth of topics, ranging from an extensive study of Aristotle via medieval and early modern philosophy to examination of contemporary developments. These writings certainly provide the subject matter for a book different from the one I have attempted to write. The situation is somewhat different in the case of the third limitation of my book. This concerns Mead's pedagogical work and his publications on educational matters. These are not ignored, but they are also not discussed as constituting a system of their own. Instead, I include them in the chapters on Mead's political biography and on his social psychology. This is because Mead's work in this area can claim no independent significance that could compete with the much more extensive and systematic work of John Dewey.[30]

The effort to follow Mead's thought, even in all the notoriously 'incomprehensible' parts of his work, might well be equally difficult to follow for some readers. The present book is thus perhaps not the ideal introduction to Mead's work for the reader who is largely unfamiliar with it. In addition, my attempt to guarantee the accuracy of my interpretation of Mead's ideas by basing them closely on his texts has inevitably made my presentation clumsy here and there. This is also true of my references to debates and empirical research being carried on at the present time. In neither case was it possible for me to achieve completeness. However, I hope that I have at least succeeded in writing a book on Mead that will foster a deeper understanding of his work. I found that the key for my entire interpretation is the concept of *practical intersubjectivity*. The significance of this concept becomes clear in its full extent only in the course of the whole book. Although it is not used by Mead himself, this term seems to me the best characterization of the core of Mead's thought and thus also of the element of that thought that attracted me so strongly to him. The concept of 'intersubjectivity' designates a structure of communicative relations between subjects, a structure that is suited for transcending, on the theoretical plane, the opposition between the individualistic bias in the theory of action and a structural theory that does not recognize subjects or human agency.[31] The political correlate of this concept is a social order in which the atomization of individuals is eliminated, not through their subordination to a collectivity, but instead through the participation of all in reasoning discussion to determine their common future.

Mead's theory of intersubjectivity is oriented neither to the *contemplative model* of a mere encountering of the other (as we find in the works of Feuerbach or Buber), nor to the linguistic model of understanding the other through language, a model which separates language and action. Rather, Mead's theory is oriented to *practical* intersubjectivity; that means, to a structure that arises and takes form in the joint activity of human subjects to achieve ends set by their life needs, a structure into which the corporeality of these subjects and external nature readily enter. *Linguistic* intersubjectivity is reconstructed by Mead from the structure of gestural communication, which is connected more closely with the body, and founded in cooperative action. The expression 'practical intersubjectivity' is intended to situate Mead in the tradition of the philosophy of praxis as well as in that of approaches to social analysis based on theories of intersubjectivity, and also to point out his importance for the further development of both traditions.

2

The Development of a Radically Democratic Intellectual: George Herbert Mead, 1863–1931

George Herbert Mead was born to the family of a Protestant clergyman in New England, entering the world on February 27, 1863, as the son of the minister of South Hadley, Massachusetts. After moving to another parish in New Hampshire in 1867,[1] Mead's father was appointed professor of homiletics (the history and theory of preaching) at Oberlin College in 1869. There he taught until his death in 1881. This college was the formative influence on Mead's childhood and youth; he matriculated there himself in 1879. Oberlin College was, on the one hand, well known for religious orthodoxy and dogmatic narrow-mindedness; on the other, it distinguished itself by an extraordinary emphasis on the social obligations implicit in living as a Christian and by a thoroughly radical commitment to the emancipation of Blacks and women.

Mead studied at Oberlin College during a period when the natural sciences were first able to gain entry into church-dominated higher education in the USA, but in doing so came into conflict with religion's dogmatic claims to provide an explanation of the world. Against the background of this conflict, grappling with the Darwinian theory of evolution as the compelling proof of the merely mythological character of the Christian doctrine of creation became a crucial turning point in the lives of an entire generation. And yet the young Mead was not at all attracted to a deterministic conception of the world that could ostensibly be proven scientifically, or by Social Darwinist views of society. Rather, he was faced with the problem of how the moral values of a socially committed Christianity could be conserved without theological dogma and outside the narrow bounds of a puritanical way of living. This period of Mead's life is characterized by an interest in finding his own identity unrestrained by moral

15

precepts, an interest which led him to literature and psychology, by an open-mindedness similar to that of the Enlightenment philosophers, and by faith in the liberating effects of scientific methods.[2] Mead himself marked the spring of 1882 as the time when he awakened from his 'dogmatic slumber' and essayed his first independent efforts in the realm of philosophy. Against the narrowness and the insipidity of the established Scottish philosophy of intuition, he placed his hopes in Kant and post-Kantian German idealism.

In 1883 Mead finished his studies at Oberlin College, which he had to pay for through his own work after the death of his father. At first he took employment as a secondary-school teacher, but after only a few months he had to resign from his post. In the following years he worked in railroad construction, as a surveyor for different railroad companies and as a private tutor. This first-hand experience of the technical application of the natural sciences reinforced his life-long openness to all developments in this area. As for Mead's personal development during these years, his correspondence with his college friend Henry Castle provides precise information.[3] Mead felt that his poverty forced him to take bread-and-butter employment in an occupation from which he could gain no satisfaction. He lamented his inability to embark on a bourgeois career and become a 'money getting animal'.[4] Even the classical alternative careers for young middle-class men at that time seemed to be barred to him. If he could believe, he would become a minister, he wrote to his friend in March 1884.[5] Loss of faith in the teachings of Christianity was for him also the loss of all certainty of a metaphysical meaning of the world and human existence. The feeling that life is absurd brought about a long-lasting existential crisis and left Mead with no guidance in his selection of professional and personal goals. The way by which he could turn his search for meaning into a profession – becoming a teacher of philosophy – was also blocked by the clerical control of teaching and research at institutions of higher learning. On the advice of his closest friend, and guided both by his desire to find meaning and by his longing to be active and socially useful, Mead decided to enter upon graduate study at Harvard University in 1887, in spite of all the attendant financial risks.

Mead's choice fell on Harvard partly because it was, alongside the Johns Hopkins University, the most intellectually free university in the USA at that time, but also because of a man to whom Mead, during his entire life, paid the highest tribute of admiration for his excellence as an academic teacher. This man was the Christian neo-Hegelian Josiah Royce, who became important particularly for Mead's view of German idealism, and who transmitted to him the basic model of a philosophy of history that interpreted the kingdom of God as the historical realization of a community of all human beings brought about by universal communication. Mead especially hoped to deepen his understanding of Kant, who, in Mead's lonely years of self-instruction, had assumed immense importance for him both as the destroyer of theological dogma and as the incarnation of the postulate of moral freedom.[6] On account of his still inadequate command of the German language, Mead was not able to follow Royce's seminar on Kant. However, he enrolled in courses on Spinoza and Spencer taught by Royce and in one on ethics taught by Palmer,[7] who accepted Mead's thesis entitled 'How large a share has the subject in the object world?'[8] Mead did not study with William James, as is frequently claimed, but he did come into personal contact with James as the tutor of the philosopher's children.[9]

All sources of information testify to Mead's overwhelming fascination with Royce; yet Mead's discontent with the merely speculative treatment of problems and with philosophy's remoteness from science and social problems drove him to search further. In Mead's eyes Royce stood for the liberation of thought, but he nevertheless soon felt that the latter's philosophy, like American neo-idealism in general, was the product of another culture grafted onto American culture, not an authentic interpretation of American life and a guide for action in the conditions of his American present.[10]

In 1888 Mead arrived at the decision to specialize not in philosophy, but instead in physiological psychology. His decision was motivated on the one hand by the insight that only empirical research could lead beyond mere elucidation of concepts to new knowledge.[11] There was, however, also a second motive. Mead thought that in the field of physiological psychology it would be possible to pursue his ideas and interests without continually coming into conflict with the Christian churches that still almost totally controlled the universities, financially as well as ideologically, and thereby losing all prospects of carrying on scientific research.[12] Thus physiological psychology was for Mead a consciously chosen means to disguise philosophically rebellious ideas that also offered the advantage of being able to contribute to the concretization and testing of those ideas.

The centre of research in physiological psychology and in the development of an experimental psychology was Germany, principally Leipzig, where Wilhelm Wundt had established the first laboratory for that purpose. Mead studied at the University of Leipzig in the winter semester of 1888/89, hindered certainly by his difficulties with the German language, which he had not yet overcome.[13] Perhaps for that reason Mead, despite his decision to study psychology, occupied himself only with philosophy during this semester. He enrolled in Wundt's course 'Fundamentals of Metaphysics', Heinze's 'History of More Recent Modern Philosophy', and Rudolf Seydel's 'The Relationship of German Philosophy to Christianity since Kant'.[14] This information from the archives of the University of Leipzig confirms that, as has frequently been suspected, Mead himself did in fact attend Wundt's lectures, not in psychology though, but rather in philosophy. Wundt by no means thought of himself as a specialist whose competence was limited to psychology; through Wundt, Mead could thus become familiar with the broader horizons of 'voluntaristic' psychology precisely through the metaphysics of 'voluntaristic monism', which was linked with that psychology. Through the lectures of Heinze, and especially those of Seydel, Mead became acquainted with important forms of the controversy between religion and a scientifically determined conception of the world. During his lifetime, Seydel was well known as a representative of a speculative Christian philosophy that drew on Schelling while distancing itself from Hegel.

After only one semester in Leipzig Mead transferred to Berlin, in all likelihood because the range of philosophical activity was much broader at the latter university. As the records of course enrolments in the archives of the University of Berlin show, Mead became a student of Dilthey, Ebbinghaus, Paulsen and Schmoller.[15] This fact is of essential importance for an understanding of Mead's intellectual roots. For through these teachers Mead was made aware of a conflict between two positions which was soon to explode in a famous controversy. This was the controversy between an 'explanatory' psychology oriented to the natural sciences and employing reductionistic procedures, with Ebbinghaus as its partisan, and a 'descriptive' psychology using the interpretative methods of the humanistic sciences, represented by Dilthey.[16] Mead's concerns do not place him on either side of this argument, the consequences of which are numerous and extend as far as the separation between phenomenological and experimental psychology. Rather, for him an anthropogenetic analysis of the interpretative accomplishments of the human 'soul', done with the methods of the natural sciences, constituted a critical problem.

Mead undertook to write a dissertation under Dilthey's direction; the topic was to be a critique of the empiricist concept of space. As letters testify, in this dissertation Mead intended to replicate for a limited problem the achievement of Kant that had played such an important role in Mead's intellectual biography; but he also proposed going beyond Kant in several respects. Unlike Kant, Mead did not understand space as a form of intuition, but rather as a constructional product of the cooperation of hand and eye. This would not only open the way for determining more precisely the corporeal preconditions of spatial perception and the constitution of space and for utilizing the empirical psychological research that had been done on this topic; it would also be a step towards escaping from Kant's phenomenalism. Mead believed that the answer to the question of the relation of human beings to nature and their position in nature could be found not through limiting, but rather through radicalizing the problems of constitution by considering them in the framework of intrinsic, fundamental characteristics of the human species. From this standpoint then, cognitive universality is no longer guaranteed by the common organic endowment of all human beings; it is rather a task that must be carried out in an active and constructional manner. Mead's insights are suggestive of philosophical themes that he was unable to develop at this time for lack of the appropriate conceptual tools, but that would occupy him throughout his life. The ambitiously conceived dissertation itself was never written.

Probably also owing to Dilthey's influence, Mead became interested in another area of research: the psychological treatment of ethical questions. Mead attended Dilthey's famous lectures on ethics, in which the latter attempted such an approach.[18] Mead asserted that the psychology of the child's early moral development was then the most important of all fields of research,[19] and he planned to publish in the USA a volume of translations of articles on this subject.[20]

In addition to these influences and his thorough study of the classics of German idealism, there was another formative experience during Mead's years in Berlin. That was the impression made on him by the social-democratic German labour movement. Mead's longing to engage socially useful tasks became politicized by this encounter, and his letters during this period expressed confidence that he would be needed in America and that he would be able to be useful there after he had finished his studies in Germany. The complementary bases of Mead's confidence are, on the one hand, the conviction that in the USA social reforms, or, as Mead unequivocally wrote during this period, socialism, would have to begin at the local level because of the weakness of the central government, and on the other hand the efficient local organization and the favorable prospects of the Social Democratic Party in local politics which he observed in Germany. Mead believed that after his return to the USA he would be able to contribute to the efforts to give a rational form to American society. His conception of socialism was informed as much by the ideals from his Christian and Roycean phases, as by his hope that he would be able to achieve the practical realization of those ideals in everyday life through his activity as a reformist intellectual.[21]

In 1891 Mead received an offer of a post as instructor of psychology at the University of Michigan in Ann Arbor and left Berlin precipitously. The new position obliged him to give courses on physiological psychology, the history of philosophy, Kant and the theory of evolution.[22] Here he attempted for the first time to draw from the theory of evolution its implications for psychology and to make the relation between an organism and its environment the basic model for psychological research. He entered in earnest upon experimental research and concerned himself with problems of attention and of the relationship between perception of pressure and perception of temperature.[23] However, it was by no means Mead's intention to allow his experimental research to be haphazard; he expressed in strong terms his need for a fundamental theoretical clarification of his standpoint. In particular, he hoped to obtain this clarification from thorough study of Hegel's thought, a hope that seemed all the more likely to be realized since two eminent colleagues in Michigan were Hegelians: John Dewey and Alfred Lloyd, with whom Mead soon became a personal friend.[24] It seemed to Mead at first that the link between German idealism and physiological psychology would be forged by developing the notion of 'life', the analytic and explanatory power of which was then only suspected.

From the time he spent in Michigan only a single instance of political activity has come to light. He was involved in the affair – known from research on Dewey – that arose in connection with the founding of a new newspaper, initiated by the syndicalist socialists Franklin and Corydon Ford, which was intended to serve as a counterweight to the commercial press. However, this project for the improvement of society through improvement of the information available to its members, which was envisaged on a gigantic scale, collapsed before it had really begun.[25] The intention to make academic intellectuals useful for social reform that was implicit in this project is also contained in the most extensive theoretical text that has been preserved from this phase of Mead's intellectual evolution. The work in question is an interpretation of the Christian notion of love against the background of William James's theory of emotion.[26]

At first glance, this seems to be an undertaking that has little to do with Mead's philosophical and psychological concerns. To the reader of this text, however, it soon becomes clear that Mead is attempting here, by means of his psychology, to take an important step toward secularizing and politicizing a central Christian notion. He interprets love as the impulse to establish a community of brotherhood encompassing all humanity, an impulse that overcomes all rituals and all legislation. Love as emotion, that is, the sentimental celebration of a Christian feeling, Mead sees as nothing more than an expression of the fact that love as an impulse to action is being thwarted.

> To sit back and enjoy this emotion must be more unallowable than in the case of any other because it should [be (H. J.)] the supreme emotion of life that calls for the most unceasing and most supreme action of which we are capable ... In so far as any experience of religion is given up to sentiment, in so far as the arousing of states of emotion for their own sake is the aim of any church in any sense in so far she confesses that she does not know what her appropriate activity is.[27]

In a manner comparable to the Young Hegelians' critique of religion, this passage expresses the strong desire to free the ethical core of Christianity as an ethics of brotherhood from the action-impeding forms of ritual and to translate it into social praxis.

In 1894 Dewey was offered the chairmanship of the Department of Philosophy and Psychology of the newly founded University of Chicago. When he accepted, one of his conditions was that he could bring Mead with him as an assistant professor.[28] Thus began the work of both men at one of the most ambitious of universities in one of the most gigantic and turbulent cities of that epoch. Here one did not find the calm and rarefied atmosphere of a New England university; nor was it possible in Chicago to have a naive understanding of democracy without posing the question of its realization in an industrial society. Chicago was one of the metropolises of capitalist industrialization; its population consisted for the greater part of first-generation immigrants, unskilled or semi-skilled workers and its growth was so rapid that every attempt at urban planning was frustrated. In the 1890s Chicago was also the centre of efforts to bring about radical social reform. Programmatically, the new university was strongly oriented towards practical tasks such as the scientific analysis and solution of problems in the local community. To the general orientation to social reform of sociology at the University of Chicago there corresponded the many-faceted commitment of philosophers and psychologists such as Mead and Dewey. I shall list these activities only in a summary fashion.

Both men, for example, were very closely linked with Hull House, the exemplary model for the settlement-house movement. For many years Mead served as its treasurer. The settlement houses were located in the problem-areas of a city, and in them social workers were lodged. Their purpose was to provide a communication centre for the population of the urban slums. Social work was not to take the form of external intervention by persons whose own life was spent in security and comfort outside the areas in which their clients lived and worked, and whose contacts with these clients were only those defined by their profession. The settlement houses offered to the members of the different nationalities then streaming into American cities, to women workers, and so on, free possibilities of activity in groups based on common interest. They also made available informal counselling by social workers. Moreover, Hull House was a discussion centre for Chicago's radical intelligentsia.[29] Its fundamental underlying notion was that democracy could not be understood simply as a particular form of political institution, and that education in democracy was not to be conceived of as the Americanization of the immigrants. Rather, democracy changed from a guarantee of freedom to an instrument of legalistic oppression when it was not developed as a form of living connected to existing forms of social organization.

Mead committed himself strongly to the struggle for women's rights and for reform of the juvenile penal code.[30] He was a member of several strike-arbitration committees and belonged to various public or quasi-public commissions on reform.[31] For decades Mead was a member of the City Club; for a time he served as its president. The City Club was an association of reform-minded intellectuals and businessmen with great influence on local politics, who advanced the political part'~ipation of immigrants, the democratization of urban planning, and the reform of municipal health services and of vocational training. Mead presided over the Club's committee on educational problems. He published a report in book form on the state of vocational training in the USA,[32] and in numerous articles he took a position on the side of the labour unions which wanted public vocational training, removed from the control of the employers, and integration of general education and vocational training. He was unreservedly interested in all questions of education and educational politics. For a while he was editor of the journal *Elementary School Teacher*. He taught at the Laboratory School of the University of Chicago, where educational reform was implemented through emphasis on the child's own activities and informal group-life for the purpose of developing the child's intellectual, practical and social abilities. He was also the president of the board of trustees of an experimental school for emotionally disturbed children.[33] In 1914 he joined in the political controversy over the progressive policies of the University of Wisconsin at Madison with a long article; spurious financial and political arguments were being made for holding the university in tutelage in a reactionary manner.[34]

All of these activities make up a part of Mead's life's work that has received very little attention. Yet Mead's multifarious practical involvement in education and politics exercised a very great influence on his theoretical evolution. It is surely no accident that he called for the development of a social psychology precisely because of its importance for a scientific theory of education,[35] and that the long series of articles beginning in 1909, in which he made the essential steps towards such a social psychology, followed upon a phase taken up almost exclusively by publications on education.

The First World War brought a new high point in Mead's political and journalistic activities. He became an ardent defender of President Wilson's advocacy of the United States' entry into the war. He argued for the issuing of war loans,[36] defended in newspaper articles the unselfish character of American participation in the war, and attempted to contribute to the patriotic education of his countrymen by means of an ethical discussion of the moral questions posed by conscientious objection.[37] In this pamphlet he demands recognition of the right to refuse to perform military service for reasons of conscience, because to do so would violate one's religious convictions or pacifist principles. Mead rejects, however, politically motivated refusal. The argument he advances is classic: in a democracy the individual citizen has only the right to work towards changing the laws; not the right to refuse to obey the laws, or to exhort others to such disobedience, or to hinder them in their obedience of the laws. This injunction is valid on condition that in the society in question there exist democratic forms of decision-making, and it is possible to effect social reform by democratic means. Under this presupposition Mead legitimates even a limiting of democracy and of freedom of speech that is the result of military considerations, and that should of course – as Mead said in his appeal to the national government – be combined with respect for democratic values, as a matter of principle.

This somewhat helpless call for giving a democratic direction to a policy that is not democratically controlled makes clear what kind of *cul de sac* Mead had been led into by his support of Wilson's foreign policy. As for his rejection of politically motivated refusal to serve in the military forces, the problem was not whether a formal right to such a refusal could be recognized, but rather that in this regard Mead, in contradiction of his own postulates, did not take up and discuss the rationally argued content of the motives of those opposed to the war for political reasons, rejecting instead on moral grounds their refusal to do military service. Mead's position on this matter, however, prevented two important questions from arising for him, namely whether decisions regarding the United States' foreign policy were made in a truly democratic manner, and what interests lay behind this foreign policy.

Taking this position was certainly not an occurrence unique to Mead's political development. It was, rather, an about-face that was common to an entire generation of progressive American intellectuals. The war was not understood as the result of global political and economic causes and of the conflicting interests of competing imperialist powers, but instead as a conflict between the principles of democracy and autocracy. According to this view, the causes of the war lay in the expansionism of German 'autocracy'; and the battle against this autocracy was not merely opposition to a competitor, but rather a morally justified and heroic act for the purpose of safeguarding democracy in the world. As worthy war goals Mead names the democratization of Prussianized Germany, and the development of non-violent mechanisms for the resolution of international conflicts, and especially the establishment of the League of Nations.

In expressing this opinion, Mead addressed himself to the American labour movement, since only it could assure that militarism in the USA would exclusively serve these worthwhile goals. Mead's belief that only through the commitment of the masses to a victory could militarism be eliminated in the USA and the continuation of a national policy of social reform rendered possible, was characteristic of his thinking.

> The masses of the allied nations must make this war their own, and the American workingmen who have been spared as yet the martyrdom of the trenches are bound to recognize that only by the ending of the war in the interests of democracy can they be freed from the evils of militarism in America.[38]

With these words Mead adopts the very stance for which he had criticized the German Social Democrats, and which had led to their willingness to go to war 'for the Kaiser' and to betray the internationalism of the labour movement. The fall of the internationalist Mead into the sin of nationalism was concealed behind an argument which attempted to surpass the internationalism of the labour movement. According to this argument, the socialist movement was only the battle formation of the working-class and not an expression of the whole human community; the internationalism of the socialist movement was therefore limited to only one class and did not succeed in coping with the real problems of national identities and of their relationships to one another.

Mead's attitude to the First World War, which he shared with his generation of pragmatist, social-reformist intellectuals, casts light on the secret roots as well as the limits of his radical reformism. He was far from being overcome by chauvinist enthusiasm for the war like a considerable proportion of European scientists; rather, he tried to understand the psychological and moral roots of militarism and of aggressive patriotism in order to combat them. Yet his efforts do not go beyond such attempts to find psychological and moral explanations for these phenomena.

Mead's acceptance of Wilson's foreign policy was possible only because it rested on a profound naivety regarding the economic motives behind American foreign policy. This naivety came above all from Mead's firm belief that the United States, because of the anti-colonialist history of its origin, and because of its democratic traditions, was an intrinsically non-imperialist, indeed an anti-imperialist nation.[39] Mead's comments on the question of annexing Hawaii in 1895, a step which he could not explain from the need to safeguard militarily America's foreign trade,[40] his statements on governmental policy toward Cuba and the Philippines,[41] his approval of Wilson's policy vis-à-vis Mexico,[42] and his endorsement in 1922 of the Open Door Policy with regard to China, were all filled with confidence in the just and liberating role of the USA in the world. For Mead, imperialism was only a problem of the political relations among states, not an economic one.

Here lies the secret of the authentic progressiveness of bourgeois thought in the USA and of its relatively long duration. Pragmatism was based on the possibility of integrating advances in science and technology and their social consequences into the bourgeoisie's optimistic belief in progress. In the USA the bourgeoisie had not yet been driven by fear of a revolution to renounce this optimism. The hegemony over the labour movement of progressive bourgeois intellectuals and even of reformist sectors of the entrepreneurs had been preserved and had prevented the emergence of a socialist alternative that threatened the reigning socio-economic system in the USA. The continuance of this hegemony had been made possible by the American economy's persisting tendency to prosperity, which was interrupted only briefly during the period in question. That the secret cause of this prosperity lay in the USA's policy of expansion was, however, not understood by Mead and other bourgeois intellectuals. What had been, during the 'Progressive Era', only a limitation on his understanding of the material conditions of his own political position, changed its function as a result of the First World War and necessarily made Mead incapable of grasping the reasons for the disappearance, in the decade after the war, of the social conditions that provided a favourable framework for reform.

It would be incorrect, though, to conclude from Mead's advocacy of American participation in the war and from the way he justified such participation that his commitment to social reform had slackened. There is considerable evidence from just these years, from 1918–19, that, if anything, his position with respect to social reform became slightly more radical during this time. In letters as well as in his review of Thorstein Veblen's book on the economic prerequisites of an enduring world peace,[43] Mead proclaimed his approval of the British Labour Party's new programme, which expressed its left-ward development by declaring 'the evolutionary establishment of a socialist society by means of precisely planned transitional measures to be the official goal of the party'.[44] Mead pondered the question whether a comparable organization was necessary in the USA, and what its chances for success would be, or whether a shift to the left by the Democratic Party would be sufficient to secure social change.[45] But in either case Woodrow Wilson was to be the political leader, and the fulfilment of the 'American mission' would be the goal.

By his approval of the United States' foreign policy, Mead was compelled to accept the domestic preconditions required by that policy, and to confine struggles for social reform within limits which maintained those conditions.[46] Whereas John Dewey subsequently sought to revise his position on the war after the Treaty of Versailles, and at least retained a sympathetic openness to the gigantic social experiment of the Russian Revolution, Mead showed no signs of doing either. Rather, he opposed the path followed by the Soviet Union with very abstract objections, such as, for example, that it was doubtful that efficient production could be organized without taking into consideration the profit motive.[47] Mead could therefore only react defensively to the sudden and extreme change of the national political mood in the 1920s, the 'fat, intolerant years'.[48] His political publications and political activity ceased almost completely. The topics with which he concerned himself shifted away from the domain of the social sciences and approached closer to natural philosophy and cosmology. The single exception is formed by his important contributions on the question of international-minded-ness versus national-mindedness.

In these writings Mead argued for the necessity of making possible international relations that are free from violence by establishing mechanisms for the rational resolution of conflicts. These mechanisms, however, presupposed that such democratic forms already existed in the individual nations and that glaring class antagonisms had been overcome in the individual nations.[49]

Compared with the tendencies of bourgeois thinkers in that era, in Europe and subsequently in the USA too, to abandon, out of aggressive nationalism or in scepticism and resignation, the Enlightenment ideal of a civilization embracing all of humanity, Mead's position was a humanistic exception. The increasing 'abstractness' of Mead's thought mentioned above, the concentration of his interests on the possibility of attaining objective values and knowledge while taking into consideration the undeniable plurality and relativity of individual perspectives – these came to pass in a social situation in which the self-evident validity of humanistic values was direly threatened, and no other way remained open to Mead than to defend the validity of these values with the means provided by his philosophy. His student T. V. Smith[50] interprets the turning of Mead's reflections to problems of natural philosophy as an attempt to found the pathos of universal understanding among individuals, of sociality, in the cosmos, inasmuch as the social power of this principle did not prove to be compellingly evident.

Towards the end of the twenties, the wave of reaction menaced even the remnants of pragmatist thought at the University of Chicago. After teaching for almost 40 years at this university, George Herbert Mead did on April 26, 1931, generally unknown, esteemed by some colleagues and students as an extraordinary thinker, and deeply embittered by controversial changes in the university's internal politics that threatened to alter the nature of philosophy there, making it Catholic and reactionary in character.[51] So great was Mead's bitterness that shortly before his death he decided to leave the institution and the city that had been his field of action. It is probably not going too far to see a connection between this turn of events and Mead's death.

The alleged opportunist adjustment of the pragmatist, social-reformist intellectuals to the changed circumstances was a crucial experience for their students, and the cause of the rift between the latter and their teachers. One of Dewey's most gifted students, Randolph Bourne, searched for the causes of this adjustment in a polemical essay,[52] which today's reader still finds gripping, and discovered them in pragmatism's central concept of adaptation. In Bourne's view, the technocratic consequences of pragmatist philosophy issued from its programmatic confinement to ad hoc reforms and its refusal to conceive of utopian alternatives to existing society. He readily admits that Dewey's 'instrumentalism' was not an ideology of value-free technical knowledge, the use of which is to be guided only by arbitrarily chosen values, but that it was, rather, implicitly founded on humanistic values. However, Bourne argues, the implicitness of these values had not sufficed. In Bourne's essay, political radicalization is combined with a willingness to give up pragmatism in favour of a philosophy of *a priori* values. What emerges in this text is a conflict that is of essential importance for understanding pragmatism. Bourne rejects a philosophy of adaptation, since its inherent limitation prevents it from making full use even of the available framework for social reforms.

> The defect of any philosophy of 'adaptation' or 'adjustment', even when it means adjustment to changing, living experience, is that there is no provision for thought or experience getting beyond itself . . . opportunist efforts usually achieve less even than what seemed obviously possible . . . A philosophy of adjustment will not even make for adjustment. If you try merely to 'meet' situations as they come, you will not even meet them.[53]

Bourne's criticisms lead us into the heart of Mead's political philosophy. For, in fact, the opposition between a 'chiliastic' ideology of social movements and a 'scientific' policy of gradual and controlled reforms was crucial to Mead's understanding of the politics of social reform. He saw the first in the Kautskyian form taken on by the German social democracy of the Wilhelmine *Reich*; the second was, he thought, prototypically realized in British trade-unionism. It was in the light of this opposition that Mead took his political stand: he explicitly declared his solidarity with those tendencies in the labour movement that have been called 'opportunist', and in Germany 'revisionist'. Mead accepted socialist utopias only as a source of inspiration for scientific social reform, but considered them to be primarily an expression of the immaturity of social movements in their early stages, and recommended to the labour movement a secularization and rationalization of its ideals similar to those which Christianity had undergone.

> There is the same specific weakness in the program that inheres in the day-dream as a motive for action. In the nature of the case the interest in the immediate process tends to take the place of the devotion to the program. Nor is this a phenomenon that is confined to socialism.

In Christianity there is a constant transfer of attention from the dogma to the interest in immediate practical effort toward the amelioration of suffering and wrong.[54]

Mead thus defended social reform against the complete rejection of it ensuing from Le Bon's theses on crowd psychology or from philosophical criticisms of utopian thinking. For him the opposite of utopian social reform remained scientific social reform. In his essay 'The Working Hypothesis in Social Reform', he explicitly undertakes to justify including social reform among the inductive sciences, and to explain what the implications of the concept of the hypothesis are in the case of social reform. The general thesis of this essay is that in social reform, as in science, we have at our disposal only a method and the possibility of observing the repercussions of the changes we make, but we do not have knowledge of ideals and final goals, from which practical measures for their realization can be deduced. This position drew its self-confidence from the impression then prevalent that the success of social reform was continually growing:

> Here, also, this takes place, not by a statement of what either society or the individual is going to be, but by finding the point of identity between them, and controlling the process of reform by sacrificing nothing valuable in either. It is only the method we can be sure of, not the result.
>
> Now, I take it that this is but an abstract way of saying that we have, in general, given up being programists and become opportunists. We do not build any more Utopias, but we do control our immediate conduct by the assurance that we have the proper point of attack, and that we are losing nothing in the process. We are getting a stronger grip on the method of social reform every year, and are becoming proportionately careless about our ability to predict the detailed result.[55]

The social conditions that were favourable to reform did not enter Mead's field of vision; the various instances of social progress appeared, rather, to be results of advances made in transforming politics itself into a science.

For today's reader this must sound, even in the words Mead uses, like the technocratic ideology of social reform presented most clearly by Popper in his critique of historicism.[56] It is indeed true that the latter, too, distinguishes between utopian and piecemeal strategies, and ascribes rationality only to the second. Popper also warns us of the dangers of revolution, the complexity of which is so great that we cannot fully grasp it, and thereby condemns all change in the realm of fundamental social mechanisms. And yet such an equation would be a serious failure to situate Mead (and Dewey) correctly in history. For between the positions of Mead and Popper there are two differences with far-reaching consequences.

For Popper, the making of politics into a science, the rationality of political action, has to do only with the choice of means and techniques, which – as Apel,[57] for one, rightly objects – does not at all bring about an 'open society', but rather allows stable structures of domination to remain unquestioned in their implicitly accepted validity. In contrast, for Mead the claim of political action to rationality is founded on the form of social decision-making itself and on a linking of the ability with the obligation to do something. In his eulogy to Robert Hoxie, the famous scholar of the American union movement,[58] for example, Mead said that it is the task of the scientist to understand the positions of all parties to a conflict and to make it possible for them to come to an agreement. Rational social reform, then, does not consist in finding economic means for given ends, but instead in an intensification of public discussion, from which emerge constructive solutions for social problems benefiting all and in the interest of all. This statement shows the rational core of Mead's anti-utopian position. His notion of reformist action is informed by the model of intelligent action in general, and is opposed both to moral guidance by ideals and to technocratic models.

Whether Mead's conception of reformist action adequately takes into consideration the conditions obtaining in societies in which social problems arise from collisions of fundamental interests re-mains to be clarified, however. It is from this question that the second difference between Mead and Popper results. For the latter, the arguments for the primacy of piecemeal strategies depend mainly upon the impossibility of giving a completely rational form to society and the inevitability of a remnant of arbitrariness in decisions regarding social change. In Mead's case these arguments are intro-duced as the very way to this complete social rationality, a way superior to that proposed by utopian socialists. Thus, for the pragmatists an ideal goal of history is excluded much less definitively than it is for Popper.

Mead and the pragmatists, however, do not explicitly defend such a goal. The question is, rather, whether Mead's political position and its implications for his philosophy of history, his ethics, and his theory of truth make it necessary to continue Mead's thought in the direction taken by Popper, or by Bourne, or in yet a third direction. In other words: are Popper's limitation of the prospects for success of social rationality, or Bourne's return to *a priori* values, the inevitable conclusions drawn from Mead's failure, or is it possible to find a way to unfold in a consistent manner the ideals implicit in Mead's concept of intelligent action in such a way as to make possible fundamental social changes? Dewey's later development – during the Great Depression – already shows a heightened awareness that a distinction must be drawn between the normative conditions of scientific discourse and the social context in which science is translated into practice. But this distinction implies the distinction between ideal and actually existing science, between ideal and actually existing forms of discourse. Later in this work, examination of immanent problems of ethics, the theory of truth, and the philosophy of history will demonstrate that the theory of communication, which has grown out of the clear knowledge of the limits of instrumental reason and the ideal of communication free of domination by those involved in it – as this ideal has been developed by Habermas and Apel – takes these insights a step further, without, however, exhausting the fruitfulness of Mead's own efforts in this area.

3

Mead's Position in Intellectual History and his Early Philosophical Writings

There is no doubt that Mead understood and referred to himself as a pragmatist toward the end of his life. Yet this label does not immediately help a great deal in understanding his fundamental approach, since pragmatism was by no means a clearly delimited school or a distinctly differentiated paradigm. Rather, it was the name of a programme, which had still to be elaborated and required clarification in many respects. Mead's increasing use of this description for himself is, therefore, not due to a change in his views, but merely to the growing currency of the term 'pragmatism'. Since Mead's classification as a pragmatist might conceal, rather than elucidate, individual particularities of his approach, I shall, as a first step, summarize the basic concerns of his thought, as these are revealed by his biography, and generally relate them to the approaches of other pragmatists as well as to the central features of his contemporary intellectual situation. This first step will show the possible significance of Mead's work for German social theories. The second step will be to draw upon the writings on the history of philosophy and science that Mead himself submitted in order to deepen our understanding of Mead's position in intellectual history. The third step will take us to Mead's early philosophical writings and to his intellectual evolution.

The fundamental themes that can be extracted from Mead's biography can be subsumed under three headings: confidence in the emancipatory prospects of scientific rationality; a striving to root 'mind' or 'spirit' in the organism; and the attempt to elaborate a theory of intersubjectivity that would conceive of the self as socially originated. Mead's confidence in the prospects of technical and scientific progress is neither naive nor apologetic. He does not identify technical with social progress, nor does he call for the extension of technical rationality to the guidance of social processes. His categorical notion of science assumes, rather, that the freedom of scientific communication underlying scientific progress is made the model for the reform of social decision-making processes. Thus, the frequently proclaimed endeavour to transform social reform into a science, and to overcome the relative falling behind of the social sciences does not conceal the germ of positivist or technocratic ideals. And yet Mead's concept of rationality also does not take on that peculiar ambivalence, which – as in the case of Max Weber, for example – interprets rationalization as a historical process occurring supra-personally and compelling the individual's adaptation, a process for which nevertheless the name of reason is used. From this ambivalence to resignation and the abandonment of all optimism about civilization is indeed only a single step.

In contrast, for Mead and his circle rationality is the remedy for social problems. He can hold this opinion only because for him the gap between 'higher', 'spiritual', 'cultural' attainments and capacities and the 'material', 'technical', 'civilizing' dimension of society had been philosophically overcome in a fundamental way. The attempt to elaborate a 'functionalist' psychology, based on the work of Darwin, is founded on the insight that all mental operations can be embedded in the functions of the organism in a non-reductionist manner. This is important both for philosophy's founding of itself and because of individual psychological and pedagogical consequences of this insight. With regard to the founding of philosophy, the model, first proposed by Darwin, of the organism actively safeguarding its life in a given environment made it possible easily to go beyond the view advanced by transcendental philosophy, which requires the antecedent reflective certainty of the thinking ego. Thus, by means of the Darwinian model, the difficult path followed by Feuerbach, and the Young Hegelians in general, in their attempts to free themselves from transcendental philosophy, is traversed with a single bound. With regard to psychology, the acceptance of the Darwinian model resulted in a 'rehabilitation' of organismic impulses, while with respect to educational theory it led to the attaching of greater importance to physical activity, sensory-motor learning, the immediate interests of the learner, and the organically conditioned stages of maturation.

The third of the aforementioned general concerns is perhaps the most characteristic for Mead. Through the theory of the social formation of the self, one of the cornerstones of bourgeois ideology in the strict sense is eliminated, namely possessive individualism. For Mead the individual and his property is no longer a presupposition of the formation of a society, but rather individualization is a consequence of the structure of socially organized life-processes. It thereby becomes possible, despite rejection of traditional individualism, particularly that of Anglo-Saxon thought, to retain the ideal of the individual's autonomy. However, this autonomy is now no longer an original given that is to be opposed to society. Instead, it requires for its emergence a re-shaping of social life, which must be so organized that free self-determination of all is both possible and necessary. From his earliest publications on,[1] this theme can be followed in Mead's writings, even though the scientific means for carrying out the programme were only gradually elaborated, and the ethical aspects of the concept of the self only gradually freed from their close ties to religion.

Now, if we ask about the relationship of these fundamental concerns to pragmatism in general, then it quickly becomes clear that the first two are, to a large extent, shared by all pragmatists, whereas the third is peculiar to Mead. This is the reason why the designation of Mead as a 'consequentialist intersubjective pragmatist' seems to me a perhaps clumsy but precise description of his position. The roots of pragmatism are to be found in the attempt, as Mead put it, to 'logically generalize' the procedures of the experimental natural sciences,[2] and in the train of Darwinism to relate all human cognitive processes to life-processes. To be sure, both of these endeavours, impressive and humanistic as they are, do not appear at all in the widespread picture of pragmatism. Rather, pragmatism is thought to be a cynical justification for acting without ultimate goals and firm principles, according to the precept that what is true is what is useful. This distorted picture of pragmatism has often occasioned imputations about its connection with the American national character, or criticism of it as an ideology. From this perspective pragmatism appears as the ideology of the adaptation of intellectuals to the formation of monopoly capitalism or as the expression of the American fetishism of success and money.[3] Even during his lifetime, Mead had to oppose these distortions; he did so ironically:

> Now this assumption of the pragmatist that the individual only thinks in order that he may continue an interrupted action, that the criterion of the correctness of his thinking is found in his ability to carry on, and

that the significant goal of his thinking or research is found not in the ordered presentation of the subject matter of his research but in the uses to which it may be put, is very offensive to many people, and, I am afraid, particularly so to the historian. Pragmatism is regarded as a pseudo-philosophic formulation of that most obnoxious American trait, the worship of success; as the endowment of the four-flusher with a faked philosophic passport; the contemptuous swagger of a glib and restless upstart in the company of the mighty but reverent spirits worshipping at the shrine of subsistent entities and timeless truth; a blackleg pacemaker introduced into the leisurely workshop of the spirit to speed up the processes of thinking *sub specie aeternitatis*; a Ford efficiency engineer bent on the mass production of philosophical tin lizzies. These disparagements are all boomerangs, but I will not constitute this a clinic in which to demonstrate the contusions which those who have hurled them have suffered, but will address myself to the single charge that this philosophy would dispossess men of the leisured contemplation and enjoyment of the past.[4]

Such misrepresentations concealed even from Marxists the extra-ordinary proximity between Marx's philosophy of praxis and the fundamental principle of pragmatism. And this, although the relation-ship of the terms 'praxis' and 'pragmatism' – extending even to their common linguistic root – was not accidental. For Peirce, the founder of pragmatism, had justified the choice of this name precisely as an attempt to overcome the Kantian distinction between 'practical' and 'pragmatic':

But for one who had learned philosophy out of Kant . . ., 'practical' and 'pragmatical' were as far apart as the two poles, the former belonging in a region of thought where no mind of the experimentalist type can ever make sure of solid ground under his feet, the latter expressing relation to some definite human purpose. Now quite the most striking feature of the new theory was its recognition of an inseparable connection between rational cognition and rational pur-poses; and that consideration it was which determined the preference for the name 'pragmatism'.[5]

Overcoming the separation between practical and theoretical reason and the primary of praxis are, however, very much fundamental principles of historical materialism, even if they have not been elaborated in much detail by the adherents of this theory.

The superficial misunderstandings of pragmatism are only gradually being dissipated by the general renaissance of pragmatism in the USA, and in the Federal Republic of Germany through the reception of Peirce's work initiated by Apel and Habermas. Concomitant to this better understanding is an increasingly clear awareness that in pragmatism at least two different large strands must be distinguished; one of them aims at objective cognitive truth and correctness of behaviour, while the other is subjectivist in character. The latter strand of pragmatist thought is represented by William James, who, to be sure, also did not reduce truth to usefulness, but did consider it – taking the individualistic point of view – merely as an instrument at the service of the individual's existence and spiritual welfare. Mead distanced himself as unequivocally from James's theory of truth as from his psychological notions.[6] Mead did in some instances employ the same terms as James, for example, 'I', 'me', and 'self', but for Mead these expressions denoted concepts that were quite different from those of James. For Mead, James's psychology only demarcated the terrain on which he made his attempt to recover objectivity and universality.

Although there is, then, objective agreement of Mead's intentions with those of Peirce, it would be erroneous to conclude from this fact that there was a direct influence by Peirce on Mead. Such an influence simply cannot be documented. In an article written in the last year of his life Mead mentions Peirce only briefly, without discussing his work even cursorily.[7] At the present time the only other instance of a greater contact by Mead with Peirce's thought is to be found in a fragment written during Mead's early years,[8] in which he drew upon Peirce's critique of 'necessitarian', that is deterministic, metaphysics in an attempt to develop various sociological trains of thought. The influence unquestionably exercised by Peirce's theory of signs on Mead's conception of the significant symbol was indirect, and came to Mead via Royce's late writings.[9] Even taking into consideration the generally small degree to which Peirce's work was known prior to the publication of his *Collected Papers* (beginning in 1928), the extent to which Mead ignored this thinker, with whom he shared so many intellectual concerns, is still really surprising.

The reasons for this probably lie in Mead's slight interest in problems of scientific logic in the narrower sense, and especially in Peirce's rejection of attempts to apply scientific procedures to social processes and of the practical utilization of 'pure' science in general. If Mead's dominant interest can be described as *a refounding of pragmatism as a theory based on the biological and social sciences*, then Peirce's confidence in the salutary effects of the natural human instincts, his optimistic anthropology, necessarily remained alien to Mead and seemed superficial to him. Apparently for that reason he did not see how extensively the basic model of cognition as the solution of problems arising from action, as the way of making possible the continuation of action – a model that he traced back to Dewey's paradigmatic essay 'The Reflex Arc Concept in Psychology' – had already been implicitly elaborated, even from a psychological point of view, in the writings of Peirce. As is well known, the latter had attempted to criticize Cartesianism also from a psychological perspective and had adapted for this purpose the 'belief-doubt' theory of Alexander Bain. Apel summarizes this theory as follows:

> 'Doubt' as the irritation of a secure form of behaviour, and 'belief' as the reinstitution of security in behaviour constitute a *terminus post quem* and a *terminus ante quem* of the cognition process in time; in a way they stake out in each case a finite functional unity in the infinite process of cognition.[10]

Although it cannot by any means be maintained that Peirce really drew all the psychological conclusions implicit in this view, or that he developed a comprehensive concept of action,[11] it is nevertheless very clear that Peirce and Mead were in the same tradition. For Dewey communicated with Peirce and had been directly influenced by him.

Although these connections have shed some light on Mead's relationship to James and Peirce as eminent representatives of the aforementioned strands of pragmatism, it is still necessary to make a few remarks about Mead's relationship to the third famous representative of pragmatism, John Dewey. This relationship is often presented as one-sided, with Mead in the role of student or collaborator. Yet it can be shown – and was stressed by Dewey's daughter in a biographical recollection – that both the central theoretical elements used by Mead in his definition of the 'psychical' and in his explanation of the social formation of the self originate with him and were only taken over by Dewey and employed in the latter's writings often in a rather superficial manner.[12] With regard to ethics and the theory of science, the two philosophers also differ from one another, with Mead generally taking the more strongly 'objective' position.

The superficial, popular misunderstandings about pragmatism unquestionably have their analogues in serious philosophical thought. Thus the critique of pragmatism using as a criterion the ideal of pure theory, such as Max Scheler undertook, as well as the subsumption of neopositivism and pragmatism under the rubric of 'instrumental reason', which we find in Max Horkheimer's critique of this kind of thinking, are characterized by a superficial and biased interpretation of pragmatism and by counter-notions of dubious merit.[13] The most interesting phenomenon in European thought in this connection, and the one that testifies most strongly to Mead's importance for German intellectual history, is the fact that when the insights of American pragmatism were arrived at independently by European philosophers, as in Nietzsche's or Bergson's *Lebensphilosophie*, they occur with a characteristic modification. Alongside the pragmatist notion of the cognition of reality there was maintained a contemplative notion of cognition, and this was done in such a manner that the world constituted in the action of human actors appears to be deficient in comparison with the world that is accessible only through abstinence from action. The logical impossibility of this 'fictionalist' pragmatism has been rightly demonstrated many times, especially in more recent Nietzsche scholarship.[14] For Mead, Nietzsche was without significance; the position described was familiar to him, however, and thoroughly discussed by him with Bergson as the example.[15]

In his critical examination of Le Bon's crowd psychology, Mead had already posed the question: from which perspective is the thesis of the necessary distortion of reality by all perception advanced?[16] This question then becomes more precise in Mead's reflections on Bergson. In significant psychological analyses Bergson had attempted to show that all conceptual cognition arises from problems posed by action and forces the world into a framework that causes all freedom and spontaneity to disappear. Bergson's primary example was his analysis of the 'spatialization of time', that is his proof that our thinking can grasp the internal experiencing of time only in categories of the external, physical world, but thereby obliterates its specific features. To the mechanistic image of the world characterized by restriction and coercion, Bergson emphatically opposed a world of change and freedom. This world is accessible through intuition – a counter-notion to conceptual cognition – which alone opens the portal leading to creative evolution.

Mead saw in Bergson's influential analyses a justified, but irrationalist critique of scientism. In his earliest discussion of Bergson's work he asked how it was possible that Bergson attributed a creative character only to intuition and to the unplanned becoming of 'life', but not to science. He saw in Bergson's position the reverse of the positivist misunderstanding of science, according to which science consists merely of interrelated propositions about facts, not the process of discovering these facts.[17] In Bergson's view, freedom derived from the essential impossibility of exhaustively predicting the future, from which fact he concluded the superfluity of the intellect. To Bergson's position Mead opposed scientific procedure understood as a readiness continually to revise hypotheses and to make the map of the future progressively more precise. In Mead's opinion, Bergson's irrationalist tendencies were rooted in his inadequate understanding of the scientific method. The appropriate remedy for this irrationalism was, Mead believed, to work out correctly the implications of the insight into the construct-character of scientific objects, to analyse the way in which scientific knowledge is constituted. What had been only suggestively associated in Bergson's writings and in the largest part of *Lebensphilosophie* – the implications of the notion of life with regard to the natural sciences on the one hand and the critique of culture on the other hand, the directing of attention to the biological foundations of the mind, and the protest against reification and rigidification of culture – these and their interrelationships had to be developed with extreme clarity in order to oppose irrationalism. But to do so, a non-irrationalist notion of life was required. By 'life' Mead does not understand the organism's creative and complete self-regulation as a counter-notion to the intellect, but rather the continual solving of problems. Reflective experience is for him both a product and a functional necessity of human life; science is the opportunity for humanity to replace the blind rule of evolutionary laws with the self-reflective shaping of its own conditions of life. Thus the notion of life held by Mead, and other pragmatists, allows them to appropriate the achievements of *Lebensphilosophie* rather than dismissing them together with its undeniable irrationalism. By contrasting Mead with Bergson, the thesis can perhaps be made more plausible that in many respects Mead's thought offers an alternative to the course taken by German and European intellectual history since the late 19th century, inasmuch as it permits one to link together, in a synthesis, moments which seem to be mutually exclusive in the German tradition. I myself see in Mead's work a possibility of escaping aporiae which occurred in the development of German philosophy from Dilthey and Husserl to Heidegger and Philosophical Anthropology, and which are important for the grounding of the social sciences. However, I will confine myself here to pointing out this possibility rather than presenting it in detail, as that would require close discussion of the aforementioned thinkers.

The fact that Mead studied with Dilthey and was familiar with the latter's intellectual aims is not an inconsequential aspect of Mead's biography, since both had certain concerns in common. For example, they both attempted to make possible a grounding of the human or social sciences by revealing how the objects of these sciences are constituted in the communicative life-praxis of human beings. This undertaking was in contrast to materialist or idealist reductionism and stood at a critical distance from the mere resuscitation of Kant in neo-Kantianism. Also common to both – contrary to misjudgements which are widespread in the history of Dilthey scholarship – was the intention of establishing a basis for objective knowledge and an open-mindedness towards the natural sciences.[18] The immediate difference between them in this regard is only a matter of accentuation, in so far as Mead was certainly more sympathetic to the natural sciences than was Dilthey. Experimental psychology, and not, as for Dilthey, historical-philological research, typified for Mead the field of non-natural-scientific investigation.

Thus, in Dilthey's eyes the approaches used by experimental psychology were all suspected of being reductionist, and he was compelled to set against 'explanatory' psychology, which he rejected, the 'descriptive' psychology that he himself had founded. The latter was directed towards answering the question of the nature of the constitutive achievements of the mind that made possible the products of the 'objective spirit'. Mead shared this concern, and, like Dilthey, held unwaveringly to the singularity of historical existence in opposition to the absolutist claims of the idealist philosophy of history, as his early writings show. The crucial difference, and the cause of the development of Mead's thought in another direction, lay in the fact that at the very beginning of his work Mead overcame the obstacle on which Dilthey's enterprise came to grief: unlike Dilthey, Mead does not maintain that the self or the structure of the psyche is in itself originally given to the actor. Despite the many fundamental premises he held in common with the pragmatists, Dilthey did not attain the same degree of philosophical radicalism and start to conceive of the self as the product of a complex of social relationships.[19] In his *Ideas Concerning a Descriptive and Analytical Psychology (Ideen über eine beschreibende und zergliedernde Psychologie)*, he clearly fails to recognize that inner experience, too, is socially mediated; it is only this failure that allows him to oppose the absolute certainty of 'inner experience' to the merely hypothetical character of 'external experience'. In *Toward a Solution of the Question Concerning the Origin of our Belief in the Reality of the External World (Beiträge zur Lösung der Frage vom Ursprung unseres Glaubens an die Realität der Außenwelt)*, Dilthey certainly made significant steps in the direction of a theory of the 'practical constitution' of the world; however, he treated the problem of the reality of other persons only in a way parallel to the problem of the constitution of physical objects, and did not go beyond the assumption that the other is inferred analogically on the basis of the self's interior experience of itself. Thus the solution offered by Dilthey surmounted Cartesianism only through its inclusion of 'life', not, however, through its inclusion of an inter-subjectivity that would ground the reality and the constitution of others.

Since this deficiency is to be found also, and to an even greater degree, in Husserl's thought, Dilthey was unable to solve this problem by drawing on Husserl, who became very important for Dilthey's later work. Although Dilthey was led to Husserl because the latter's concept of 'meaning' *(Bedeutung)* seemed to provide a safeguard against the relativist dangers of a purely psychological foundation of the human sciences and to open the way to their 'hermeneutic' grounding, which Dilthey subsequently sketched out with his theory of expression,[20] there was nevertheless an aporia implicit in this progress. Despite a common interest in a theory of the constitution of scientific knowledge, Husserl's approach was radically different from pragmatism and also from the pragmatist features of Dilthey's thought:

on the one hand, there is an appeal to intuitive evidence, an eidetic theory of meaning, the seeing of essences [*Wesensschau*], and a radical absence of presuppositions; on the other hand, there is an appeal to the ability to make or to do something, an operational theory of meaning, Constructionism, and the recognition of the presuppositions in the language and situational context of the praxis of life.[21]

Since Husserl's concept of meaning did not stem from linguistic theory or – taking a broader view – from a theory of intersubjectivity, Dilthey was not able to attain, by means of this concept, a theory that preserved the range of problems posed by the question of the truth and validity of assertions, and that belonged as well to the realm of social psychology.[22] And conversely, Husserl's idealism and transcendentalism grew out of his belief that they offered the only escape from the dissolution of all values in historicism and naturalism.[23] Husserl's later transcendentalism seems to me to be the other side of Dilthey's inability to solve the problem of relativism. The concept of meaning, arrived at by way of the phenomenology of essences, blocked precisely those possibilities of elucidating the anthropological presuppositions of communicatively mediated human life-praxis that were implicit in Dilthey's theories.

What was thereby left undone was also not accomplished in subsequent attempts. The most important attempt to escape from the framework of transcendental philosophy and to find a point of departure other than the self-certainty of the experiencing ego was the ontological turn which Heidegger gave to phenomenology. Admittedly, his modification of phenomenology introduced into it intersubjectivity in the form of 'being-with' (*Mit-Sein*), praxis in the form of 'care' (*Sorge*), and the structure of the relation between the organism and its environment in the form of 'being-in-the-world' (*In-der-Welt-Sein*). But this was done at the price of the possibility of posing the question of the validity of the notions of the true and the good, and by means of the philosophically arrogant claim to provide a basis for the sciences, rather than giving an elucidation of what the sciences are and how they proceed. Existential hermeneutics enunciates in philosophical language insights that, according to their entire content and for their real implementation, require the integration of philosophy and the sciences. For Heidegger, surmounting Husserl's transcendentalism is synonymous with renunciation of the critical claims of subjectivity.[24] Although in Heidegger's ontological phenomenology the proximity of philosophy and empirical science achieved by Dilthey is lost, it is restored in the various attempts to develop a Philosophical Anthropology. But these attempts, too, founder on the problem under discussion.

Let us consider only the two most highly elaborated and most significant variants of Philosophical Anthropology, namely those developed by Arnold Gehlen und Helmuth Plessner. It can be shown that Gehlen's anthropology suffers generally from an inadequate notion of intersubjectivity and that the substantial deficiencies of his theory of language, conceptions of perception, ethics, and theory of institutions can be accounted for by the politically motivated rejection of democratic intersubjectivity.[25] Plessner's theory, on the other hand, correctly focuses on human expressivity as an area of essential importance and performs significant preparatory work for an anthropological founding of hermeneutics. He restricts hermeneutics, however, through the connection of his theory with the framework of transcendental phenomenology, inasmuch as he grounds intersubjectivity in the fundamental organic structure of the human being, conceived of as 'excentric positionality', rather than arriving at an understanding of human self-reflectivity – which is to be found, Plessner shows, even in 'sensuousness' itself – from the structures of intersubjectivity.[26] What was thereby not achieved in the German tradition is a theory of the fundamental structure of human sociality that is based in a thoroughgoing way on intersubjectivity and is not apriorist and transcendentalist,[27] that is non-relativist, and draws upon and is consistent with the findings of natural and social science. To such a theory, I believe, Mead made a significant contribution.

Neither German sociology[28] nor historical materialism can offer an alternative to Mead's contribution to a theory of human sociality. It is impossible to discuss here Max Weber's critical deficiences with regard to the theory of action or the failure of perhaps the only Marxist who reached the level of this complex of problems, Georg Lukács.[29] As for the development of Mead's theory, in my opinion it was made possible by the positive relationship of the American pragmatists to the ethical implications of a categorical notion of democracy and to the emancipatory prospects of progress in technology and the natural sciences.[30] In Mead's and Dewey's hands this notion of democracy did not become a formalist ideology legitimating certain institutions and election procedures; nor was it undermined by the insight that the democratic ideal is often used for the purposes of such a legitimating ideology. For them, the ideal of democracy is not replaced by an opposing notion of the dictatorship of the proletariat, for which it is no longer possible to conceive of criteria for assessing its inherently democratic character. The conception of democracy as the only value that is self-legitimated and as the path followed by historical progress allows one to eliminate the fictions of transcendental philosophy, without falling into a relativism of values or taking the position that it is necessary to simply accept one's fate. The notion of the democratically structured community of experimentation and communication as the quintessence of the scientific method makes it possible to abandon the separation between a philosophy that conserves values and an instrumentally curtailed science. The insight into the effects on personality structure of the democratic organization of interpersonal relations makes it possible radically to conceive of the self as socially constituted. It is my impression that access to Mead's thought is best obtained through an understanding of his relationship to the 'categorical' notion of democracy.

These assertions can be developed further through examination of Mead's own views on the history of philosophy and science. In doing this I make use exclusively of his statements about philosophical and scientific developments since the Enlightenment, although a wide range of material on ancient, mediaeval, and early modern philosophy is also available, the last period being represented mainly by Galileo, Descartes and Leibniz.[31] Mead's frequent study of Aristotle appears to have been carried out chiefly for propaedeutic reasons; in Aristotle's writings he found a theory of nature that was free of assumptions considered self-evidently valid by modern thinkers, and that threw precisely these assumptions into clearer relief. Mead's attention was frequently directed to Galileo because he saw in the latter's theories and work some of the sources of the mechanistic view of the world and the subjectification of the question of the meaning of reality which is linked with that world view. Mead's project was to undo this subjectification of meaning. His posthumously published book on the intellectual history of the 19th century does not contain these parts of his work nor his original reconstruction of the controversy between rationalism and empiricism. In this reconstruction he criticized both schools of thought from the standpoint of 'experimentalism', finding fault with them for an insufficient mediation of the particular and the universal, and for a false generalization in each case of a certain phase of experience, of the acquisition of data in the case of empiricism, or of interpretation of data in the case of rationalism.[32] Mead's views on rationalism and empiricism also make it clear that, unlike James, he did not at all consider himself a defender of empiricism, but rather that for him the synthesis of these two philosophical theories by Kant and post-Kantian idealism was of decisive importance.

Although the published material presents, then, only part of Mead's interests and research, it nevertheless illustrates both of the methodological characteristics of his historiography of philosophy. These are, first, strong emphasis on the social-historical contexts to which philosophical and scientific thought is related, and second, constant consideration of the development of the empirical sciences. These are viewed in their connection with the development of social production and as both an object and problem for global philosophical interpretations. The execution of this undertaking, or more exactly the record we have of it – since this consists entirely of students' lecture notes – is admittedly of quite varying quality. That is the reason why this material is used here only to aid in interpreting Mead's position in intellectual history, and not regarded as an area of Mead's research in its own right. In his history of 19th century philosophy, one finds historical mistakes, the assignment of Hegel to Romanticism, which in all likelihood stems from Royce, on whose book on modern philosophy Mead obviously drew,[33] and a superficial discussion of Marx, standing in contrast to thoroughgoing and inspired interpretations like those of Fichte and of Bergson and French philosophy of the 19th century.

In Mead's history of philosophy, Rousseau and Smith appear as the two most important thinkers of the latter part of the 18th century. Rousseau was the first philosopher to escape from the dilemma of having to choose between the unsatisfactory alternatives of pessimistic anthropology, with its tendency toward justifying the 'strong state' and optimistic anthropology with its tendency to naive confidence in the creation of general benefits from the action of numerous separate individuals. He accomplished this by thinking out to its conclusion the possibility of reasonable agreement among human beings. For Rousseau democracy was collective self-determination, the dissolution of dominance, rendered possible by individuals' mutual recognition of one another's rights and by universally binding laws. Again and again Mead has recourse to this rudimentary intersubjectivist notion of right implicit in Rousseau's concept of property. As for Adam Smith, in Mead's opinion he was the first thinker to work out the cooperative association of members of society as the real foundation for their making decisions in common. Despite his criticism of the individualist features of Smith's ideas and of the hedonist psychology to which they gave rise, Mead called the Scottish philosopher's oeuvre 'the source of social psychology'.[34] Mead's critical but openminded consideration of the British utilitarians continued this line of reflection.

Kant, however, whom he held to be the pivotal thinker who alone could make the philosophical problematic of the 19th century comprehensible, was treated by Mead in a manner not at all taken for granted by contemporary American intellectuals. He stressed the roots of Kant's thought in that of Rousseau and candidly bestowed on him the title 'the philosopher of the revolution'. Rousseau's insight into the possibility of rational institutions was transformed by Kant into the question of the conditions for the possibility of universally valid knowledge and the moral orientation of human individuals. Kant finds this universality in the conditions of all cognition, which are inherent in the cognizing subject prior to all experience, and in a pure postulate of free and responsible action, oriented in accordance with generally binding legislation and not directed by the individual's own inclinations.

Mead shared unqualifiedly the universalist orientation of the question Kant posed, but he finds his predecessor's answer to the question unsatisfactory. If the conditions of objective knowledge are to be found in the knowing subject prior to all experience, then they stand outside all communality and precede all development of the human subject. If the basis for the possibility of responsible action cannot be found in reality, and if that possibility remains a pure postulate, then we are in danger of abandoning ourselves permanently to a self-deception. Mead opposed to Kant's transcendental subject the community of acting and communicating human beings. According to Mead's view, knowledge arises from the practical engagement of members of society with an environment that they must reshape, and from their communicative collaboration and exchange of opinions. Knowledge undergoes development in the process of reaching agreement carried out by those collaboratively striving after knowledge, in the process of the individual's education and experience, and in the formation of the foundations of know-

ledge in the human subjects in the course of natural history. Should it
not also be possible to divest the possibility of free action of its
character of a mere postulate by abandoning as one's point of
departure the solitary subject, considered in isolation from all human
community and in abstraction from its interaction with a natural
environment?

It is from this perspective that Mead regards the development of
German idealism beyond Kant's philosophy by Fichte, Schelling
and Hegel. Common to all three, according to Mead, is that they
make the self an object of possible knowledge, of possible experience,
and of genetic development. They thereby go beyond Descartes'
self-experience, which merely gives evidence of the subject's own
existence, and pose the problem of joining Kant's two notions of the
self, the one linked with the structuring of the world in pure reason,
the other with moral action in practical reason:

> What took place in the Romantic period along a philosophical line was
> to take this transcendental unity of apperception, which was for Kant
> a bare logical function, together with the postulation of the self which
> we could not possibly know but which Kant said we could not help
> assuming, and compose them into the new romantic self.[35]

Fichte, says Mead, does this by taking recourse to moral action
and to the development of the self through the internalization of
duties. Schelling, in contrast, shows through examination of aesthetic
activity that the artist does not bring an idea to the material from
without, but instead finds it in the material and in so doing unfolds
himself. Lastly, according to Mead, the theme of Hegel's philosophy
is the reflective overcoming of contradictions in experience and their
final resolution in absolute knowledge. The interpretations of these
three philosophers differ greatly in their fullness and thoroughness.
The best lecture, in my opinion, is the one on Fichte.[36]

Mead argues that Fichte's central concern is to demonstrate
analytically that the constitution of the world is founded in moral
praxis, and that the main problem for Fichte is the question of how
the world, which is independent of the self, can enter into immediate
self-experience. From his discussion of Fichte it becomes clear that
Mead's conception of the situation in which action occurs can in large
measure be elucidated by the German philosopher's theories. Of
critical significance, however, are two theses of Mead's interpretation of Fichte, to which he attaches special importance. The first is

that Fichte shows that the formation of the self – to use a contemporary phrase – is dependent on the objectifications of our praxis, and cannot be achieved through mere introspection that does not lead the subject's attention to the external world.

> One does not get at himself simply by turning upon himself the eye of introspection. One realizes himself in what he does, in the ends which he sets up, and in the means he takes to accomplish those ends. He gets the rational organization out of it, sees a relationship between means and ends, puts it all together as a plan; and then he realizes that the plan of action presented in this situation is an expression of his own reason, of himself. And it is not until one has such a field of action that he does secure himself. This process, according to Fichte, is what is continually taking place. The self throws up the world as a field within which action must take place; and, in setting up the world as a field of action, it realizes itself.[37]

The second thesis is that there is a dialectical relationship between the delimitation of the self and its embeddedness. Fichte develops this dialectic by demonstrating that the constitution of a finite self is possible only within the framework of an overarching unity which has the character of a self; he thereby arrives at his notion of the absolute self. For Mead, this absolute self is analogous to, or is an idealist anticipation of, his own concept of society.

> Now what the philosophical imagination of Fichte did was to go beyond this conception which united man with society, and to conceive of the man as an integral part of the universal Self, that Self which created the universe . . . Now, what Fichte did was to conceive of an Absolute Self which is just such an organization of all selves; an infinite Self which is the organization of all finite selves. Then, just as society sets its tasks in terms of the act of all its members, so this infinite and Absolute Self sets the task for itself in terms of all the functions of all the finite selves that go to make it up. The universe as such is, then, the creation of this Absolute Self in the same sense as cultivated areas and great metropolitan areas are created by the society that lives in them . . . In this view we are all parts of God. We each have a finite part in an infinite creative power. Organized in the one Self we, together with an infinite number of other selves, create the universe. And for Fichte this creation is moral, for he conceives of the world as an obligation, as a task which the Absolute Self has to carry out, has to fulfil.[38]

In Mead's view, Fichte's limitation as an idealist could be seen in his attempt to interpret the evolution of the world as a phase of human moral experience; he failed at the task of conceiving of the evolutionary emergence of human beings from a pre-human age of the world's development.[39] However, his insight into the constructional character of the self, his conception of the moral problems confronting the self, which served as a paradigm for the theory of action, his thesis that self-reflectivity is related to action, the dialectic of individual and collective self contained in his notion of the absolute self, and the relationship of this dialectic to the collective transformation of the world – all of these features of Fichte's philosophy make him an important precursor of a concept of 'practical intersubjectivity', or of a philosophy of praxis that theoretically accounts for intersubjectivity.[40]

The philosophical dignity which Mead accords to the approaches to a theory of evolution in the 19th century, especially to that of Darwin, but to Lamarck's as well, is implied by his criticism of Fichte. The chapter on Schelling is disappointing, as Mead's interpretation of this philosopher focuses on the aesthetic aspect of his thought to the exclusion of all others, and does not develop the significance, for the problems addressed by Mead, of Schelling's attempt to found the concept of self-consciousness in a speculative philosophy of nature. The chapter on Hegel, too, is completely insufficient. The most striking thing about it is the contrast with the subtle understanding of Hegel to be found in Mead's early philosophical writings, to which we will turn our attention shortly. In *Movements of Thought* Hegel is presented as a speculative precursor of evolutionism, inasmuch as he tried to conceive of the categories as developing in the history of the individual human and of humanity. This interpretation of Hegel's thought could have very explosive implications, but appears in a quite clumsy form in this transcription of Mead's lectures. Considering the quality of this text, there would be no point in discussing it in detail. Nevertheless, leaving aside the question of the significance of Mead's presentation of Hegel, the arguments which are central to Mead's critique of Hegel are of interest.

Above all, Mead finds fault with Hegel for not having formulated adequate concepts of the individual and of the future. Hegel's philosophy is thus incapable of grasping individuality in its concreteness, which cannot be decomposed into the relationships dealt with by the philosophy of history. That is exactly the argument which Dilthey, too, benefiting from the empirical historical science of the 19th century, brings into play against the system-building of German idealism. But neither for Dilthey nor for Mead does this criticism of idealism give rise to a sort of existentialist protest. Rather, it led them to undertake investigation of the constitutive role of the individual's experiences and creative accomplishments for society, history and 'objective spirit'.

Mead saw a link between this deficiency in Hegel's philosophy and the latter's inadequate understanding of a history that is open to the future and that is still to be given shape. The American philosopher emphatically refused to accept the notion of absolute knowledge or of an end of history that had been reached, or even one that could only be definitively anticipated. This is an argument that has played an important role from the Left Hegelian critique of Hegel's philosophical system – especially that of Moses Hess – onward to the attempts to formulate a non-scientistic conception of historical materialism,[41] of which Merleau-Ponty's work is an example. However, Mead develops both arguments, not primarily by drawing them from political and social relationships, but rather from his conception of the procedure used by the experimental sciences:

> The grandiose undertaking of Absolute Idealism to bring the whole of reality within experience failed. It failed because it left the perspective of the finite ego hopelessly infected with subjectivity, and consequently unreal. From its point of view, the theoretical and practical life of the individual had no part in the creative advance of nature. It failed also because scientific method, with its achievements of discovery and invention, could find no adequate statement in its dialectic. It recognized the two dominant forces of modern life, the creative individual and creative science, only to abrogate them as falsifications of the experience of the absolute ego. The task remained unfulfilled, the task of restoring to nature the characters and qualities which a metaphysics of mind and a science of matter and motion had concurred in relegating to consciousness, and of finding such a place for mind in nature that nature could appear in experience.[42]

Thus, in the philosophies of the three chief representatives of post-Kantian German idealism, the realization of the self by means of the non-self and the problem of the self-reflectivity of the actor were given central importance, while Schelling and Hegel, in addition, put the transcendental problematic of consciousness back into the world that is to be known. All this was done, however, by clinging ultimately to a process of consciousness conceived of in the manner of transcendental philosophy, and not by actually abandoning the use of the consciousness of the solitary subject as the final basis for their lines of argument.[43] As a consequence of this approach, it became impossible for these philosophers to answer certain central questions. The question of how individual perspectives could be combined into a common one was supplanted by the fiction of a divinely absolute self that occupied completely the place in these philosophers' systems that otherwise would have been given over to the decision-making of communities. The question of the historical conditions of cognition which are independent of cognition was not posed, since history and even natural history had now to be interpreted using the categories of aesthetic creation or reflection, or the categories applicable to matters of obligation. The question of the openness and plasticity of the future was eliminated, since now absolute knowledge and the supposition of an end of history would clear away uncertainty and empirical science would become a subordinate component of knowledge.

In order to overcome these aporiae Mead does not turn for help to the Left Hegelians, who seem to have been completely unknown to him, and hence also not to Marx. The presentation of the latter's thought, which obviously has only a narrow textual basis, in particular the *Communist Manifesto*, is a delineation of the Kautskyian 'Marxism' of the period of the Second International, rather than of the analyses and theories of Marx himself. Mead's emphasis on Marx's proximity to Hegel signifies that he imputes to both of them a quasi-religious philosophy of history that is deterministic in its certainty of history's goal, and a repressive tendency to subordinate the individual to the claims of the collective body. What Mead opposes to these positions can be described approximately as an anti-bureaucratic and impassioned argument for the possibility of self-determination by the producers in a society, and is indeed much closer to authentic Marxism than Mead knew. This is certainly due to the state of knowledge of Marx's works at that time: aside from Lukács's brilliant anticipation, in *History and Class Consciousness*, of a new view on Marx, Marx's philosophical relevance became apparent only with the publication of Marx's principal early writings towards the end of the twenties. Be that as it may, Mead had complete sympathy with the universalist features of a class-conscious movement of the international proletariat as a class.[44] He held Marxism to be one of the fundamental elements of truly modern thought, along with German and British neo-Hegelianism, that of T. H. Green, for example, or of F. H. Bradley, with its stress on the individual, and along with the scientific turn given to the questions of mind in physiological psychology.[45]

For Mead, though, the key figure for a new beginning in philosophy was Darwin. Darwin's model of an organism in an environment, to which it must adapt in order to survive, provides the means for founding all knowledge in behaviour and all behaviour in the necessary conditions set by nature on the organism's reproduction of itself and its kind, in contrast to the attempt to deduce the subject's behaviour and the external world from a self that is preordinate to them. Darwin's theory about the origin of species offered an escape from the dilemma of the alternative mechanistic and teleological explanations of evolution, since his theory emphasizes, anti-mechanistically, the possibility of qualitatively new forms of organisms, without having to take recourse to an immutable teleological principle that precedes and governs all history.

For Mead, and for pragmatism in its entirety, Darwin's theory was not at all decisive proof of a deterministic view of evolution and adaptation, in the manner either of a psychology of instincts or of Social Darwinism. Instead, the pragmatists undertook to conceive of the basic structure of animals' adaptive accomplishments as a primitive analogue to the intelligent behaviour of human beings and to the procedure of the experimental sciences, and to take care in doing so that they did not efface the differences between them. In the pragmatists' opinion, these differences lay in the structure of human material reproduction, which is based on a system of impulses different from that of other kinds of organism, and which becomes, by means of the active reshaping of the environment, the self-reflective control of the principles of organic evolution and liberation from their dominion.

In the synthesis that Mead sought to achieve there can be seen the outlines of a theory of society which takes into account both the natural basis of human sociality as well as the concrete forms that human societies have historically taken and the role of the unique individual. In Mead's later writings, all of these various efforts fall under the hegemony of his concern not to allow stress on the particular individual to result in the elimination of objectivity and universality, but rather to arrive at an understanding of it as the true precondition of the latter. In Mead's thought this enterprise primarily assumed the forms of a philosophy of nature and of a theory of science. It was because of their relevance to this undertaking that Whitehead's work and the discussion of the theory of relativity became important for Mead. He formulated this task in the following words:

> Stating it in as broad a form as I can, this is the philosophical problem that faces the community at the present time: how are we to get the universality involved, the general statement which must go with any interpretation of the world, and still make use of the differences which belong to the individual as an individual?[46]

Mead's early philosophical writings, that is the texts prior to 'The Definition of the Psychical', published in 1903, have a strongly programmatic character and are linked to their quite accidental provenance: most of them are book reviews. The single exception is perhaps 'Suggestions Toward a Theory of the Philosophical Disciplines', which appeared in 1900. Thus, they are chiefly useful here because they reveal the circumstances in which Mead's later ideas had their origin. In addition, in my examination of Mead's intellectual development, they also serve to document my thesis that Mead went through a Hegelian phase before he founded his intersubjectivist pragmatism.

When I say that Mead went through a Hegelian phase, I do not mean that he specialized in philosophical studies about Hegel, or that he elaborated a position with regard to Hegel's work which was carefully considered in all its details. Rather, my statement repeats a self-characterization by Mead, the meaning of which must be correctly understood if we are to appreciate its significance. The claim that Hegel was important for Mead of course appears incredible and absurd to those who are accustomed to regard Mead as a social behaviourist.[47] But for Mead's students this was by no means the case; Sidney Hook, for example, in a review of *Movements of Thought*, bluntly stated that Mead was 'out of the school of Hegel'.[48] Mead's retrospective remarks on Royce and Dewey show how strongly the liberation from the dualism of subject and object, of matter and mind, of the divine and the human, which Hegel offered, and which Royce and Dewey had stressed, had also influenced him.[49] The form taken by this influence is shown by Mead's early writings.

Admittedly, the first two do not contribute much in this respect. They are short articles on the attempt by Kurt Lasswitz, a German neo-Kantian theoretician of the natural sciences and historian of natural philosophy, to draw the epistemological implications from the theory of energy proposed by the physics of the latter half of the 19th century.[50] The first of Mead's articles is more of a summary of Lasswitz's book; the second develops its psychological implications. From these articles it becomes clear why Mead was interested in Lasswitz's undertaking. According to Lasswitz, the theory of energy put forward by contemporary physics advanced beyond the model of the earlier physics, for which mechanics was the ultimate basis of explanation, and thus presented a 'critical theory of experience' – the expression is Lasswitz's – with new opportunities and new problems. Lasswitz is referring to the question of the constitution of science in immediate experience, and the question of the relationship between qualitative sensory experience and the quantifying treatment of this experience by physics.

In his articles on this book, Mead does not develop positions of his own, but he does announce themes and points of view that run through his own work. One example is the question of an adequate understanding of the unifying function of the self, the question of a psychological reformulation of Kant's transcendental unity of ap-perception. Other examples are the attempt to define, for the first time, the concept of the object in categories of action, and to this end to investigate the coordination of the contact senses and those which perceive objects at a distance, and Mead's insistence that qualities are not merely subjective in character, in contrast to the ostensibly objective character of quantities. However, perhaps most important is the passage in which Mead clearly states that the absurdity of a psychology modelled on physics can be demonstrated with the aid of a theory of the constitution of science.

In a word, the physicist has abstracted the entire mathematically statable content of the sensation – and only this; and for the psycho-physicist to strive to use that which is left for the same purpose is to make it evident that he does not comprehend the relations of the two fields. We trust with Herr Lasswitz that the substitution of energy for mass in the physicist's statement will carry home the nature of the scientist's abstraction.[51]

Thus reductionist psychology and natural sciences that have forgotten how they are constituted are considered as two sides of a single development, the development that Husserl would later call the 'crisis of the European sciences'. Mead's articles on Lasswitz show how inconceivable it would be to classify him as the proponent of a reductionist psychology.[52]

The next article by Mead is a discussion of a book by the German neo-idealist Gustav Class that appeared in 1896, entitled *Toward a Phenomenology and Ontology of the Human Mind (Untersuchungen zur Phänomenologie und Ontologie des menschlichen Geistes)*. Class programmatically undertook to achieve a synthesis of Hegel's notion of the 'objective spirit' and Schleiermacher's concept of 'personal individuality' *(persönliche Eigentümlichkeit)*. Hegel's 'objective spirit' represents recognition of the dependence of the mental life of human individuals on cultural formations, on the objectifications of their activity. Schleiermacher's concept, however, demands that the human individual be understood not only as an example of the species, but rather that 'every man shall present humanity in his own peculiar manner'.[53] Schleiermacher's concept thus contains a claim to the right of individuation that was far in advance of his time, and that, in Mead's view, had to be matched by a theory of the social formation of the self. The conceptual means for elaborating this theory, wrote Mead, have been provided by Hegel, whose 'method' could be fully restated and applied to the entire content of life only upon the basis of the revelation of processes of development that had been made by the modern physical, biological, and social sciences. Only when every substance-centred metaphysics has been rejected, and one has attained the notion of 'organic activity', is it possible to form a conception of how 'the individual can be completely individualized and yet present simply the whole'.[54]

It is very characteristic of Mead that he links here the speculative notion of life, which underlies Hegel's statements, with the biological concept of life. In his review of Class's book, Mead places the problem of a social conception of the self, formulated in philosophical terms, in the context of the religious and political problematic of his era. He regards the notion of the soul, or personality, as an unchanging substantial entity to be a serious obstacle to solving this problem, since this notion is drawn from the assumption of an exclusive relationship of the individual to the Deity, beyond the individual's fellow human beings and his natural environment.

> To such an individual all the social relationships here can be only of a purely superficial character except in so far as they react upon a nature [i.e. the God-given nature of the individual, (H.J.)] that is independent of them. It would be impossible to regard such a nature as the expression of the social relationships within which it finds itself. There would be no meaning in arousing a consciousness of these relations as the essence of the self. The most that could take place would be a judgement from without as to our duty with reference to them. But if I am not mistaken the tendency not only of our social sciences but also of the forces of society itself is to substitute in the individual a vivid immediate consciousness of himself as a nodal point in the operation of these social forces, for the conception of an individual who stands outside of the processes and enters in or strays out as his conscience dictates or his desires demand.[55]

As a political example of the point he is arguing in the passage quoted, Mead gives the right of the workers to form labour unions, a hotly debated topic in the USA in that period. He sees no merit in the objection that unions destroy the worker's independence; rather, he regards them as a means to a new and more profound individuality. The development of the individual personality is only possible through extension and intensification of social relations; 'personality is an *achievement* rather than a given fact'.[56] Mead criticizes Class for merely postulating individualities and the formation of the self and not being able to ground them scientifically. Class's inability to do so, says Mead, making an implicit reference to his own philosophical programme, lies in the fact that he incorrectly distinguished between a realm of mere facts *(das Tatsächliche)* and a realm of the spiritual, or that which expressed the meaning of the world *(das Sachliche)*. To be sure, Class conceives of the spiritual itself as pragmatic, that is in its function as the universalization of the particular, but he forcibly separates this universalization from all that is material or belongs to nature. This means that there is a gaping chasm between material civilization and the cultural conditions of individuation, as though the two had nothing in common, instead of individuation being firmly attached to and having its roots in the social structure of human beings' material reproduction. From his discussion of Class's book it becomes clear that Mead hoped that non-reductionist psychology, based on physiology, would provide just this theoretical mooring for his conception of the formation of the self.

The programmatic joining of Hegel's thought with that of Schlei-ermacher, which is suggestive of Dilthey's philosophical enter-prise, anticipates in some respects Mead's theory of the social formation of the self. However, Mead's detailed discussion of the interpretation and critique of Hegel given by the British theologian Charles F. D'Arcy in his book, *Idealism and Theology*, provides a still deeper insight into the roots of Mead's social psychology. D'Arcy's book is a strange attempt to combine the philosophies of Hegel and Berkeley: he conceives of a Hegelian subject-object-world that is itself held together in a higher subjectivity; as this subjectivity he posits the triune God who can be reached through an act of faith. This book appears to have been not only a provocation to Mead's secularized Hegelianism, but also to have raised the question of the point in Hegel's philosophy, or in the interpretation of that philos-ophy, which would provide the starting point for D'Arcy's theory. At first it seems that D'Arcy's concerns are identical with those of British neo-Hegelians, inasmuch as these, too, were always talking about the irreducibility of the individual. Mead, however, quickly shows that, in the case of D'Arcy, this irreducibility of the individual is limited to the postulation of the individual personality as the source of the contingent, the arbitrary, the bad. To Mead's way of thinking though, this is not enough to keep the concept of personality from being an Hegelian abstraction. Underlying D'Arcy's notion of the individual personality is, says Mead, more the 18th century's individualist concept of the person, which isolated the individual from society, than Hegel's. And if D'Arcy's book has not even reached the conceptual level of Hegel's thought, then it can hardly go beyond it. The question is, rather, how that which is individual can be 'saved' by demonstrating its positive functions, its necessity for the community.

> The problem, then, comes to this: Is it possible to express the positive element in personality in terms of rationality, law, and goodness? I think the author is right in identifying the problem with the question of chasm between individuals. The freedom of the will is not a problem of the spiritual economy of an isolated individual, it is the problem of fixing responsibility within a community of individuals

who isolate themselves in certain phases of their conduct. It is a social, not an individual, problem . . . It is the working together of individuals, the mutual dependence which is involved in the social ends and means, that presents the something which always resists the complete necessary formulation of our world. Finally, the problem of evil is not one of its existence or its reality, but of its social significance, and the possibility and duty of overcoming it. If the self is in its reflective processes isolated, there is no solution of these problems possible. No such individual can fix responsibility upon another or accept it when fixed by another. If the means and ends are not identical, there can be no community in meeting the problems of social existence. If the suffering of another is not a reality in my own world and is not identified with myself, there is no possibility of giving to the instinctive reaction against it the large social meaning and value which we feel it should have. The chasms between individuals in a social consciousness represent, not insoluble epistemological problems, but points at which reorganization needs to take place.[57]

In what respects then does D'Arcy fail to understand Hegel? First, by maintaining that individuality manifests itself in an impassable chasm and irreducible alienness between individuals. D'Arcy tries to admit the possibility of objective knowledge of nature, but to deny that knowledge of other persons, and hence the social sciences, can be rational to the same degree. Mead argues against any possibility of making this distinction, since the claim that there can be objectively valid knowledge originally has nothing at all to do with the kind of object which is to be known. A more serious objection, though, is that D'Arcy's thesis flagrantly contradicts our immediate experience, in which other persons are more certain than physical things are.

There is nothing more immediate than the personalities of our fellows. There is nothing so clearly conceived, so distinctly thought out, as those elements of our world. We depend as surely upon the rational organization of the social world as upon that of the material, and there is the same source for this rational organization as subsists for the world of the physical sciences.[58]

Mead's insistence on a unitary and uncurtailed notion of rationality, his acknowledgement of a chasm between individuals as a social fact and as a practical task, and his refusal to accept this chasm as humanity's ineluctable metaphysical fate – these all show how well pondered the foundations of his social psychology are. However, the manner of his critique of the English theologian's work makes it clear that he is still far from carrying out the project of a theory of the social formation of the self and from demonstrating the primacy of the constitution of social objects over that of physical objects.

For Mead, the way to the realization of this programme seems to be offered by the Hegelian 'method', and his second principal criticism of D'Arcy is that the latter has completely failed to comprehend the character of this method. D'Arcy understands Hegel's philosophy as a metaphysical system that substitutes the category of the subject for that of substance. What D'Arcy does not grasp is that this transformation precludes a metaphysics of fundamental entities and makes philosophy a method of thought. Mead shows his understanding of Hegel's procedure in his interpretation of the situation in which a moral decision is made and that in which a new thought is developed. In both cases the problem is solved by a synthesis, which the individual must constructively and creatively effect, and which philosophy must reconstructively match in an analogous act. Entities are formulations of certain stages of this process; they must not be considered separately from the process of reflection that constitutes them. To Mead, Hegel's dialectical method was a discovery, the significance of which Hegel himself did not fully understand, and one which reveals that the procedure of the experimental sciences, correctly understood, is the fundamental structure of human reflection in its highest form. For Mead, therefore, the pragmatist interpretation of the situation of action and Hegel's dialectic of reflection converge. Philosophy, then, is

> not a formulation of entities . . . not in search of being, but is a statement of the method by which the self in its full cognitive and social content meets and solves its difficulties.[59]

The most ambitious and most systematic of Mead's early writings is his attempt to establish a classification of the philosophical disciplines, published in 1900. In this article Mead undertakes nothing less than laying the groundwork for a new logic in the sense in which Hegel used this term, that is, a theory encompassing all of the fundamental determinations of thought. Going beyond Hegel, Mead projects this new logic as a general theory of intelligent action. He bases his undertaking on Dewey's essay about the reflex-arc concept, in which the latter construes all thought as an attempt to solve problems in immediate experience, and more specifically in situations of action. It would be inappropriate to discuss this thesis here in detail, since Mead does not defend it, but only presupposes it in this text. The comprehensive 'logic' is, then, the theory of the reconstruction of objects, the validity of which has been made uncertain, and Mead seeks to assign to each of the philosophical disciplines its own particular origin in the action-situation. Metaphysics is not rejected as meaningless, in the manner of positivism, but instead has the role of the keeper of problems which cannot be solved at the present time.

> Metaphysics I wish to identify with the statement of the problem. It may take psychological form or not. If the result of the recognition of the problem is only to bring to consciousness the meaning of the object in terms of past experience, we get the universal – the ideal – and the use of the object thus defined can be systematized in a manner which is described in deductive logic. If, on the contrary, we abandon the old universals – the interpretations involved in the objects as we have constructed them – and frankly look forward to a new meaning, the immediate experience can claim only subjective validity, and we have the subject matter with which psychology deals. The use of this material to reach the new universal is evidently the procedure of inductive logic. The application of either of these methods to conduct as a whole, in their relation to the ideal or to the larger self to be attained, fulfils the function of ethics, while aesthetics deals with the artistic representations of the object either as ideal or as a phase in the process of development. Finally, the general theory of the intelligent act as a whole would fall within that of logic as treated in works such as that of Hegel.[60]

What this formulation contains in condensed form is developed in the course of the article. Mead's interpretation of deduction and induction from the perspective of the theory of action – reminiscent of Piaget's interpretation of deduction as a correlate of accommodation and of induction as correlative of assimilation[61] – or his interpretation of aesthetics as the field of activity in which unresolvable contradictions or unattained goals are expressed in given objects – these must be particularly stressed as original and as indicating fruitful lines of reflection. However, one can sense that, in addition to the principle of his general theory of intelligent action,

Mead is primarily concerned in this article with one phase of the act and with one of the philosophical disciplines: with the psychical and with psychology, which he still understands as a philosophical discipline here. These he treats at remarkable length. By the psychical Mead means that phase of the act in which hypotheses are formed, in which the old validities of objects have become uncertain and new ones have not yet established themselves; in which a free play of subjectivity is necessary for the origination of new hypotheses. What Peirce discussed as 'abduction' in his logic of scientific research and placed alongside deduction and induction, becomes the 'psychical' in Mead's refounding of pragmatism as a theory based on the biological and social sciences. Mead does not draw here upon Peirce, though, but only on Dewey's psychology, and, with respect to the logic of scientific research, also on Whewell, whom Peirce, too, held in high esteem.[62]

In opposition to a simplifying interpretation of the psychical as merely intensified attentiveness, Mead stresses that the critical characteristic of this phase of the act consists in the fact that here attention is not directed to objects whose validity is recognized, but instead to the generating of such validity. From this sketchily presented notion of the psychical Mead develops a critique of the received form of the elementarist and associationalist psychology, derived from empiricism. This critique leads him to a train of thought, already implicit in the articles on Lasswitz, and its conclusion that a physicalist reduction of human perception does not solve the real problem of comprehending the givenness of the world for perceiving subjects, but rather bars the way to its solution.

> Parallelism is pure epistemology, and does not get within the realm of the psychical. The distinction between the immediate content of the world of perception, and the physical theory of these perceptions, does not touch that distinction which lies between the world of unquestioned validity, and the state of consciousness which supervenes when it has lost that validity and there is nothing left but the subjectivity out of which a new world may arise.[63]

Psychology is thus divided into two fields, each with a different task: into the theory of the constitution of experience, which Mead understands in the sense of the analyses undertaken by Kant and continued by Hegel in his *Phenomenology of Mind*; and into the analysis of the psychical situation which is prototypically represented by William James's examination of the stream of consciousness.

The significance of Mead's internally consistent attempt to elaborate a pragmatist classification of the philosophical disciplines has to date remained completely unrecognized, especially as it contrasts with Peirce's efforts late in his philosophical career to establish a hierarchy of the philosophical disciplines, and with the danger that these efforts might require for their basis a 'phenomenology' that Peirce's initial premises make wholly impossible. It appears that Mead did not pursue this project further in this form. His interest turned to the notion of the psychical and to the grounding of psychology in a comprehensive theory of action. What he developed in a rudimentary fashion in 'Suggestions Toward a Theory of the Philosophical Disciplines' in 1900, Mead soon dealt with again more thoroughly and comprehensively in 'The Definition of the Psychical'. With this paper Mead's mature work begins.

4

The Definition of the Psychical

Mead's article 'The Definition of the Psychical' is certainly his most significant work prior to the development of his fundamental premises for a theory of interaction and a social psychology.[1] Moreover, it is one of the most concentrated and intensive investigations which Mead himself ever prepared for publication. Yet this work remains almost entirely unknown. Appearing in 1903 in a somewhat obscure publication – a commemorative volume marking the University of Chicago's tenth year of existence – the article elicited hardly any response from the contemporary scholarly community and to the present day has never been reprinted in its entirety.[2] Even in the circles of functionalist psychologists, to which Mead considered himself to belong at that time, and one of whose spokesmen he was,[3] a text that pointed out, with extreme philosophical radicalism, the necessity of reflecting on the object of psychology in general before engaging in psychological studies, and that was thus directed to the definition of the psychical, was clearly in large measure incomprehensible. That seems to have been the case even for Mead's friend and colleague, John Dewey, whose comment to William James on the article betrays some perplexity.[4] This is in spite of the fact that Dewey's critique of the reflex-arc model,[5] published in 1896, had given the impetus to and been the point of departure for Mead's arguments. In 1910, when Mead was already distancing himself from functionalist psychology because of its tendencies to lapse back into psycho-physical parallelism, he looked back with self-irony on the probably somewhat 'obscure and ineffectual' character of his exposition.[6]

It cannot be claimed that matters have improved in this regard since then. Without exception, the literature on Mead does not discuss 'The Definition of the Psychical'. Among the authors of shorter studies of Mead, only Gary Allan Cook has asserted in three articles that,[7] as a matter of principle, Mead's work must be understood with the aid of the guiding thread provided by his early writings, and not retrospectively from the standpoint of a meta-physical interpretation of his late writings. Up to now there has literally not been a single interpretation of this important, although certainly difficult text.

In the above-mentioned retrospective commentary, Mead himself stated that the purpose of the exposition given in this article was to demonstrate that 'psychical consciousness' should not be conceived of as a substance or sphere *sui generis* corresponding to the external world in a parallel way, but rather that it is 'a particular phase in development of reality'.[8] In other words, what Mead undertook in this article was a critique of all forms of mentalistic psychology of consciousness and their apparent objective supersession by psycho-physical parallelism. In contrast to these, Mead envisaged a conception of consciousness which would define the psychical in its functionality within objective reality, without falling prey to the dangers of reductionism. In order to make the nature of the problem and the attempted solution fully understandable, it is necessary to sketch the context of Mead's analysis in the history of psychology and philosophy.

Mead's article belongs to a transitional phase in this history. The acceptance of psychology as a science of the facts of consciousness and the dominance of introspective methods of psychological research associated with that conception of psychology had been shaken. Watson's behaviourist 'psychology without consciousness', and the predominance of experimental research methods that excluded the understanding of meaning had not yet been established. It is quite unjust to regard the theoretical endeavours of this period of transition – as is often done – merely as degenerate forms of the mentalistic psychology of consciousness or as inconsistent precursors of behaviourism. For during this period many attempts were made to overcome in a fundamental manner the mind-body dualism implicit under various guises in the received theoretical pseudo-alternatives. In the field of the mentalistic psychology of consciousness, on the one hand, both Wundt's 'voluntaristic' psychology and the 'psychology of acts of consciousness' elaborated by Franz Brentano, Husserl's teacher, with its concept of intentionality, made advances towards overcoming the atomism and the elementarism of received empiricist psychology, deficient though the form taken by these advances may have been. On the other hand, the influence of Darwinism on psychology offered the opportunity of liberating physiological psychology from reductionist tendencies by making it possible to relate consciousness and the psychical to the organism and to its behaviour in an environment and to recognize their biological significance.

Thus in many ways, and with additional support from the persuasive philosophical critiques of empiricism then being made by pragmatists and neo-idealists, an effort was made completely to redefine the psychical and the appropriate method for investigating it. In American psychology the most productive attempt proved at first to be that of the functionalist school.[9]

Dewey's article 'The Reflex Arc Concept in Psychology' can be considered the manifesto marking the founding of this school. In this paper Dewey makes a devastating critique of a psychology that believes it has found its goal in the apprehension of causal, law-like relations between stimuli and responses. Stimuli are understood by this psychology as independent variables which trigger in the organism a determinate instinctive or acquired processing and a motor discharge that is a consequence of this processing. Taking this view, external stimulus, internal processing, and external response appear as independent entities, clearly delimited from one another. Dewey finds no part of this model convincing. In the external distinctions between stimulus and response, or between stimulus and internal processing of the stimulus, he sees the old separations of body and soul (or mind), of sensations and ideas (or mental presentations). He denies that stimuli and responses exist at all in their specific qualities, without having been previously constituted as parts of a unitary action. According to the reflex-arc model, an action is composed additively from its phases. In contrast, according to Dewey, unless we make an anticipatory judgement about the action in which stimuli and responses are joined together, we can speak only of a temporal succession and not of the causal relation implied by the stimulus-response model.

Dewey demonstrates that the action as a whole precedes the discrimination of stimuli and responses by showing how crucial phenomena of perception cannot be accounted for by the stimulus-response model. He stresses the active character of perception, which first makes a selection among stimuli, rather than being passively subject to them; the directing of attention by the character of an action; and sensitization with respect to certain stimuli and the dulling of sensitivity for others. Underlying these assertions is the assumption that perception, too, is action, and is a part of a more comprehensive action-nexus. As his next step, Dewey demonstrates through an examination of learning phenomena that learning cannot be understood as simply the substitution of new stimuli for ones previously experienced and retained, but rather, it must be conceived of as the incorporation of new experiences into previously elaborated or acquired action-schemata.

Dewey comes to the conclusion that the expression 'reflex arc' is unsuitable in both its parts and proposes that it be replaced with the concept of the 'organic circuit'. In this conception of action, the elements differentiated in the reflex-arc model can no longer be discerned as fixed entities, but instead as functional distinctions. The question of when the functionality of these distinctions appears, when one can meaningfully decompose the unity of an action into its components, leads Dewey finally to an idea with far-reaching implications, namely that the internal parts of a unitary action are seen as segmented only when the performance of the action is interrupted. We become aware of sensation as external stimulus when its character is unknown; and we become aware of the necessity of a reaction as such only when we do *not* know how we should react. In the case of actions which are executed without interruption, the actor himself cannot meaningfully speak of stimuli and responses; only an external observer is able to interpret these concepts into the action. For this procedure Dewey coined the term 'psychological fallacy,' since positing and analysing consciousness precisely where it cannot exist for the actor is, in his opinion, the constitutive fallacy of the psychology which had to be refuted and supplanted.

It would be completely wrong to consider Dewey's article, with its wealth of ideas, as antiquated because the crude forms of stimulus-response determinism such as Dewey attacked, and as they found full expression in the behaviourism that was to come only later, are today increasingly less seriously advocated. Its continuing relevance also does not lie simply in the fact that Dewey, by intimately linking 'perception' and 'movement', succeeded in anticipating scientific advances of this century: the principle of reafference in biology,[10] and the anthropological approaches, presented in different conceptual forms, to explain perception and movement as two aspects of action, namely those of Piaget ('sensory-motor assimilation schemata'), of Gehlen ('elementary circular processes'), of Merleau-Ponty ('circular causality'), and of von Weizsäcker ('Gestalt circle').[11] Of even greater importance for the larger perspectives in which these scientific advances are to be seen is the fact that Dewey's critique of contemporary psychology and his suggestions for the further development of that discipline result from his concept of *action*, and that this concept of action is clearly taken from ethics, transposed into logic, interpreted in the context of organismic life-functions, and thus made useful for answering the question of how psychology is constituted.

Indications of the recognition of these connections found early expression in the writings of the father of pragmatism, Charles Peirce.[12] Here the mere mention of these connections suffices to make clear that the topic of Mead's article does not have to do only with psychology, but ultimately is concerned with the logical position of subjectivity, with its general philosophical definition.

This is also the question with which Mead introduces his exposition of the 'definition of the psychical'. To the relative clarity of the concept of 'objectivity' he opposes the complicated history and current polysemy of the concept of 'subjectivity'. Mead's definition of objectivity is derived from action: Objectivity is that which stands the test of action, that which – to give a very crude formulation – allows an action to be successfully performed.[13] While this definition is, from the standpoint of philosophy, relatively non-controversial, since it presents itself as an obvious implication of practical action, the concept of 'subjectivity' has been defined in quite different ways. Its function as the conceptual opposite of objectivity confers on it a more precise meaning only against the particular background of the analysis of how subjective consciousness attains objective truth. For all the various definitions of subjectivity contain as a common element reference to the individual: . . . 'the subjective is that which is identified with the consciousness of the individual *qua* individual'.[14] However, this assertion does not suffice to delimit clearly a field of investigation:

> As subjectivity refers to the consciousness of the individual, and as the phase of consciousness which is peculiar to [the (H. J.)] individual as

such is generally placed within the process of reflection, the definition of subjectivity will depend upon the function which a theory of logic ascribes to the individual consciousness in the formation of the judgement.[15]

It is important to note at first that Mead does in fact insist upon clarification of this question. He directs his attack against the objectivist understanding of psychology, whose adherents naively conceive the object of psychology to be given in reality and do not reflect on the process of abstraction by which only this object is produced.

'The Definition of the Psychical' can be described as *an attempt to introduce into the constitution of scientific psychology an unabridged notion of subjectivity*. Mead's critique is aimed at the different forms of such an endeavour. As a critique, Mead's paper can be compared in its reflective profundity and the sharpness with which the problem is formulated with only one contemporary counterpart: Husserl's critique of objectivist psychology (for example, in *Philosophy as Rigorous Science*).[16] As similar in some respects as the two critiques are, they differ quite markedly in their attempts to solve the problem and in the suggestions they make for changing psychology. Although it cannot be denied that Mead's study has the form of a philosophical reflection on a fundamental scientific problem, his concern is precisely not to abandon subjectivity to a philosophical (or 'phenomenological') psychology which is different from scientific psychology, and which has its own methodology and apriorist, 'eidetic' or transcendentalist claims. Rather his aim is to argue compellingly that the investigation of subjectivity can be made completely the concern of the empirical biological and social sciences. Although Mead and Husserl are in agreement that the psychical, unlike a natural object, does not exist independently of a subject, but is rather linked to the self and bound to the moment, they part company in the questions they are led to pose by this postulate.[17] For his part, Mead asks: what is the function of such a phase of consciousness within action in a common world? His arguments offer a continuous stream of objections to the phenomenological enterprise.[18]

With what positions does Mead take issue in his endeavour to define the psychical, and what is the still valid and relevant significance of this controversy? Among the positions criticized and mutually related to one another, pride of place falls to the theory of Wilhelm Wundt, to whom the discussion also repeatedly returns.[19]

In his postulation of 'two points of view' or of '*two types of experience*', Wundt made an attempt to escape from the dualistic conception of psychology as a science based on inner experience, in contrast to the natural sciences which are founded on external experience, by defining the subject's total experience and the content of that experience as psychical. The effect of this measure is to make the question of how the object of psychology is constituted appear superfluous and meaningless, since psychology is thus presented as the science that has its object immediately given, as, in Wundt's words, the 'immediate science'. In contrast to psychology, the natural sciences are merely 'mediate sciences', since they only arise through a process of abstraction from the same experience that provides psychology's object, by means of logical correction of experience and by means of the construction of concepts. But the assertion that the object of psychology is immediately given cannot be meant with complete literalness, for Mead is able to cite passages from Wundt's works in which the latter says that the physical sciences and psychology are two different kinds of abstraction, two possible points of view of the same unitary experience. Just what these statements mean, however, becomes clearer only when one does not consider solely the definition of the realms of different scientific disciplines, but in addition the determination of the function of subjectivity underlying that definition.

For Wundt, there exists a sphere of original subjectivity, comprehending the emotions and volition. Alongside this original subjectivity there is also a mediated or derived subjectivity which arises when contradictions appear in the mental presentations representing the object-world; then, on the one hand, conceptual objects are constructed, while on the other hand the mental presentations, which have been understood to be 'merely subjective', are not simply destroyed, but rather employed further as sensuous representations of the content of the concepts constructed, as symbols for concepts. Psychology thus has two kinds of objects: the originarily subjective one and the content remaining as a residue of the processes of abstraction. Mead's critique is directed against this doubling of the psychical; in his opinion, this doubling does not accomplish the overcoming of the dualism of body and psyche promised by Wundt, but instead only transposes it onto another plane.[20]

Mead subsequently identifies as the causes of this deficiency

Wundt's insufficient concept of reconstruction and an empiricist self-deception about the character of his voluntaristic psychology. Wundt fails to develop a sufficient concept of reconstruction because he assumes that the form of the content of an object of a mental presentation can be preserved when its validity has been lost: 'He denies the mutual dependence of the validity and the form of the content'.[21] Wundt thus does not recognize that a genuine problem arising in the course of an action does not leave unaffected in subjective experience the qualities of the object which has been called into question, that such a problem, rather, is just what makes it necessary creatively to recompose the lost certainty about the character of the object out of the certitudes which are still at the actor's disposal. Wundt falls victim to an empiricist self-deception, inasmuch as he introduces the concept of volition but treats this concept as an immediately psychical given. To this Mead replies:

> . . . instead of the presentation becoming psychical by being withdrawn into the field of the unquestioned subjectivity of the will and the emotions, the will and the emotions have received psychological treatment in so far as they have been drawn or withdrawn into the field of the presentations.[22]

The implication of Mead's observation is that the givenness of the will in consciousness raises the question of its constitution just as much as do all other data of consciousness. A first conclusion yielded by Mead's critique of Wundt is, then, that mind-body dualism can be successfully overcome only if the constitutive and reconstructive character of subjectivity is taken seriously.

Before this point can be pursued further, the question must be asked whether this dualism could not be supplanted more simply – at least for the purposes of science, if not for those of 'metaphysics' – by psycho-physical materialism. Mead discusses this possibility primarily with reference to the writings of Oswald Külpe, whose treatment by Mead does not, as the latter very well knew, do justice to all the ramifications of his thought. Rather, Külpe serves merely as the representative of a possible position.[23] This position conceives of subjectivity as dependence of facts of experience on the corporeality of individuals. The fact that a physiological correspondence to psychical processes cannot be denied serves here to justify construing the physiological processes as the true reality and declaring the object of psychology to be what corresponds to such processes. Certainly, the way is thereby opened for a science that is clear in the definition of its object, and that proceeds objectively and experimentally. The question, though, is whether the definition of subjectivity given is at all possible, whether the assumed function of the psychical is at all conceivable.

Mead examines this question by using as his example the problem of the 'error of observation'. He asks whether the individual variation of measurement expressed in the error of observation can itself be made into an object of study by the natural sciences. If this is the case, then the psychical and the subjective are only inadequate stopgap aids temporarily useful to an insufficiently developed natural science. If this is not the case, then a simple extension of the natural sciences does not suffice for the investigation of the subjective and the psychical, and the different structure of this other object-field must be taken into account in its specificity. Now, for psycho-physical materialism it is a given that the individual variations of measurement can be made an object of study by the natural sciences. Mead formulates this position very graphically:

> From this scientific standpoint the animal organism is simply a fearfully and wonderfully complicated piece of apparatus whose numerous mean variations must be determined.[24]

When all psychical processes have been translated into physiological ones, then

> . . . it is evident that we have reduced this mechanism to the level of the apparatus and theoretically can determine not only the accuracy of the observation but also of the scientific reasoning.[25]

This apparatus could be ignored, if perception offered complete objectivity. The psychical is an object of scientific interest for psycho-physical materialism merely because the universe is mirrored only imperfectly in the individual.

In order to refute this attenuation of subjectivity to a remnant of individual perceptions in science that cannot yet be eliminated, Mead introduces the important distinction between three planes of perception: the plane of the physical interaction of things and sense organs, the plane of everyday perception with reference to meaning, and that of the scientific registration of data. This distinction suggests that the reduction of ordinary, everyday perception to its physiological bases is itself a scientific construct, which bypasses clarification of the proper structure of this perception, and is unable to explain just what its function is. Later in this article – and in many subsequent writings – Mead takes up again the thesis that sense-experience is the basis of all science.[26] If this is true, then physiological reductionism can be warded off, while the relationship of the psychical to the organism can be preserved by the very question that reductionism cannot answer, namely, what is the function of the psychical. Thus Mead's critical examination of Wundt's and Külpe's positions yields as a result that the definition of the psychical requires that an unabridged concept of subjectivity be rooted in a determination of the functionality of the psychical for living organisms.

The discussion of Hugo Münsterberg's psychology that follows next[27] adds only a further small aspect to the requirements for a definition of the psychical as they have emerged thus far. Münsterberg recognizes not only the model of the physical sciences, but also that of the social sciences, which he regards as being as valid as the first kind.

> The first are causally and the second teleologically organized. Now in neither of these [systems of sciences (H. J.)] does the psychical appear. It does not form a part of the mathematically determined order of nature nor is that which the social sciences treat psychical. These sciences treat the whole individual and his methods of conduct.[28]

The psychical is, then, only that which is left over by the processes of abstraction that must be gone through in entering the world of science. According to Münsterberg, science is purposeless-purposeful, that is, it can fulfil its task only if it liberates itself from all the purposes of the 'actual ego'. What science leaves behind as belonging to the prescientific world of the actual ego is now itself made the object of a science by psychology. How little this conception of the object of psychology implies ideas about the function of the psychical and its investigation is shown by Münsterberg's explicit declaration that the motive for establishing this new science of psychology is to be found in a kind of spontaneous diffusion of the curiosity underlying scientific research.

In his next step, Mead turns his attention to the conception of the psychical advanced by the eminent British neo-idealists and opponents of empiricism, F. H. Bradley and Bernard Bosanquet.[29] Mead's examination of their theories is more significant for the argument he is elaborating than his treatment of Münsterberg was. In many respects the British philosophers represent the exact opposite of psycho-physical materialism. Their resolution of mind-body dualism proceeds in the opposite direction: they completely disconnect the psychical from the corporeal. Like the representatives of the emerging psychology who were oriented to the natural sciences, Bradley called for a strict separation between metaphysics and logic, on the one side, and psychology on the other. He did so, however, for the sake of metaphysics. For Bradley denied to the psychical a proper structure of its own that could be investigated and apprehended; for him the psychical is merely the phenomenal appearance of the material, which as such can never be found in cognitive consciousness in its own form. If the psychical is nothing more than the raw material for thinking, then a theory of thinking is justified in so structuring the psychical that it corresponds to the requirements of thinking. Bradley recalls that the formation of concepts in the natural sciences is operational rather than essentialist in character, and demands that psychology do the same. His logic or metaphysics is, then, not subject to the supervisory control of a discipline of psychology.

In Bradley's case, Mead's critique is very restrained. He can be confident that the continuation of classical German idealism without the conceptual instruments of psychology will be found convincing only by those who hold fast to the notion of 'absolute knowledge'.[30] If this Hegelian claim of the identity of consciousness and its object, of the self-reflective presentation of the entire history of the mind, falls as a result of insight into the finite character of all human knowledge, then it becomes clear that knowledge is not completely identical with its genesis, nor is the relation between them one of mutual exclusivity. Only on the premises of absolute idealism can Bradley simply subordinate psychology to logic, determine the object of psychology in a purely phenomenalistic manner, and, while taking great interest in the *evolution* of consciousness, programmatically reject a theory of its *origination*. From his examination of Bradley's position Mead draws the conclusion that psycho-physical dualism can be overcome neither by a materialist nor by an idealist monism. More important for Mead than this negative conclusion, however, is a positive one. He comments favourably on Bradley's non-individualist concept of the individual, which originated with Hegel.

One further advantage of the attitude is that it is not even bound to regard the psychical as peculiarly the consciousness of the empirical individual. That is, this type of consciousness is not psychical because it is that of the individual as such, but under certain conditions the particularity of the individual is expressed by the fact that for the time being he identifies his consciousness with these psychical contents.[31]

The psychical content is thus not conceived of as locked within the inviolable privacy of the individual, but rather as directed to universality and embedded in a common world. Further, a relationship is established between the psychical and the dimension of truth or validity in logic and ethics. In Mead's discussion of Bradley, then, the question of the correct determination of the relation of the psychical to the individual in the definition of the psychical is added to the problems posed by mind-body dualism.

This question provides the guiding thread for Mead's scrutiny of the position taken by the British psychologists and philosophers Ward and Stout.[32] Both regard the individual as the locus of the psychical, and the history of individual consciousness as the object of psychology. These definitions of the psychical and psychology are, of all those that Mead has discussed so far, the closest to the contemporary common understanding of these matters; but the price of the apparently clear starting point of the individual as he is given is the exclusion from psychology of the question of the cognitive validity of the facts of consciousness. Mead's criticism of the naivety of this procedure and of the avoidance of the question of how that which is individual is constituted is intended to demonstrate that it is impossible to eliminate from psychology, especially from a genetic psychology, the question of the validity of the facts of consciousness which are its object. The difficulty in this regard begins for such a psychology with the concept of subjectivity.

In so far as states of consciousness are referred to the subject as distinct from the object they cannot be cognitive. The psychological individual then never does attain to knowledge. As long as the states of consciousness may be termed subjective, he does not know, and when they become objective, he is no longer the individual with which psychology deals.[33]

Mead does not fail to recognize that indifference to the question of the validity of data of consciousness is not to be equated with a focusing of attention on what is merely subjective, in contrast to objective cognition. He argues, however, that abstraction from the question of validity has the consequence that the individual as immediately experienced is no longer the starting point of our theory. For there can be no doubt that this individual claims that his states of consciousness have cognitive validity.

> If it is the real individual of unanalyzed experience, and our psychology deals with the genesis of his knowledge and conduct, there is a passage from the subjective to the objective, and the canons of logic and ethics will have forced their way into psychology, even if metaphysics is not introduced with them. And this cannot be avoided by prefacing that psychology deals with these processes simply as data, not with their validity (see Stout, *Analytical Psychology*, p. 12). For the nature of the steps is going to be determined by the goal toward which they are moving, and no treatment of the steps will be adequate which overlooks this relation. Furthermore, if it is a development, no sharp line can be drawn between the genesis and the result. The phases and the sciences that treat them will shade into each other as do morphology and general biology. These authors slur over a difficulty with which Bradley has dealt with subtlety and acumen.[34]

Against Ward's theory Mead makes the objection that the transformation of the determinations of the transcendental ego of the idealist philosophical tradition into those of the empirical ego of psychology is not possible in such a simple way. For such a transformation has to confront the question of the cognitive validity of states or processes of consciousness. Critical examination of Ward's and Stout's position leads to the conclusion that the relation of the psychical to the individual fails if that relation is not conceived of as a relation to the individual's reflection. Psychology is neither simply subordinated to logic, as it is for Bradley, nor is it completely separated from logic, as in the case of Ward and Stout. Accordingly, the definition of the psychical has the task of clarifying the psychical in its relation to individual reflection.

The last of the positions treated by Mead is expressed in the very influential psychology of William James and consists in the phenomenalist rehabilitation of the notion of the soul. For James, the notion of the soul – leaving aside its metaphysical implication, or the criticism of that implication since Kant – is a possible and useful tool for describing psychical facts. Mead admits that James thereby abandons the pseudo-precision of elementarist psychology and makes it possible easily to conceive of the unity of consciousness, a relation with the body, and a relation to the concept of personality. Of James's analysis of the 'stream of consciousness', Mead says that it is 'by all odds the richest statement of the psychical consciousness that philosophic literature has yet presented'.[35]

Mead's attitude toward James's success is marked by irritation that such a fruitful approach can follow from such an unsatisfactory methodological position. For James openly accepts the dualism of the knowing mind and the thing known, and that psychology is psychology of consciousness.[36] The conclusion that Mead draws from this state of affairs is that what James apprehended intuitively will have to be reconstructed after the development of an adequate concept of the psychical. The notion of the 'stream of consciousness' is for Mead, in contrast to phenomenology, which was profoundly influenced by James in just this point, not an ultimate given, but rather it must itself be subjected to interrogation about how it is constituted and what its function is. Just how Mead envisaged doing this can be shown only after we have followed the formulation of his definition of the psychical.

Having considered the positions discussed by Mead, which were supposed to contribute positively or negatively to a clearer grasp of the problems posed by definition of the psychical, we can now formulate the requirements for such a concept. What would a concept of the psychical look like that neither limited the psychical to physical or physiological processes in the manner of reductionistic materialism, nor dismissed it as trifling, as a merely accidental phenomenal form that could be sublated in the concept in the manner of an absolute idealism; that, however, was also not constrained by a clinging to the traditional dualism of the corporeal and the psychical, or vitiated by a spurious overcoming of this dualism in theories of two types of experience or of two different linguistic systems?[37] What would a concept of the psychical look like that did not permit the connection of the psychical with the individual to be swallowed up in a notion of the universal or collective, but also did not safeguard this connection by eliminating the dimension of the cognitive validity of states and processes of consciousness, by abstracting from the individual's claims to have valid knowledge of his world? What would a concept of the psychical look like that takes into account the fact that the psychical is bound up with the instant by regarding

> . . . the psychical, not as a permanent phase, nor even a permanent possible aspect of consciousness, but as a 'moment' of consciousness or in a conscious process, and which has therefore cognitive value for that process.[38]

Mead claims that he has solved these three problems: overcoming dualism, formulating a non-individualist concept of the individual, and determining the cognitive value of individual knowledge, in a single, unitary concept. The solution to the problem of dualism is provided by the concept of conduct or action; the solution to the problem of cognitive validity is to be found in the notion of reconstruction; and, lastly, the solution to the problem posed by the role of the individual is given by an understanding of the necessarily subjective character of the formulation of a problem and of the necessarily general validity of the solution found to the problem. According to the definition which Mead arrives at in this article, and which is intended to join together these three problem-complexes, the psychical is

> . . . that phase of experience within which we are immediately conscious of conflicting impulses which rob the object of its character as object-stimulus, leaving us in so far in an attitude of subjectivity; but during which a new object-stimulus appears due to the recon-structive activity which is identified with the subject 'I' as distinct from the object 'me'.[39]

Now, this definition clearly contains some components – the emphasis on immediate consciousness and the distinction between 'I' and 'me' – that have not yet appeared in our exposition of Mead's argument. The difficulty of presenting Mead's train of thought in this article lies in the fact that, after surveying the competing positions regarding the definition of psychology's object, Mead does not proceed in a straight line to arrive at his own definition. Instead, he demonstrates the fruitfulness of the change of paradigm he is proposing through a wealth of critiques consisting of retroactive interpretations and reconstructions. For the time being let us continue to follow the steps of Mead's argumentation.

Mead's point of departure is the transferral of the pragmatist analysis of reflection to the question of the psychical. The psychical does not appear 'until critical reflection in the process of knowledge analyses our world'.[40] Prior to reflection, the subjective and the objective cannot be disentangled. Reflection, however, is not something that as such has a value in and of itself. It is, rather, embedded in action-nexuses and concomitant of these as preparation for them, as accompanying supervision, or as a retrospective accounting for them. Mead first asks himself whether the notion of the immediacy of experience can at all be a meaningful component of the definition of the psychical when this relation to reflection has been effected, and empirical psychology's belief in the immediate givenness of elementary sensations has been lost. In considering this question, too, Mead begins by scrutinizing Wundt's ideas, since with the notion of the immediacy of the will and his conception of immediate, constructive and synthetic operations of consciousness, the latter appeared to have in his voluntaristic psychology a concept of immediacy that went beyond empiricism. We have already spoken of Wundt's inconsistency with regard to the immediacy of the will in connection with Mead's criticism of his notion of 'two types of experience'. The appearance of the will in consciousness – to recall the conclusion drawn there – has to be subjected to the question of how it is constituted just as does the appearance of any other datum of consciousness. And this holds true also for all other determinations of subjectivity.

> The assertion that the subject to which these activities are referred along with other states is there because it must be there, or because the subject-object relation can't be got rid of, does not enable us to materialize anything more than corresponding elements.[41]

This passage means that the mere reference to underlying operations of a creative subjectivity does not say anything about the conditions under which this subjectivity can itself be experienced and thus does not change in a fundamental way the traditional empiricist definition of the object-field of psychology.

If, however, the attempt to introduce a notion of immediate experience within a theory of reflection should be unsuccessful, then Mead sees no escape from slipping into psycho-physical parallelism. For if we, in defining the psychical, cannot discover its roots in an immediate experience of the actor, then we must regard it – in the manner of the 'psychological fallacy' – as a permanent 'property' of the individual. Then, however, the only way leading to the apprehension of the psychical is not examining the phase of acts in which the psychical is present in the self-awareness of the actor, but rather continually correlating acts of thinking, sensing, willing, etc., with the 'objective' conditions of these acts. In Mead's view, psychophysical parallelism in science is linked even more strongly to this methodological constraint than to philosophical traditions and ideological compulsions that necessitate adherence to mind-body dualism. Under this methodological constraint the psychologist compares that which he considers to be the objective givens of a situation with that which the actor in this situation appears to perceive. When this method is employed, the analysis of the psychical makes use of concepts proper to the assumed objective reality; and the psychical appears as the refraction in the individual of objectively real states of affairs.

> This whole type of psychology can do no more than state the objective conditions under which the criticised act of cognition with its content of feel, emotion, and effort took place. That these psychologists have not confined themselves to this is undoubtedly true, but their scientific method can only assume psychical elements that correspond to definite conditions of objective experience.[42]

According to Mead, the origin of this misunderstanding of its own methodology in psychology is to be found in an objectivist conception of science.[43] What the psychologist opposes to the experience of the individual as the objective world is not independent of constitution by the subject. For it arises upon the basis of controlled sensuous experience. If we take the standpoint of this type of psychology, we forget that the world of conceptual objects is not originary, but rather the product of abstraction; that therefore the apparently objective world of physical and physiological facts is to be understood as a 'common world', as a 'thesis' about an objective world having intersubjectively a strong claim to validity. Mead touches here upon the theme that will be of central importance for his mature work from 1920 on, namely the question of the experiential basis of natural science, of the constitution of scientific experience in everyday experience.[44] In the context of 'The Definition of the Psychical', though, these questions only serve to demonstrate the impossibility of founding psychology upon the abstractions of natural science. For if one does, then sensuous experience does not appear as the primary experiential basis of all science, but instead as deficient in comparison with the world of science and as accessible only from this world.

> The *ex post facto* legislation by which we transfer this analysis back to the objects, whose immediacy was a precondition to it, is certainly out of place in a science which is supposed to deal with immediate experience. That is, it is not justifiable to demand of psychology that it regard all sensuous contents as psychical because analysis has shown certain of them not to be objective, while in the same experience other sensuous contents are necessarily regarded as objective.[45]

If, therefore, the psychical or consciousness is understood simply as a 'property' of subjects, then the postulate of the immediacy of the psychical and the postulate of subjectivity would enter into conflict with one another. For the merely subjective is then the product of a reflection that has eliminated the objective validities of the facts of consciousness.

This contradiction can be resolved only if conditions can be stated in which the psychical, in its restriction to a subject and in its immediacy, is itself functional. This is, of course, only possible if the psychical is not thought of as a permanent concomitant phenomenon of, but rather – in Mead's words – as 'organic phases in the cognitive act'.[46] Accordingly, there would have to be a phase of reflection or of action, in which the individual himself necessarily disregards any and every objective validity of certain data of his consciousness and experiences himself as thrown back upon his subjectivity. The psychical, says Mead, is thus to be located where action threatens to miscarry because of problems it has encountered.

At this point Mead adduces Dewey's criticism of the reflex-arc model as the classical critique of objectivist psychology and also as the introduction into psychology of the concepts of action and of crisis in an action. Where a problem for action makes its appearance, there a part of our world is deprived of its objectivity, is disorganized; the effort we make then is directed to the reconstruction of this objectivity, which, however, can only be achieved by a creative operation performed by the subject himself.

'The question then arises: In what form do these contents appear when this disintegration and reconstitution takes place?'[47] If the psychical is to have its moorings in this phase of the creative resolution of problems for action, then we cannot presuppose, when we analyse the psychical, the concepts of those very objects whose validity has become doubtful. Interpreting an actor's problems as only subjective inadequacy, and not as genuine doubts, that is, as formulations of problems aimed at an improved interpretation of the action-situation, would be again to misunderstand the actor's problems in an objectivist fashion. At this point in his exposition Mead takes recourse to James's presentation of the 'stream of consciousness' in order to obtain an acceptable point of attack for the analysis of the psychical. At Mead's hands the stream of consciousness undergoes a reinterpretation. No longer is it, as for James or for phenomenology, the foundational form of consciousness out of which the individual acts of consciousness and the individual actions emerge; rather, it is the expression of a liquefaction of previously stable validities. The 'psychological fallacy', as Dewey, and Mead with him, called the transferral of features of consciousness to precisely those situations in which consciousness cannot occur, proves to be harmless in the case of James's analysis because he is unwittingly analysing just that consciousness which is familiar to us in our self-experience from the formation of hypotheses and attempts to solve problems.

> The kaleidoscopic flash of suggestion, and intrusion of the inapt, the unceasing flow of odds and ends of possible objects that will not fit, together with the continuous collision with the hard, unshakable objective conditions of the problem, the transitive feelings of effort and anticipation when we feel that we are on the right track and substantive points of rest, as the idea becomes definite, the welcoming and rejecting, especially the identification of the meaning of the whole idea with the different steps in its coming to consciousness – there are none of these that are not almost oppressively present on the surface of consciousness during just the periods which Dewey describes as those of disintegration and reconstitution of the stimulus – the object.[48]

To the foregoing must be added that the situation of crisis in action is, of course, not to be conceived of as a state of rest or inactivity, but as a highly active effort to bring together in a higher-level unity habits of conduct and perceptions that conflict with one another. Mead explicitly points out that this unquestionably takes place during action by means of continual re-orientation of the actor's attention; thus, the existence of a consciousness that accompanies action is no argument against an interpretation of consciousness based on the interruption of action.

There remains one component of Mead's definition of the psychical which still requires more clarification: the relation of the psychical to the individual. In providing this clarification, Mead begins by differentiating his position from other, competing ones. To this end he makes use of the distinction between 'I' and 'me', originally drawn by William James, according to which the 'me' is the individual as an object of consciousness, while the 'I' is the individual as having consciousness. Mead stresses that it is first of all necessary, in opposition to the concept of the ego of a great number of the contemporary psychologists, to insist on the constitutive, quasi-transcendental character of the self. Yet this would be insufficient, if this self were conceived of merely as the unifying function of 'thinking' in the manner of Kant. For Mead, the solutions of this problem attempted in the manner of post-Kantian German idealism are also inadequate; these are the concept of the self as an ethical ideal and the notion of the self as the bearer of absolute knowledge. Mead tries to find a concept of the self that retains a complete determination of subjectivity, without relapsing into the idealism of the determinations of transcendental philosophy. It is precisely the requirement of an immediate givenness of this self in the psychical phase of action that compels us not to allow the concreteness of the subjectivity and individuality, which is in each instance different and unique, to perish in our analysis of the psychical.

Mead finds two starting points for his attempt to arrive at an empirical concept of constitutive subjectivity. The one consists in the scattered and weak vestiges left behind in empirical psychology by the 'transcendental ego': phenomena such as those of attention, of the active focalizing of the sense organs, of the feelings of effort and activity. The other starting point lies in Baldwin's project for a genetic and social psychology.[49] The latter had presented an important contribution to a theory of the social genesis of the self.

Mead, who of course shared the goal of Baldwin's theory, stresses the importance of this analysis which traces the stages of development from a 'protoplasmic' initial state of consciousness, in which what is subjective and what is objective are not distinguished from one another, on to the constitution of persons and things, then to the reactive formation of a self-reflective identity, and finally to the capacity to distinguish between mind and body. Mead considers this model important, because through it a foundational dimension of subjectivity had been linked with a theory of the social formation of the self. Nevertheless, in this article[50] Mead criticizes Baldwin because he permits the development to end in a dualism of mind and body and confines 'protoplasmic' subjectivity to early childhood. In Baldwin's analysis reflectivity and foundational subjectivity exclude each other. Mead, however, claims that he can combine both approaches to elaborating a concept of subjectivity and explain the functionality in reflection of Baldwin's 'protoplasmic' phase of consciousness by rooting the psychical in the stage of the disintegration and reconstruction of objects and of impulses to action.

> Thus, in the theories we have criticised, the subject is represented in two aspects, neither of which can presumably be present in the material with which the science deals; first as a content, the original subjectivity out of whose 'projection' or 'imitative introjection' arise not only the others' selves, but reactively our own, and second the 'activities' that answer to attention or apperception; but in this phase of disintegration and reconstruction both these aspects *are* immediately given. The disintegration of the object means a return, with reference to a certain field, to the original phase of protoplasmic consciousness, and within these limits there is neither mind nor body, only subjectivity.[51]

To make this concept of subjectivity and the situation of the disintegration and reconstruction of objects and impulses to action more vivid for the reader, Mead gives a detailed description of the reconstruction process. He emphasizes most strongly that what is called in question is always only relative in character. Every conflict between tendencies to action divides the data of the situation into two fields. The one field forms the problem area, in which new objects must be constituted. In contrast, the other field remains intact, that is does not undergo reconstitution, and forms the background of conditions for the elaboration of hypotheses about these 'new objects'. Mead illustrates this process with a detailed account of a problem encountered in the course of action. The example he gives is an instance of social interaction in which the ideas we hold about the character of an acquaintance have been contradicted by his conduct and hence suspended, and no new ideas have yet become established. He underscores that doubt about someone else always implies a doubt also about oneself, at least about one's capacity for judging the other person. The resolution of this situation, the simultaneous constituting of a new subject and a new predicate, necessitates creative individuality.

> And it is in this phase of subjectivity, with its activities of attention in the solution of the problem, i.e., in the construction of the hypothesis of the new world, that the individual *qua* individual has his functional expression or rather is that function.[52]

> But it is evident that, as the function of the world is to provide data for the solution, so it is the function of the individual to provide the hypothesis for that solution . . . It is the self of unnecessitated choice, of undreamt hypotheses, of inventions that change the whole face of nature.[53]

With these statements Mead concludes the elaboration of his definition of psychology's object-field. He goes on to give, in a kind of appendix, an interpretation of the empiricist psychology of sensations and of the voluntaristic psychology of mental presentations, which is intended to elucidate the relative validity of these psychologies. According to Mead, the psychology of sensations grasps only one side of the process he has described, namely that of the conditions in which the reconstruction takes place, while the psychology of mental presentations grasps only the other side, that which is directed toward the reconstruction, the formation of hypotheses. However, both abstract precisely from the situation of the interruption of action and therefore come to an incorrect understanding of the givens or of the new interpretations of the situation, for these appear in the psychologies as firm facts and not as forms that are in flux. In conclusion, Mead concedes that the objectivist varieties of psychology have a pragmatic utility which, however, can only be properly assessed if these varieties of psychology are comprehended in a functionalist psychology, in an adequate concept of the psychical.

We have now reached the point where we can ask whether Mead succeeded both in attaining the goals which he set himself and in making a contribution to the definition of the psychical that is still relevant today. Looking back on Mead's various arguments, one notices that some of the parts of his analyses which bear the principal burden of their proof are merely stated and not well founded through detailed explanation. Perhaps for this reason Mead's exposition is predominantly given over to criticism of the internal contradictions and inadequacies of the positions he examines. The observation just made is especially true for the concept of action, which is supposed to describe the specific structure of the relation between the organism and its environment in the particular case of the human being, but which is not at all phylogenetically arrived at. The observation is also true, though, for the theses about the constitution of all science in sensuous experience and about the relationship between individual cognition and collective acceptance of that cognition as valid. These are thematic complexes in whose investigation and clarification Mead remained interested to the end of his life. The further development of Mead's thought did not bring about revisions of these theses, but did produce numerous and better attempts to ground them.[54]

This cannot be said for 'The Definition of the Psychical' in its entirety, however. In the passages on the logical function of individual cognition one can hear as an undertone not only the pathos of the individual's importance for the progress of knowledge and humanity, but also Mead's polemic against the individual who is imprisoned within private experience and shut off from public discussion. With his thesis about new perceptions and ideas of individuals which need to be transformed into a common language in order to acquire validity, Mead is continuing that polemic on the epistemological plane, and with his rejection of the belief in the 'private' character of mental presentations, on the psychological plane. To be sure, both theses are based on the intuitive insight into the essentially linguistically or intersubjectively constituted character of the predicates used for self-interpretation. Only while Mead had not yet clearly grasped the implications of this insight could the contradiction between this position and his belief that the 'I' could be immediately experienced remain hidden from him. A similar contradiction appeared between the theory of the social genesis of the self, regarded approvingly even in 'The Definition of the Psychical', and Mead's claim that the self is directly accessible to reflection. However, both the status of the immediacy of experience and that of the psychical as essentially bound up with the moment were insufficiently clarified. It was an open question whether human action was at all to be qualified as conscious action outside of the phases of subjectivity in which, or the points at which, the human individual becomes aware of his action. If the answer to this question is yes, then one would also have to be able to differentiate clearly human conduct from animal behaviour in these phases.[55]

The two problems required of the philosopher further, crucially important, steps: the first pressed him to take into consideration, in a consistent manner, the social genesis of self-reflectivity; the second urged him towards a concept of intersubjectively constituted meaning. In order for this undertaking to succeed, the whole frame of reference of 'The Definition of the Psychical' had first to be broken asunder. Thus Mead's article of 1903 proved to suffice from the standpoint of a functionalist treatment of reflective consciousness, but not from that of an investigation of human sociality. In this article, therefore, Mead could still remain within the essentially monologic framework of functionalist psychology and place the individual organism and its actions in the centre of his study. But once Mead had grasped that self-reflectivity is an individual precipitate of sociality, then central importance had to be accorded to the structure of groups of organisms and to social activity as the all-embracing unity of individual actions. What Mead had to learn, and the analytical advances he had to make, in order to achieve this understanding and the resulting conclusion are the subject of the following chapter.

The reasons that drove Mead to move beyond the theoretical position he took in 1903 are, of course, also limitations on the validity of the definition of the psychical which he offered. Nonetheless, we can ask at this point what the significance is of that definition. Its importance seems to me to lie in the fact *that Mead linked the objective rootedness of the psychical in the structure of human action with the insight that psychology is essentially self-reflective in character.* Just as Piaget, with his definition of the psychical as *functional* adaptation, or Leontief, who defined it as the function of the subjectification of objective meanings in the framework of instrumental activity, so too did Mead, with his rooting of the psychical in the crisis in an action that can be mastered only creatively, not oppose the psychical to the world, but rather situate it within the world. For Mead, though, in contrast to Piaget and Leontief, the objective action-nexus does not thereby turn objectivistic. The reduction of the subjective achievements in the constitution of meaning to the mirroring in consciousness of objectively given meanings or to their mere assimilation by consciousness, which is to be found in Marxist psychology from Rubinstein through Leontief and on to Holzkamp, simply breaks the point of the real thorn of the problem of subjectivity. Linguistic theory and the shaping of communicative relations by the individuals participating in them are thereby made unimportant as topics for investigation, while it becomes possible to continue to cling to the copy theory of knowledge and to an objectivist notion of history.[56]

Although Piaget assigns a central place in his theories to the necessity of constructively overcoming states of disequilibrium of accommodation and assimilation, this fact does not suffice to answer the question whether he thereby addresses only the genesis of self-regulating systems, or also the liberation of subjectivity. There is nothing new in pointing out the conflict between these two conceptions, both of which are to be found in Piaget's work, and the preponderance of the objectivist conception.[57] On the other hand, Mead, unlike Husserl, does not ascribe the essentially self-reflective character of psychology to its transcendental grounding. Whereas Husserl asserts that subjectivity is accessible to the philosopher through methodical preparation, but remains inaccessible to the practically active individual,[58] Mead identifies that phase of an action in which subjectivity shows itself to the actor. Consequently, the investigation of this subjectivity is the task of a science which is itself embedded in the relational complexes of practical activity, and which is not possible without the aid of the self-interpretations of the individuals which it studies.

That psychology can lose its 'impersonality', to use Titchener's term, without thereby ceasing to be a 'rigorous science', if it joins the insight into the intentionality of the psychical with a non-individualist concept of mind – this is what recent studies seek to demonstrate, those of Theodore Mischel, for example, which originated from a thorough examination of the development of psychology from behaviourism to cognitivist psychology. Mischel's penetrating insight is that cognitivist psychology does not add another dimension of variability to the received explanatory model of psychology, but rather makes a fundamental revision of psychology necessary.[59]

Studies such as these make it clear that 'The Definition of the Psychical' is not merely the intra-psychological preparation of Mead's social-psychological approach, but also offers, in rudimentary form, an understanding of psychology from the standpoint of a theory of communicative action that to the present day has not been entirely equalled elsewhere, nor been fully developed.[60]

5

The Origin of the Concept of Symbolic Interaction

There are two reasons why exact knowledge of the history of the origin of Mead's anthropological theory of symbolic interaction and of the social psychology based on that theory is necessary.[1] The first arises from the unfinished and accidental form in which Mead's mature work has been handed on to us. It has been overlooked again and again that *Mind, Self, and Society*, posthumously composed from students' lecture notes, suffers from a diminished precision of the individual arguments and formulations because of the originally oral nature of the texts on which the book is based, and that the structure and content of the work were influenced by the institutional context in which it was to be used, namely as a university lecture course for particular courses of study. For example, Mead's student and colleague, Ellsworth Faris,[2] has pointed out that, due to a kind of division of labour between an introductory and the principal lecture course on social psychology, the general fundamentals of psychology, which Mead continued to consider important, were no longer taught in detail by him personally after 1920. Therefore, they are not to be found, or are contained only in a very inadequate form, in the work that has shaped the generally held image of Mead.[3] For that reason, I have attempted here to bring together and to systematize all of the material contained in the relevant articles written by Mead himself.

The second reason why it is necessary to know the history of the origin of Mead's theory is that it can also, I believe, be a path to a better understanding of his ideas. Mead developed his conception of symbolic interaction in distinct steps, which can be reconstructed as steps in reflection necessary to reach that goal. By following the evolution of Mead's thought after 'The Definition of the Psychical',

90

which appeared in 1903, through a series of articles which ended in 1913, the reader can observe the emergence of a concept from which implications were to be drawn and utilized only much later, in symbolic interactionism and in a reconstruction of historical materialism influenced by interaction theory.[4]

An attempt to characterize, in a preliminary fashion, the process of the origination of Mead's theory yields the following description. Mead's approach to a social psychology was guided by the conviction that the social conditions and functions of the self-reflectivity of human individuals had to be elucidated. To accomplish this, he had to demonstrate the conditions of the possibility of this self-reflectivity in the most fundamental features of human sociality: in the distinction of the basic structure of human sociality from all animal social forms. This was the purpose of Mead's anthropological theory of communication. This approach is derived from Darwin's analysis of the expressive behaviour of animals and especially from Wundt's conception of language and gesture; in Mead's anthropological theory of communication, however, Darwin's analysis and Wundt's theory are transformed into a different conception of communication in steps that can be precisely retraced. This transformation was determined by three approaches, the significance of which Mead acknowledges in an article from that period,[5] but each of which he finds insufficient when taken alone. These are Baldwin's theory of the social origin of the self, Royce's thesis on the essentially social character of linguistic meaning and consequently of reflection, which necessarily makes use of symbols, and McDougall's doctrine of the existence of social instincts. In all three cases, it is not a matter of theories which Mead is prepared to make his own, but rather of problem-areas that Mead designates, symbolically, with the names of these men.

Mead's critical reading and discussion of the writings of Draghiscesco, which have since been forgotten, and of McDougall's influential social psychology made more precise the theory of the social formation of the self that he envisaged. Draghiscesco, too, claimed to deduce genetically the individual consciousness from a social or collective consciousness, but he did not make clear whether he understood by the latter a specific medium of social organization or the expression of an objectively given functional interdependence of the actions of the society's members. Nevertheless, this lack of clarity, with which Mead finds fault, is not the real target of his criticism. This is, rather, Draghiscesco's attempt to escape from the epiphenomenalist theory of consciousness by positing the totally deterministic character of the natural world and the definitive character of the natural sciences, in contrast to the teleological and conscious character of social phenomena and the persistent mutability of the social sciences. For Draghiscesco, consciousness, of which certitude is given by self-experience, is a part of that higher region of the social which is not determined by nature, while unreflected action is a result of physiological mechanisms. Thus the social character of reflective consciousness is also maintained with this theory, although at the same time it opposes reflective consciousness to the physical bases of human behaviour. This is the starting point for Mead's objections.

He begins by attacking Draghiscesco's conceptions of nature and the natural sciences. The difference between these and the social world and social science does not, says Mead, lie in the deterministic character of nature, nor in the non-teleological character of natural-scientific knowledge; instead, the rational core of this distinction consists in the difference in the ways in which social and physical objects are given to the human actor. For social objects are themselves also perceiving subjects,[6] and Mead asks whether the implications of this state of affairs are as significant for the psychology of perception as they are for ethics, for which Kant founded the character of the other subject as an end in itself, in contrast to being a mere means to an end, as are physical objects, on just this circumstance. In this review article, printed in 1905, Mead denies to this circumstance such implications. It is obvious, though, that what his assertions are intended to deny is a quite particular conclusion from the state of affairs in question, namely that drawn by Draghiscesco. The latter concludes to the essentially necessary introspective certainty of the self, in contrast to the physical object, which is accessible to us only through analysis. Of this matter Mead writes:

From the psychological point of view the question becomes this: does introspection present the knowing self to the knower, as a social content implying necessarily other selves, while the known physical object is subject to analysis into states that must be referred to this self? If this were the case, we might indeed deduce the whole cognitive process out of a consciousness which was primarily social and secondarily physical. But the fact is that this self which our introspection reveals is the so-called empirical self, and is just as much a construct as the physical object. A constructing self never appears as the object of introspection. He can no more be got on to the dissecting table than Kant's transcendental ego. It is true that we cannot construct empirical selves without constructing other selves. It is equally true that we cannot construct our physical bodies as objects without constructing other physical objects, and it is a piece of Berkeleyan idealism to refer the consciousness of physical objects to the consciousness of the empirical self, giving precedence in reality to the latter over the former.[7]

Mead's discussion in this passage is noteworthy in three regards. First of all, Mead argues here, for the first time and in contrast to his own position in 'The Definition of the Psychical', against the claim that the constitutive operations of the self can be immediately experienced, by pointing out the self's quasi-transcendental character. Second, Mead reasons that the formation of self-consciousness is linked with the constitution of a reflective relationship to our body, and that this constitution can only be successfully effected concomitantly with the constitution of other physical objects. It thus becomes impossible for Mead, in opposition to Draghiscesco, to separate the social origin of the self from corporeality, from both the organic processes of maturation and the relation of the actor to his body. Third, in this phase of the development of his thought, Mead does not yet have the conceptual instruments which would allow him to assess the difference between social and physical objects without relapsing into belief in originary, introspective self-certainty. In summary, the conclusions that can be drawn from Mead's critique of Draghiscesco are that in this article he is endeavouring to leave behind the residue of solipsism in the theories of the social formation of the self, including those of Cooley and Baldwin, and is seeking to link the formation of the self with the whole development of the human organism; that, however, he still lacks the concrete means for carrying out this program, and therefore retracts, in a self-contradictory manner, the definition of the difference between social and physical objects which he has advanced.

McDougall's social psychology[8] is famous even today because its approach is founded on a theory of social instincts. This approach promised an objective, natural-scientific foundation for social psychology, but was frustrated by the difficulties encountered in applying the concept of instinct to human beings. Mead, too, later dissociated himself from the psychology of instincts and became an adherent of the weaker version of this theory which held that the impulses are the remnants of instincts in human beings. Initially, though, the psychology of instincts seemed to him a weapon against all forms of the mentalistic psychology of consciousness and an important step toward a psychology taking a concept of action or conduct as its point of departure.[9] His criticism was thus not directed at the concept of instinct as such, but rather against a simplifying model of human perception and emotion, such as that proposed by McDougall. On the other hand, Mead was able to gain an important idea from McDougall's theory of *social* instincts. The existence of social instincts, whether that of parental care, of courting, of combat, or of spontaneous cooperation, is important for Mead as evidence of the existence of social objects. The theory of social instincts offers an alternative to the anthropology of an egotistical human nature, which makes sociality inconceivable or restricts it to the form of a common will, excluding the content.

Mead is then all the more disappointed when he subjects McDougall's own theory of the development of self-consciousness to scrutiny. He criticizes McDougall for beginning with an instinctual drive to self-preservation which is postulated as original, and for his inability to conceive of a social consciousness in which others do not appear as a mental presentation of the self, but rather the self appears as a datum on the same plane as the others. This failing leaves the question of the social character of morality or of the moral implications of sociality in its traditional form, namely, how an individual with egotistical drives can become an altruist. It seems that, because of his critical examination of McDougall's theory, Mead recognized the necessity of joining a theory of the social formation of the self with a theory of the social character of human impulses, but that in this phase of the eevolution of his thought he does not yet have at his disposal the means to retain the essentially social character of the impulses as well as their organismic basis, while relinquishing the notion of social instincts.

The problem-area within which Mead's intellectual development took place has been sketched and the relative worth of two of the four strands of theory that were mentioned has been elucidated, namely that of Baldwin and Draghiscesco and that of McDougall. The two other strands – Wundt's theory of language and Royce's concept of meaning – will lead us into the domain in which Mead's attempt to solve the above-mentioned problem was developed. Mead's first, and for the most part uncritical, discussion of Wundt's theory of language is to be found in an article published in 1904, bearing the title 'The Relations of Psychology and Philology'. Two years later, in accord with the structure of Wundt's *Völkerpsychologie*, this article was followed by a short study of the latter's treatment of myth and imagination.

Wundt's *Völkerpsychologie*, a book in which he accounts for the cultural life of nations or peoples, can be regarded as a precursor of the attempts to found a social psychology, which differs from these in that a notion of the 'objective spirit' still echoes in it and makes cultural objectifications one of the central objects of this psychology. In language and myth, Wundt, as well as Mead, believed that they had found exemplary cases demonstrating the insufficiency of an individualistic psychology and hence the necessity of a folk psychology *(Völkerpsychologie)*, of a collective or social psychology. Language and myth cannot be made understandable as matters of the individual psyche, of the individual human being. Mead accepts Wundt's claim to have established a psychological theory of language; his discussion of the relationship between philology and psychology has the primary purpose of defending Wundt's claim against philology and against the associationist psychology of the Herbartian tradition. Mead stresses repeatedly that only psychology can open the path to a correct theory of language, since this path is barred to philologists by their concern with the details of individual languages. Philology, says Mead, cannot of itself lead to a theory of language in the sense of a theory of linguistic competence intended to account for the species-specific language capacity of the human being. On the other hand, such a theory of language must also prove its fruitfulness for the philologies of individual languages.

The question of the origin of human language is the touchstone, according to Mead, which demonstrates most clearly the superiority of the 'psychological' procedure, as it was called by both Mead and Wundt, in comparison with the philological tradition as well as with associationist psychology. In response to the question of the origin of language, the latter psychology can only offer the absurd hypothesis that human language was invented. Philology, on the other hand, had entangled itself in complicated research to determine the structure of proto-Indo-European, or of the *Ursprache*, the single primordial language. In contrast, Wundt's voluntaristic psychology took a decisive step toward an effortless solution of the problem by locating the origin of language in primitive impulses to expression, and by conceiving of these expressions as one of the various forms of movement.

> The sound is at first but a gesture (*Lautgebärden* in Wundt). Articulation, as a muscular process, is explained in the same way that movements of the face, of the hands, of the whole body are accounted for under the influence of emotional tension. Instead, therefore, of having to assume unknown or exceptional conditions as the antecedents of the origin of speech, we can find the conditions present in our own movements, in the first activities of children, in the gesture languages of primitive peoples or the deaf-mutes.[10]

This is the first passage in Mead's writings in which the theory of language is linked, albeit in a very crude way, to the corporeal expressive movements of the human organism. In this article of 1904, Mead summarizes completely uncritically, not only Wundt's interpretation of the gesture as an affective expression, but also the further implications of his conception of language. Wundt conceives of communication as having arisen out of a mechanism by means of which gestures call forth in a fellow species-member feelings that are identical with the affects triggering those gestures. Gradually – according to Wundt – the identical sympathetic movements became transformed into answering movements, and there originated 'a common thought process, taking place through the exchange of gesture expression'.[11] Mead does not question the plausibility of the details of this explanation, for his initial reception of Wundt's theory is pervaded by enthusiasm over this approach to a theory of language in general and over the scientific harvest promised by the supplanting of elementarist psychology with a theory of action.

> Perhaps there is no better illustration of the importance of psychology to the comprehension of language than such a natural and simple presentation of the beginning of the interchange of ideas through the simple sympathetic interaction of gesture expression within a common emotional situation. There could be no better illustration of the advantage of beginning one's psychological analysis with the act in its primitive form of the impulse, instead of being forced to build it up out of intellectual elements.[12]

Speech is an act and like any other act has its natural history which psychology can undertake to give us from a study of its nature and its analogy to other acts. It is, in its primitive form, emotional expression, not because primitive languages are more emotional, but because gestures and cries are the external parts of emotional acts.[13]

Reading this article, one has the feeling that Mead has found in Wundt's work a text of key importance for him, similar to Dewey's essay on the reflex-arc concept, a text whose ideas he will henceforth continuously elaborate and rework, in order to adapt them for his own purposes, and at the same time to give his own undertaking a scientifically tenable form.

In his second article on Wundt's *Völkerpsychologie*, Mead is much more critical and in many respects makes use of arguments which he presented in 'The Definition of the Psychical' to show the inconsistencies of Wundt's voluntaristic psychology. Examining two of Wundt's notions, Mead demonstrates that, while the former does go a step beyond associationist psychology, he also exhibits strong tendencies to fall back into that psychology. The first of these notions is Wundt's concept of apperception, a term used to designate the operations of consciousness going beyond association. However, Wundt ultimately explains these apperceptions by means of the associations, rather than accounting for associations by means of the selective operations of the action-nexus of consciousness, which is the only way that an adequate concept of consciousness could be arrived at. Second, Mead shows that there is an unresolved contradiction between Wundt's concept of feeling as a content of consciousness and as a kinesthetic sensation directly connected with movement and action. Because the foundation of his reflections is insufficient, Wundt does not succeed in employing for the theory of imagination the productive approach of his theory of myth. Instead, he projects backward in time the autonomous art of his own epoch and interprets artistic production according to the explanatory schema of individual desire to express emotional experiences independently of the social and practical context of the artistic production. Mead, however, does not draw from these notions implications for the further development of Wundt's theory of language, even though this would have been possible in the case of the concepts of feeling and consciousness, as will be shown below.

Not until 1909 did Mead publish the first in a series of articles which, appearing in rapid succession, and each referring to a large extent directly to its predecessors, presented the crucial steps in Mead's elaboration of his conception of symbolic interaction. The purpose of the first of these articles, entitled 'Social Psychology as Counterpart to Physiological Psychology', was to demonstrate that soical science is not a field of application for psychology, but is rather presupposed by psychology as much as biology or physiology is generally recognized to be. Mead's thesis has two goals. First, it combats psychologists' understanding of their discipline as a constitutive science which, as Wundt maintained, can serve to found both the natural and the human sciences. Second, Mead's thesis counters the position that social psychology is to be understood as the application of psychology to the social interrelations of human beings or to the uniformities of their behaviour. In arguing for his thesis, Mead directs his irony especially at the influential treatise on social psychology authored by E. A. Ross.[14] Mead's unremitting concern to bring to light and to comprehend the profoundly social character of consciousness and of the psychical guides the survey of the attempts to elaborate a social psychology that he gives in this article. This concern also leads him to caution sociologists, who had overcome the hostility to psychology prevalent in their field since Comte, to determine what the value of the social character of human consciousness is in any psychology that they attempt to use.

But what is the step towards the development of the concept of symbolic interaction that Mead makes in this article? For the first time Mead uses the concept of *meaning*, and attempts to combine this concept which he had introduced in the philosophical formulation given by Royce, with Wundt's anthropological theory of language. Royce, whom Mead esteemed most highly of all his academic teachers, and who was one of the few scholars who were familiar with Peirce's writings and also understood them, had attempted to provide a stronger foundation for his theses on the communitarian character of thought by making recourse to Peirce's theory of signs. Royce's enterprise drew Mead's attention, although even in this article of 1909 his dissatisfaction with Royce's way of thinking, which did not go beyond philosophical speculation, is clear and expresses itself in specific objections. However, from the standpoint of the history of social theory, it is most interesting to see that the frequently noted intrinsic kinship between Mead's linguistic theory and Peirce's 'semiotic transformation of transcendental philosophy'

(Karl-Otto Apel) does not appear to be due to a direct influence, but instead came about through Josiah Royce's intermediation. Nevertheless, Peirce's theory had its effect on Mead, and because of the article under discussion the time of this effect can be determined with relative exactness.

Mead's chief criticism of Royce also reveals the manner in which Mead's project goes beyond Royce's position and the role played by Wundt's theory in that project. Mead objects to Royce's theory of imitation. For the latter, imitation is the presupposition of understanding meaning. In Mead's opinion though, Royce is 'putting the cart before the horse'.[15] For it is rather the case that imitation presupposes that there is already social consciousness. It is not through imitation, says Mead, that we obtain the internal representations of actions which are necessary for grasping the meaning of actions; on the contrary, it is our capacity for these internal representations that permits us both to understand actions and consciously to imitate them. Later, we will consider more closely Mead's constant struggle against the postulation of primitive imitation which, as a pseudo-explanation, more obfuscated than clarified the question of the emergence of the individual consciousness in numerous contemporary theories. What he wants to accomplish with his argument against Royce in the article we are discussing is to penetrate through the explanation given by Royce to the social, collective processes of action that underlie meaning-constituting linguistic communication. When viewed from this perspective, the theory of imitation is seen to be an individualistic subterfuge, since it assumes originary individual intentions with regard to actions, or reduces collective action to mere series of individual actions. To these implications of the theory of imitation Mead opposes the necessity of human cooperation based on division of labour and the probable role of this cooperation.

> The important character of social organization of conduct or behaviour through instincts is not that one form in a social group does what the others do, but that the conduct of one form is a stimulus to another to a certain act, and that this act again becomes a stimulus to [the (H. J.)] first to a certain reaction, and so on in ceaseless interaction. The likeness of the actions is of minimal importance compared with the fact that the actions of one form have the implicit meaning of a certain response to another form. The probable begin-

ning of human communication was in cooperation, not in imitation, where conduct differed and yet where the act of the one answered to and called out the act of the other. The conception of imitation as it has functioned in social psychology needs to be developed into a theory of social stimulation and response and of the social situations which these stimulations and responses create. Here we have the matter and the form of the social object, and here we have also the medium of communication and reflection.[16]

The sphere of cooperative actions is thus opened to the efforts to explain the origin of the individual consciousness and of communication. In addition, Mead's exposition in the passage quoted makes it possible to connect the concept of meaning with Wundt's theory of vocal gestures, according to which these are truncated, syncopated actions serving to express emotions. The theory of signs is thereby related to the social actions of individuals, and on the other hand the social character of the meaningfulness of vocal gestures, which Wundt does not at all make clear in a consequent fashion, is made manifest.

It is evident that but for the original situation of social interaction the bodily and vocal gestures could never have attained their signification. It is their reference to other individuals that has turned expression, as a mere outflow of nervous excitement, into meaning, and this meaning was the value of the act for the other individual . . .[17]

For Mead, then, 'meaning' has its roots in the relations among actors that are established through their actions. Here, however, he defines meaning objectivistically: namely, with reference to the reaction of the other actor. The empirical advantage over Royce's theory gained by this conception of meaning is paid for at first by the loss of a basis for enquiry into an 'ideal' or 'universal' character of meanings transcending the immediate response to a stimulus.

In the next and perhaps most important article of this series, however, the definition of meaning given above has already entered into flux. As indicated by its title, 'Social Consciousness and the Consciousness of Meaning', Mead gives in this article a more refined formulation of the concept of meaning. In doing this, he makes decisive changes in three areas in the previously accepted conception of meaning. He undertakes to pass beyond Wundt's ideas about the connection between gestures and emotions and hence also the latter's notion of human communication, to elaborate a version of the concept of meaning that is no longer objectivist, and to determine more precisely the action-situation in which meaning is constituted.

Mead begins the article by giving a succinct account of communication by means of gestures, which are defined as the early phases of social actions. He explicitly stresses the initially non-intentional character of these gestures and the fact that they play an important role even in the social behaviour of animals. Through this embedding of gestural language in the continuity of human with animal sociality, the anthropomorphism that originated with Darwin is overcome.[18] According to Darwin, gestures serve to express emotions. Wundt had already gone a step further by construing gestures as the initial phases of actions, and as such they were, according to his theory, psychological counterparts to emotional states of consciousness. In opposition to Wundt's position, Mead asserts that while gestures do indeed reveal emotions to the observer, this fact does not at all mean that their function consists in giving expression to emotions. It is, rather, the inhibition of the immediate impulses, which is caused by the compulsion to orient oneself to the beginnings of the acts of other individuals, that brings about an accumulation of dammed-up emotions seeking discharge. In other words, Mead, in contrast to Wundt, is now trying, not to explain gestural communication by means of isolated mental acts, but to ground meaning in the tasks towards which actions are directed, that is to say, in natural problems and the cooperative mastering of them.

> The first function of the gesture is the mutual adjustment of changing social response to changing social stimulation . . .[19]

Harbingers of this critique can be found already in Mead's comments on Wundt's theory of emotions both in 'The Definition of the Psychical' and in the article on Wundt's theory of myth. In both cases Mead found fault with Wundt because of a remnant of the mentalistic psychology of consciousness in the latter's concept of emotion, that is to say, because Wundt did not adequately comprehend the relation between 'action' and 'emotion'. Mead himself draws a sharp distinction between the immediate impulses and the emotions, as these appear in the consciousness of the actor.

Here it is necessary to point out that Mead's theory of emotion is not a new creation by him *ad hoc*; it is, rather, a matter of the introduction into the problematic of language and interaction of a train of thought belonging to Mead's earliest projects in empirical psychology. Unfortunately, all that remains of this project is a short summary of a lecture delivered by Mead at the meeting of the American Psychological Association in 1894 and a reference to it by Dewey in his 'Theory of Emotions'.[20] Scant though this textual material is, it nevertheless suffices to make clear the fundamental idea of this project.

William James, in the well-known James-Lange theory of feeling, liberated, as it were, the conception of emotions from the clutches of associationist psychology and made it 'voluntaristic' by construing – somewhat too narrowly – not actions as the expression of emotions, but instead emotions as consequences of actions and their physiological mechanisms. To James's doctrine Dewey added 'the necessity of conflict in action in order for emotions to arise'.[21] Emotions are, then, to be understood as the appearance of an impulse in consciousness caused by the inhibition of an action, and Mead's central thought with regard to this conception of emotion is to construe this inhibition of an action as a phenomenon systematically included in the planning of action. In this view, emotions are the conditions of the possibility of anticipatory evaluation of an act:

> The teleology of these [emotional (H. J.)] states is that of giving the organism an evaluation of the act before the coordination that leads to the particular reaction has been completed.[22]

From this extremely interesting standpoint, Mead wanted to investigate the relationship between the vegetative and the motor functions of the human organism; as far as we know at the present time, he never carried out this plan. Be that as it may, the critique of Darwin's conception of emotions appeared as early as 1894–95 in Dewey's work, which Mead made use of, and some of whose ideas originally came from him.

Now, the implications of this changed understanding of the relation between gesture and emotion for the model of human communication taken over from Wundt are of great import. The latter had conceived of communication as arising out of the primitive imitation of gestures and the replication, triggered by those gestures, of the feelings that led to a particular triggering gesture. Mead, however, had toppled both of the pillars on which this conception was based: explanation of human communication through recourse to imitation and to expression of emotion. He nevertheless held firm to the programme of deducing human communication from the interplay of gestures and of regarding human communication as the basis of the social character of consciousness. What must now follow are steps leading to the formulation of a new description of the mechanisms of human communication that would satisfy the objections made against the previous attempts to explain its origin.

The new version of the concept of meaning is a first preparation for formulating the new description. No longer is meaning objectivistically misunderstood as the reaction of the other; now it is understood to be the consciousness of the specific readiness for response in the actor himself. Mead distinguishes with the greatest possible clarity consciousness of meanings from the mere experiential accumulation of stimulation:

> The association of one content with another content is not the symbolism of meaning. In the consciousness of meaning the symbol and that which is symbolized – the thing and what it means – must be presented separately.[23]

However, this holds true only for the consciousness of meanings, not for the existence of meanings themselves. Therefore, the distinction between meaningful actions and the making these meanings conscious becomes crucially important. On the one hand, meaning exists precisely in the perfect, completely habitualized relation between an action and an object, in the unanimous correspondence between the qualities of the stimulus and the features of the response. The notion of habitualized meaning now permits Mead to conceive for the first time of the essential difference between human action and animal behaviour, and not, as in 'The Definition of the Psychical', virtually to restrict this difference to the isolated 'luminous phases' when consciousness momentarily gleams out. However, precisely where meaning exists, says Mead, nothing brings forth a consciousness of this meaning:

> In fact it is essential to the economy of our conduct that the connection between stimulation and response should become habitual and should sink below the threshold of consciousness.[24]

How can we escape this dilemma? How can meaning as self-reflective awareness of the individual's own attitude of response originate?

The answer to this question that suggests itself, says Mead, and that at first glance would appear to be a consistent extension of the pragmatist notion of reflection and of the functionalist psychology of thinking, is the simple assertion that meaning does not originate in habitual actions, but only in conflicts in actions. Mead does not make matters so simple for himself, however. For he sees that most conflicts in actions do indeed lead to substantial intensification of the discrimination of stimuli, but do not by any means lead to heightened attention to *one's own* responses. The situation out of which meaning can arise must therefore be such that in it attention to one's own action – and not to the data of the environment – is functional for the actor. *This kind of situation is given only in the case of interaction between or among individual actors.* Only then is one's own action responded to by the immediate responses of others in such a way that one is compelled to assume an attitude of self-reflective attentiveness. Only when we are ourselves the stimulus for the responses of another, responses which are in turn stimuli for us, must we concentrate our attention on our character as a source of stimulation.

During the whole process of interaction with others we are analysing their oncoming acts by our instinctive responses to their changes of posture and other indications of developing social acts. We have seen that the ground for this lies in the fact that social conduct must be continually readjusted after it has already commenced, because the individuals to whose conduct our own answers, are themselves constantly varying their conduct as our responses become evident. Thus our adjustments to their changing reactions take place, by a process of analysis of our own responses to their stimulations. In these social situations appear not only conflicting acts with the increased definition of elements in the stimulation, but also a consciousness of one's own attitude as an interpretation of the meaning of the social stimulus. We are conscious of our attitudes because they are responsible for the changes in the conduct of other individuals. A man's reaction toward weather conditions has no influence upon the weather itself. It is of importance for the success of his conduct that he should be conscious not of his own attitudes, of his own habits of response, but of the signs of rain or fair weather. Successful social conduct brings one into a field within which a consciousness of one's own attitudes helps toward the control of the conduct of others.[25]

Mead illustrates his distinction between social conduct and an individual's reaction to his physical environment with a comparison between the state of consciousness of a man running through a forest or over broken ground and that of a man engaged in combat with an enemy. He concludes this article by stating:

> It must remain for a later paper to analyze the process of language in these terms, and to indicate the fundamental character of this consciousness of meaning in the consciousness of self, and finally to present the process of thought itself as such a play of gesture between selves, even when those selves are a part of our inner self-consciousness.[26]

The subsequent articles of the series and a large part of Mead's later intellectual effort were devoted to the execution of this program.

The next article, 'What Social Objects Must Psychology Presuppose?', admittedly represents progress in this direction only in the indications given in it, since it is chiefly a defence of Mead's whole approach, which was based on functionalist psychology, against the tendencies of this same school to lapse back into introspectionism. To this end Mead presents many of his previous analyses in new formulations. The article's principal purpose is to correct, by demonstrating the social character of self-consciousness, the erroneous understanding of introspection as an approach that begins with the isolated subject's self-certainty. In particular, Mead defends the notion of self-consciousness or of the self as the concept of an objective component of reality, as a part of material social processes. In making this defence, he directs his hopes to the further development of the social sciences, which cannot manage without recognition of the objective existence of others, and which can thus act as a counterweight to the 'solipsistic spook' in philosophy and methodology. Without waiting for this development of the social sciences to occur, however, one can combat this 'spook' by means of immanent critiques of the positions from which it emerges. More clearly than in the preceding article, where the modification was alluded to, Mead defines the concept of meaning, not with reference to the actual reaction of the other, nor to the mere awareness of one's own attitude of response, but rather as the consciousness of the relation between one's own actions and the responses of the other to them, which one can anticipate. However, the most marked advance in the substance of Mead's theory made in this article is announced in its concluding sentences, placed before the reader without supporting arguments:

> Whatever our theory may be as to the history of things, social consciousness must antedate physical consciousness. A more correct statement would be that experience in its original form became reflective in the recognition of selves, and only gradually was there differentiated a reflective experience of things which were purely physical.[27]

Mead expresses here his opposition to the merely abstract separation of our behaviour towards social objects from our behaviour towards physical objects, of communicative from instrumental activity, as much as his opposition to their unclear fusion or the reduction of the one form of activity to the other. His intent is, on the contrary, to link together the two lines of development, which do have to be analytically distinguished, of communicative and instrumental acts. He insists on the emergence of self-reflectivity out of social situations, but also stresses that this self-reflectivity is the precondition for the constitution of things in instrumental action. With this assertion Mead broaches the subject matter of one of the most important of his later areas of research.[28]

In Mead's work up to this point, two areas of unsolved problems in particular have become delimited. One of these has to do with the just-mentioned problem of the relationship between 'social' and 'physical objects'. To be sure, it is not necessary for the foundation of social psychology that the concrete linking of these two lines of development of consciousness in fact be effected. What does have to be accomplished, though, is a clear determination of the difference in the way the two kinds of 'objects' are given. The other area concerns the elaboration of an alternative conception to Wundt's mechanism of communication, which is also an application of the concept of meaning that Mead has worked out to the question of the evolution of human language from gestural communication. These two problem-areas are central to the next article in the series, 'The Mechanism of Social Consciousness'.

With regard to the first area, Mead attempts in this article to define the character of the social object in such a way that it becomes clear that every social object is also a physical object, while being at the same time more than a physical object. He describes very subtly the constitution of physical objects in the combining of stimulus and past experience, of distant stimuli and contact experiences. The social object is then initially defined in parallel fashion.

> The object was found to consist of the sensuous experience of the stimulation to an act plus the imagery from past experience of the final result of the act. The social object will then be the gestures, i.e., the early indications of an ongoing social act in another plus the imagery of our own response to that stimulation.[29]

Just as the child's feeling of having a unitary body presupposes the prior development of the notion of physical objects, so too the child's own 'self' can only arise after it has developed the notion of social objects.

> The form of the object is given [to him (H. J.)] in the experience of things, which are not his physical self. When he has synthesized his various bodily parts with the organic sensations and affective experiences, it will be upon the model of objects about him. The mere presence of experiences of pleasure and pain, together with organic sensations, will not form an object unless this material can fall into the scheme of an object . . . This is as true of the object that appears in social conduct, the self. The form of the social object must be found first of all in the experience of other selves.[30]

To this analogy Mead can easily join one between the individual parts of the unitary body, which, however, must first be apprehended in their unity, and the individual components of a self: he conceives of the 'me', which arises in every interaction as the image of my own person that I perceive in the partner to the interaction, in its dependence on the multiplicity of interaction-situations. It is then the task of the self actively to synthesize the numerous, ever new 'me's' into a unitary self-image. Persuasive as this analogy is, it can hardly be the final word on this matter. Mead has only placed two chains of developmental steps alongside each other here – the one in the sphere of the constitution of the physical object, and the other in the sphere of the formation of the self – without giving consideration to the fact that they are entwined one with the other, a fact that necessarily results from his thesis that self-reflectivity is a presupposition of the constitution of physical objects. However, this article introduces into the theory of the origination of human communication a new idea of decisive importance.

In this paper Mead adds to the theory of the necessary connection of self-perception with situations of interaction his insight into the evolutionary value of the fact that vocal gestures can be perceived by the human individual who is making them. Self-reflectivity, says Mead, can *originate* where social actions can themselves be directly perceived by the actor himself, so that – prior to the constitution of the self and hence prior to the differentiation between 'I' and 'you' – my own action can trigger in me the same responses as in the other to whom my action is directed. Only in this fashion does the structure of social interaction, of which only one of the participants in socialization initially has a real mastery, come to be internally at the disposal of both parties.[31]

> Certainly the fact that the human animal can stimulate himself as he stimulates others and can respond to his stimulations as he responds to the stimulations of others, places in his conduct the form of a social object out of which may arise a 'me' to which can be referred so-called subjective experiences.[32]

Of course, Mead does not regard self-perception of vocal gestures by the one making them as the only possibility for building up a self. He calls attention to the development of deaf-mute children and asserts that only the individual's affecting of himself is necessary.

> Any gesture by which the individual can himself be affected as others are affected, and which therefore tends to call out in him a response as it would call it out in another, will serve as a mechanism for the construction of a self.[33]

Phylogenetically, however, the development of the human self seems to have taken place by means of vocal gestures. But it is obvious, Mead continues, that the mere capacity to respond to one's own gestures is a necessary, not a sufficient condition for the emergence of self-consciousness, for the talking of a parrot, as everyone agrees, does not lead to its formation of a self. The superficial similarity conceals here the profound difference of the sphere of 'social objects', the difference between the structure of interaction between human beings and, say, the structure of interaction among birds. Within the entire complex of conditions which make hominization possible, Mead believes that in the vocal gesture, perceptible by the individual making it and therefore potentially a bearer of meaning, he has found the crucial mechanism which made possible the reshaping of animal sociality into human sociality.

Mead concludes his article 'The Mechanism of Social Consciousness' with remarks on the character of the notion of the 'I'. Having worked out, in its fundamental outlines, a complete analysis of the social origination of meaning and self-consciousness, he can now shed new light on the untenable nature of the thesis that the 'I' can be experienced directly. Mead stresses unequivocally that the 'I' can contemplate itself only through recourse to past actions, that is, through remembering these actions; however, the remembering 'I' is already changed, so that it is impossible for the knowing 'I' to be congruent with the known 'I'. This assertion is the starting point of the last paper of the series we are considering.

Making use of the distinction between 'I', 'me', and 'self', Mead demonstrates in 'The Social Self' the dialogical or dramatic structure of self-consciousness. These three concepts, which were introduced by James, are given new meanings in the context of Mead's theory of the social formation of the self. For James, the 'social self' was only one among several selves; it was the social mirroring of the self, to which he attributed influence, but did not ascribe a constitutive function. James had also assumed a self-consciousness that was, in virtue of its essential nature, constantly present. Mead identifies the experience behind this psychological thesis: the experience of a vague consciousness accompanying our actions:

> that running current of awareness of what we do which is distinguishable from the consciousness of the field of stimulation, whether that field be without or within. . . At the back of our heads we are a large part of the time more or less clearly conscious of our own replies to the remarks made to others, of innervations which would lead to attitudes and gestures answering our gestures and attitudes toward others.[34]

Mead knew that he must be able to explain this phenomenon, in order to block a lapse back into introspectionism. He models his explanation after the response of an actor to himself, which is characteristic of that sort of one's own gestures which can be perceived by the actor. While we act, not only do we stand in relation to the objects of our actions; there are also immediate repercussions of our actions on ourselves. Thus, a speaker is also one of those who hears what he says.

> The actual situation is this: The self acts with reference to others, and is immediately conscious of the objects about it. In memory it also reintegrates the self acting as well as the others acted upon. But besides these contents, the action with reference to the others calls out responses in the individual himself – there is then another 'me' criticizing, approving, and suggesting, and consciously planning, i.e., the reflective self.[35]

This self-reflective consciousness accompanying our actions cannot, however, be the necessary precondition of self-reflective action. This is shown most clearly by the fact that it recedes as we become increasingly absorbed in something and completely concentrate our attention on it.

The demonstration that the self is socially constituted also makes it possible to grasp the essence of the *per se* social structure of the self. Here Mead employs for the first time the concept of role, in order to express that our self-image results from the internal representation of others' responses to us; when we internally represent these responses of others, then we assume, so to speak, their roles.

> In this way we play the roles of all our group; indeed, it is only in so far as we do this that they become part of our social environment – to be aware of another self as a self implies that we have played his role or that of another with whose type we identify him for purposes of intercourse. The inner response to our reaction to others is therefore as varied as is our social environment.[36]

In Mead's opinion there is a continuous development, extending from the immediately dialogical structure of the self-consciousness of the child, who speaks to itself in the words of its parents, to the most abstract processes of thought. In the course of this development, the direct connection to particular persons of the individual parts of the internal process of communication, as which Mead considers all reflection, becomes weaker; but the mechanism is unchanged and remains a social one:

Until this process has been developed into the abstract process of thought, self-consciousness remains dramatic, and the self which is a fusion of the remembered actor and this accompanying chorus is somewhat loosely organized and very clearly social. Later the inner stage changes into the forum and workshop of thought. The features and intonations of the *dramatis personae* fade out and the emphasis falls upon the meaning of the inner speech, the imagery becomes merely the barely necessary cues. But the mechanism remains social, and at any moment the process may become personal.[37]

With the formulation of these insights the history of the emergence, strictly speaking, of the concept of symbolic interaction is concluded. Henceforth this conception will be expressed in different forms and various terminologies and used, above all, as the basis for Mead's argumentation in the other research fields of his later writings. The essays in which Mead's thoughts on this subject first found form do not, however, lend themselves as well to a first effort to become acquainted with Mead's central ideas as do some later ones. The brief summary 'A Behavioristic Account of the Significant Symbol',[38] for example, is especially noteworthy for the first appearance in it of Mead's description of his position as 'behaviouristic'. The paper 'The Genesis of the Self and Social Control', which appeared in 1925, offers a mature recapitulation of Mead's theory, which is presented there, however, completely with reference to the constitution of time and of physical objects. In his review of Dewey's work on social psychology, *Human Nature and Conduct*, – which, as far as I know, was never published,[39] – Mead is extremely critical of the strongly rhetorical character of Dewey's book and of the indifference to empirical evidence displayed in its arguments. Further, Mead deplores Dewey's lack of precision and logical consequence from the standpoint of a theory of intersubjectivity. Finally, in the essay on Charles Cooley, which appeared not long before Mead's death, he praises highly Cooley's attempt to elaborate a theory of the social formation of the self, but unequivocally distinguishes his own theory from that of Cooley. Mead demarcates a conception of society which is intrinsically social and takes into account the actions of the members of society from one which is individualistic and takes into consideration only direct and conscious communicative exchanges between actors. In contrast to Cooley, Mead regards a society as an objective action-nexus, and not as an interrelational complex of the subjective mental presentations which the society's members have of one another.

One of the few passages in which Mead treats problems of the methodology of empirical social research occurs in this important article. Mead clearly rejects the restriction of social research to the study and understanding of individual cases and would like to integrate the interpretations provided by social psychology and interpretative analyses of data into an objective theory of society. As the pioneers of such a theory of society Mead names the luminaries of the Chicago School, the most important of whom was William Isaac Thomas. A controversy becomes visible here, one which was not fought out then because objectivistic, quantifying methods soon gained predominance. Later, when 'interpretative' approaches to social research were rediscovered, the controversy was eclipsed by the enthusiasm for the alternative to the quantifying methods that was being delineated. However, if social scientists seek to draw from Mead's theory its methodological implications, then this state of affairs cannot be allowed to continue.[40]

Having told the story of the origin of the concept of symbolic interaction, I should now like only to recapitulate this notion, by way of summary, in the form in which Mead left it to us. This can be done briefly, as the ground for this undertaking has been prepared by the familiarity of *Mind, Self, and Society* to large numbers of my readers and by synopses of Mead's thought. Therefore, it is merely a matter here of giving a succinct systematization of the notion of symbolic interaction, while pointing out empirical confirmations of Mead's theory as well as evidence that calls it into question.

In founding his social psychology, Mead does not begin with the behaviour of a single organism or human individual, but rather with a cooperating group of specifically human organisms. For Mead the primordial given is not a 'Robinsonade', not solitary actors who must first enter into social relations with one another, and who must first constitute commonly binding values, but instead the 'social act', the complex activity of a group.

> We attempt, that is, to explain the conduct of the individual in terms of the organized conduct of the social group, rather than to account for the organized conduct of the social group in terms of the conduct of the separate individuals belonging to it. For social psychology, the

whole (society) is prior to the part (the individual), not the part to the whole; and the part is explained in terms of the whole, not the whole in terms of the part or parts.[41]

This social psychology and theory of society, is, then, behaviouristic in Mead's sense of the term when it analyses all social processes according to categories of action – which is something completely different from what reductionistic behaviourism seeks to accomplish. Unlike the various attempts of crude behaviourism to liberalize itself, Mead's approach does not consider phenomena of intentionality and self-reflectivity to be merely additional variables; rather, Mead sees in these phenomena precisely that which is distinctive of human action.

> Social psychology is behaviouristic in the sense of starting off with an observable activity – the dynamic, on-going social process, and the social acts which are its component elements – to be studied and analyzed scientifically. But it is not behaviouristic in the sense of ignoring the inner experience of the individual – the inner phase of that process or activity. On the contrary, it is particularly concerned with the rise of such experience within the process as a whole. It simply works from the outside to the inside instead of from the inside to the outside, so to speak, in its endeavour to determine how such experience does arise within the process. *The act, then, and not the tract, is the fundamental datum in both social and individual psychology when behaviouristically conceived,* and it has both an inner and an outer phase, an internal and an external aspect.[42]

Mead regards behaviourism in the reductionistic sense as empirically false – it can be refuted with anthropological and phylogenetic arguments. Of central importance for Mead's own position is the fact that he has passed beyond the view that humans are by nature non-social. He does not conceive of society as a merely historical and cultural phenomenon, which as an external bond holds together human individuals who are by their nature isolated. Instead, he conceives of human nature itself as essentially social.[43] Thus the difference between human and animal sociality becomes for him a central object of research. According to Mead, groups of human organisms are characterized by features which distinguish them essentially from organisms at pre-human levels. In contrast to the highly developed social forms of insect colonies, a rigorous division of labour cannot be guaranteed in human society by biological specialization of anatomy and differentiation of innate patterns of behaviour. The organizing principle of societies of vertebrate animals is also impossible for human society, namely the organization of group life by instinctually rigid forms of behaviour, which are modified solely through gaining a certain status in a unilinear hierarchy of dominance. In social groups of primates we can, it is true, already find rudimentary traditions, but these remain narrowly delimited, since they do not assume objectified form.[44] The development of human society requires the solution of the problem of how individual behaviour, that is not naturally fixed, can be developed into differential forms, and how these can then be integrated into a unitary group activity by means of reciprocal expectations about behaviour. With his anthropological theory of the origin of specifically human communication, Mead tries to uncover the mechanism that makes this possible. Admittedly, this yields only a logical reconstruction of the process of hominization, not a complete anthropological theory, since Mead completely neglects the ecological conditions of this process. Within the framework of this logical reconstruction, the ability to communicate occupies the focal point of the analysis:

> In man the functional differentiation through language gives an entirely different principle of organization which produces not only a different type of individual but also a different society.[45]

In Mead's view, specifically human communication is what makes possible the coordination of instrumental action-processes organized in accordance with a division of labour. To criticize Mead's concept of society for being narrowly based on communication reveals, therefore, serious misunderstanding. He states, with unequivocal clarity:

> The mechanism of human society is that of bodily selves who assist or hinder each other in their cooperative acts by the manipulation of physical things.[46]

Neither from the phylogenetic nor from the ontogenetic perspective does Mead hold the view that sociality is linguistically constituted. Rather, through his concept of intersubjectivity, which extends beyond speech to encompass and begin with gestural communication, Mead succeeds in elaborating theories showing the connectedness of developments in the interpersonal sphere and in the sphere of human activity directed to physical objects.

Mead, then, situates language in the context of 'body-related expressions', and does not conceive of it as the incarnation of an originally pure mind. For Mead, language is to be understood only as it functions in cooperative physical actions, and not on the model of expressional intentions which are fixed in the individual consciousness prior to all interaction. In rejecting this model, which he calls that of the 'prisoner in a cell', Mead gives a highly graphic description of it:

> The study of the process of language or speech – its origins and development – is a branch of social psychology, because it can be understood only in terms of the social processes of behaviour within a group of interacting organisms; because it is one of the activities of such a group. The philologist, however, has often taken the view of the prisoner in a cell. The prisoner knows that others are in a like position and he wants to get in communication with them. So he sets about some method of communication, some arbitrary affair, perhaps, such as tapping on the wall. Now, each of us, on this view, is shut up in his own cell of consciousness, and knowing that there are other people so shut up, develops ways to set up communication with them.[47]

What Mead's various analyses, which need not be repeated in detail here, come down to is that – given the human individual's constitutional uncertainty of reaction, caused by reduction of instinct in humans, and given the retardation of reaction made possible by the human nervous system – the existence of gestures which the one making them can perceive himself does not merely result in the functioning of signs as quasi-stimuli, but also has the consequence that thereby the stimulus-response schema of behaviour is broken through, something that would otherwise not occur. It has become possible for a human actor to direct his actions according to the potential responses of his partners in interaction. Human action is oriented in accordance with behavioural expectations; since the same capacity is, in principle, at the disposal of one's partner in an interaction, a shared, and binding, pattern of reciprocal behavioural expectations is the precondition of collective activity.

At this point it would be appropriate to interject with two observations on Mead's concept of meaning. The one is occasioned by the description of Mead's theory of language as lying between theories that assert a linguistic constitution of meaning and so-called copy theories of language – whether seeing language as a copy of mind or of reality makes no difference here. Meaning, in Mead's view, is not linguistically constituted, nor is it simply pre-existent. Rather, meaning exists prior to consciousness of meaning, namely in the objective structure of the active relation of an organism to a determinate component of its environment. This structure can be shaped through action and is constituted by the acting subject through his practice.

The other observation concerns the thesis that meaning does not obtain *de facto* but rather *de jure*:[48] that is, meaning is not confined to actual responses, ideal meanings, or reference to objects as such, but instead must be conceived of as a claim to validity.[49] Peirce's 'pragmatic maxim' locates meaning in instructions for action; Mead locates meaning in behavioural expectations. Both positions must be rigorously distinguished from the reduction of meanings to actually observable action.[50] Only then is an identity of meaning among actors responding in different ways understandable.

Despite certain modifications of some of Mead's ideas, which were determined by the contemporary state of knowledge, the biological components of Mead's argumentation in proof of his theory have been well confirmed empirically.[51] Although I will point out three deficiencies of Mead's theory, I do not intend thereby to weaken the foregoing assertion, but merely to indicate parts of that theory which must be worked out more precisely, if the theory is to be more than a chapter in the history of ideas and to claim to be a valid account of reality. The deficiencies in question are the following. First, Mead does not analyse the reasons for the frequency of the human being's autonomous uttering of sounds, before these sounds have taken on the function of significant symbols. On this point he should have given additional explanations, perhaps, for example, accounting for it by means of Konrad Lorenz's ethological concept of displacement movement.[52] Second, Mead does not show how the capacity to assimilate social stimuli comes into being in human ontogenesis.[53] There is no doubt that he ascribes the emergence of this capacity to an organic maturation of the perceptual apparatus, which, however, he does not define more exactly.[54] Third, in his theory of the origin of language, Mead restricts himself to the level of symbolic interactions and of elementary, one- and two-word sentences. His theory lacks an adequate concept of syntax as much as it does a semantics comprehending word fields and fields of meaning, or a taxonomy of the various ways in which language can be pragmatically used. This deficiency lessens the plausibility of Mead's analysis among linguists who are concerned with highly differentiated syntactic constructions, and it has to be supplied through reconstruction, from the standpoint of interaction theory, of the processes of language learning going beyond the level of Mead's analysis.[55]

A further area in which Mead's theory must be strengthened against present-day criticisms, and for which the prospects are good that it can be, is the significance of imitation for the child's development.[56] In Mead's view, the analysis of intersubjective phenomena using the concept of imitation is not an explanation, but rather a speculative construction that prevents approaches derived from theories of intersubjectivity from being accepted and developed further. He repeats again and again that imitation is not an impulse, but comes about only through the acquisition of role-taking abilities. However, even if one accepts Mead's rejection of an explanation of language acquisition by means of imitation, his position on the matter is not the final word on the precise definition of the function of imitation. To be sure, by using Mead's arguments one can reject explanations of language acquisition based on the behaviouristic theory of learning as well as the premature embedding of human learning in an alleged phylogenetic continuity.[57] But then one still has to establish, independently of these, the nuanced connection of the various forms of imitation with the stages of the child's development. In this respect, Piaget's theory of imitation is important and resembles Mead's rejection of the explanation of imitation phenomena by positing an originary impulse to imitation. Piaget analyses the stages of imitation according to the stages of the development of the child's intelligence. However, it has been correctly observed by a number of authors[58] that Piaget's analyses do not include investigation of the response of the partner in situations of imitation, and that they thus implicitly decide in advance against an interpretation from the viewpoint of a theory of intersubjectivity. Piaget's interpretation of imitation as an operation of the intelligence tears asunder the interaction-nexus of reciprocal imitation and makes social development merely an instance of the application of cognitive development. We will have to return to this complex of problems when we treat the constitution of physical objects and of temporality.[59]

The anthropological theory of communication provided Mead with the most important concepts for his social psychology.[60] The concept of 'role', for example, designates the 'pattern' of behavioural expectation; 'taking the role of the other' refers to the anticipation of the behaviour of the other, and not taking over his position in an organized social situation. As a result of this internal representation of the behaviour of the other, different moments take form within the individual human consciousness. Indeed, the individual now makes his own behaviour an object of his contemplation and evaluation in a similar manner as the behaviour of his partners in interaction: he sees himself from the perspective of the other. Thus, alongside the impulses there now appears a moment that can evaluate them, and that consists in the expectations of the reactions to the external expression of these impulses. In this connection Mead speaks of 'I' and 'me'. The concept of the 'I' designates for Mead not only the principle of spontaneity and creativity, as it does in the philosophical tradition, but also the endowment of the human being with impulses. The reference of this concept is seen as self-contradictory only if one associates the term 'impulse' with some natural compulsion of which the human individual is only dimly aware, in opposition to which freedom takes the form of an incorporeal mind.

In contrast to this viewpoint, Mead, like Gehlen, thinks of the human being as endowed with a 'constitutional surplus of impulses'; going beyond all the possible limits of the impulses' satiation, this surplus finds expression in fantasies, and social norms can only channel it. 'Me' refers to my mental presentation of the image that the other has of me, or, at a primitive level, to my internalization of his expectations of me. The 'me' as the precipitate within me of a person who serves as a standard of reference for me is an evaluating moment serving the structuration of spontaneous impulses, as well as an element of my emerging self-image. If I encounter several reference persons who have significance for me, then I acquire several different 'me's'. In order for consistent behaviour to be at all possible, these different 'me's' must be synthesized into a unitary self-image. If this synthesis is successful, then there originates the 'self' as a unitary self-evaluation and orientation of action, that is nevertheless flexible and open to communication with a gradually increasing number of partners. Simultaneously, there develops a personality structure that is stable and certain of its needs. Unlike Freud's, Mead's model is oriented to a dialogue of impulses and social expectations. Mead does not present us with a choice between the inescapable alternatives of repression as the price of culture and anarchic satisfaction of impulses; rather, the model he offers is one of open exchange and discussion, in which social norms are accessible to communicative modification, and the impulses to discerning and voluntary, because satisfying, re-orientation.

Mead's theory of personality passes over into an attempt to elaborate a developmental logic of the formation of the self. Central to this logic are the two kinds of children's activity which he calls 'play' and 'game'. 'Play' is the interaction of a child with an imaginary partner,in which the child mimes both parts of the interaction. In this form of play the child's capacity for anticipation of behaviour is given practice: the behaviour of the other is directly, that is through imitation, represented and complemented by the child's behaviour in his own person. The child has reached this stage as soon as it is capable of interaction with any reference person whatever, and of taking the viewpoint of the other; that is to say, when the reference person who is invested by the impulses with a high degree of significance is no longer the only one who counts. This stage of development is followed by the attainment of the capacity for 'games', for participation in group play. This ability requires more than the anticipation of the behaviour of a single partner; now the behaviour of all other partners must be taken as the guideline for the child's action. These others are not at all unconnected parts, but have functions within groups whose activities are directed to goals through division of labour. The individual actor must orient himself to a goal that is valid for all the actors concerned, which Mead, trying to express its psychological bases, calls the 'generalized other'. The behavioural expectations of this 'generalized other' are, in the case of group play, the rules of the game, and more generally the norms and values of a group, which are of course differentiated to apply to specific positions in the group and to specific situations. The orientation to a particular generalized other reproduces, certainly, on a new plane the same restriction as does the orientation to a particular concrete other. The problem implicit in this similarity: orientation to an ever more universal generalized other, then becomes, as shall be shown, one of the guiding ideas of Mead's ethics.

Admittedly, Mead is very vague when answering the question, at which age of the child do these developmental steps occur? Since it is a matter here of a developmental logic, in contrast to a developmental psychology, this is not a defect; nonetheless, the lack of precision often makes the interpretation of the examples difficult. It is clear that with the formation of the self Mead is not referring to the successful conclusion of the adolescent crisis, but at a much more elementary level to an infantile self, although many examples do provide a basis for the other interpretation. The phasing of the capacities for 'play' and 'game' gives rise to difficulties, since it is clear that the ability to participate in coordinated collectives must be acquired on several levels, and is not, for example, acquired either shortly after the end of the sensory-motor phase of development, or only when children reach school-age. I attribute the lack of more precise statements on these points in Mead's writings to the fact that he completely omitted to relate his model of development systematically to the motivational development of the child. After a period of adherence to instinct theories, Mead, under the influence of Freud and against the background of a general behaviourist victory over explanations of human conduct by means of instincts, changed over to a conceptual framework that was at bottom closely related to psychoanalytic anthropology. He assumed the existence of natural aggressive and solidary impulses, which, however, as such are only the material of the motives: the internalized community monitors them, and prescribes for them the form of expression.[61] All of the human being's instinctual impulses are reduced in strength and can be restrained; they enter into a motivational structure only through interpretation and experience, and can be subjected to examination by the individual. Mead does not restrict the sociality of the motivational structure to its being socially formed, though, but emphasizes repeatedly the intrinsically motivating character of an activity which is a communal striving to attain common goals. He did not, however, elaborate such a theory of motivation and embed it in a theory of society.

6

Ethics

Mead's ethics cannot be separated from his fundamental premises for a theory of action and from his social-psychological conceptual framework. This is true not only in the sense that Mead's ethics unavoidably names and defends explicitly the concerns informing his *oeuvre*. It has been mentioned repeatedly that the origin of Mead's and Dewey's model of action is to be found in their reflections on situations in which moral problems arise, and that Mead's interest in a theory of intersubjectivity developed through his opposition, on the one hand, to considering individual egoism to be an innate characteristic of human beings and, on the other hand, to hypostatization of collectivities, which negated the individuality of the collectivities' members. Mead's references to ethics in his early writings also make it clear that he believed that in ethics he could see revealed most directly – without as yet introducing any elements of a theory of intersubjectivity – the significance of creative, 'synthesizing' operations of the self as an Hegelian legacy.[1] Nevertheless, this apparent biographical connection for Mead between ethics and science is less important than their systematic connection in his thought. The latter consists in Mead's use of his concepts of action and interaction in order to found his ethical ideas and to uncover the psychological presuppositions of competing approaches to ethics.

Mead insists on the normative implications of his concept of action, as well as on the more than merely empirical or descriptive character of the fundamental concepts of his social psychology, such as the 'self' or role-taking. He advances and defends the thesis that action *per se* is not an ethical value, but that without action the realization of values is impossible. Although the self and role-taking are conceived of as scientifically demonstrable *specifica* of human

121

sociality, they nonetheless also have as such the status of anthropological conditions for the possibility of realizing an ideal society. Admittedly, with these assertions Mead arouses the suspicion of those who hope to safeguard science's claim to objectivity by privatizing value-relations, and it will be necessary to show how Mead himself interpreted the relatinship of ethics to science, considered as objective. In any case, complete understanding of the concept of 'practical intersubjectivity' is possible only if one also includes ethics under this concept. For in ethics is exhibited the necessarily practical character of intersubjectivity, which distinguishes rationally guided, common activity from collective self-gratification, as well as the intersubjective character of praxis, which distinguishes such activity from the destructive competition of egotistical individual human subjects.

Even more so than for other aspects of Mead's *oeuvre*, the textual foundation for an examination of his reflections on ethics is such as to cause the researcher difficulties. Such an interpretation must be based on passages in the most varied works and on the very few articles that Mead himself published on ethics, in which numerous theses are advanced but not systematically grounded.[2] Further, Mead's lectures for a course entitled 'Elementary Ethics' are available in detailed (and unpublished) student notes from 1927.[3] To be sure, these lectures are more informative with regard to Mead's demarcation of his own approach from others than with respect to a systematic carrying through of his own undertaking. In them it is clear that Mead drew very strongly on Dewey and Tuft's book on ethics,[4] to which Mead's students were referred for explication of lines of thought that Mead only mentions in passing. From this one should not, however, conclude that Mead's thought is identical to that of Dewey in the field of ethics, since Mead was driven by his much clearer adherence to a theory of intersubjectivity to emphasize objectivity and universality in ethics more strongly than Dewey.[5]

Mead and Dewey developed the premises of their own ethics through criticism of utilitarian and Kantian ethics, considering each from the standpoint of the other. Utilitarian ethics is the prototype of a morality confined to the results of action. Mead is quite willing to regard it as a refreshing antidote to a mere ethics of intention or conviction. Utilitarianism overcomes the restriction, effected by Protestant Christianity, of the good being a matter of volition and makes ethics a practical matter, having to do with changing society.

Utilitarianism succeeds in doing this only by completely severing the connection between action and the actor's motives; for utilitarianism there exists only a single, unchanging motive for action, namely 'desire for pleasure and the avoidance of pain'. In the social context the conclusion to be drawn from this premise is that the morally best conduct is that which satisfies this desire to the greatest extent; that action is good which contributes to the greatest possible happiness for the largest possible number of people.

Mead concerns himself in detail with the question of how, in the writings of the chief representatives of this school, Bentham and Mill, the social can appear in a form going beyond this external conception of it. He establishes that for Bentham the happiness of the other is only a means to one's own happiness, while the younger Mill unequivocally conceives of the direct willing of good for the other as a goal of the individual. The latter attempts to analyse the phenomenon of conscience in the framework of utilitarian theory, and to this end works out an explanation based on associationist psychology, according to which consideration of others is an habitualized property. From these lectures it becomes clear that in Mead's view the utilitarian theoreticians, who were proponents of social reform, had failed in their efforts to found altruism upon a theory of self-interest.

In contrast, Mead regards Kant's ethics as the most thoroughly thought out and impressive form of a pure ethics of conviction. It is not the result of an action that is decisive for its moral quality, but the intention out of which the action arose. Kant assumes the existence of conscience and the autonomy of the will, and sees in them, that is, in the possible rationality of the individual, the presuppositions for giving a rational form to society. In the 'categorical imperative' he formulated the principle of an ethics which grounds its universality in the motive of the actor himself. Mead shares this striving toward universality, yet he finds Kant's ethics insufficient for several reasons. Restricting the universality of moral actions to action performed from a sense of duty places duty in insurmountable opposition to inclination, and makes a truly dialogical and situation-relative character of moral action impossible. Mead mentions Schiller's critique of Kant, in which Schiller called attention to the moral quality of a good deed performed from inclination and argues that Kant's ethics was repressive of human needs and wants, as it was impossible from the standpoint of such ethics to make human needs and wants themselves the object of decision-making. A really dialogical procedure is prevented, inasmuch as the moral law in its transcendental status does not become clearly recognizable as the totality of the requirements for cooperation by individuals having equal rights. Mead stresses very strongly that the self-examination called for by the categorical imperative reaches its limit when it is not a matter of determining just what one's duty is, but of resolving a conflict of duties, or, better, of establishing a constructive way of fulfilling one's duty. The question of the correct way to do one's duty, which is not pre-ordained but has to be creatively discovered, bursts asunder the framework of a Kantian ethics.

In Mead's opinion, the deficiencies of utilitarian and Kantian ethics turn out to be complementary:

> The Utilitarian cannot make morality connect with the motive, and Kant cannot connect morality with the end.[6]

The cause for both deficiencies is to be found in a false concept of action, which artificially tears apart the motive and the object of an action.[7] A motive that is not directed to the active attaining of an object is not truly a motive. Mead interprets this separation of motive and end as an expression of the empiricist concept of experience, which at bottom also applies to Kant's notion of inclination. He responds:

> We are now free from the restrictions of the Utilitarian and Kantian if we recognize that desire is directed toward the object instead of toward pleasure. Both Kant and the Utilitarian are fundamentally hedonists, assuming that our inclinations are toward our own subjective states – the pleasure that comes from satisfaction. If that is the end, then of course our motives are all subjective affairs. From Kant's standpoint they are bad, and from the Utilitarian standpoint they are the same for all actions and so neutral. But on the present view, if the object itself is better, then the motive is better.[8]

Mead's first step toward passing beyond the unacceptable choice between the alternatives of a mere ethics of conviction and an ethics of mere responsibility for the results of one's action is a critique of the 'hedonistic fallacy':

The Hedonistic fallacy is that as soon as you give your attention to the pleasure you stop seeking it.[9]

It is hedonistic psychology and not the inadequate solution of the problematic of the theory of intersubjectivity which establishes the insurmountable particularism of the individual's inclinations and impulses. Only when the insight has been attained that not the particular individual's awareness of his own state, but the attainment of objective ends of his actions motivates him to act, does the concept of motive take on a form susceptible to universalization, so that the claim to universal validity can be examined in the intersubjective sphere.

Mead attempts to provide support for this critique of the psychological presuppositions of the ethics he criticizes by demonstrating that Kant, too, cannot avoid introducing into his consciously formal ethics a material content endowed with value. In Mead's words, Kant states

that there is no content, but by setting the human being up as an end in himself, and so society as a higher end, he introduces content.

This picture of a kingdom of ends is hardly to be distinguished from Mill's doctrine, since both set up society as an end. Each of them has to get to some sort of an end that can be universal. The Utilitarian reaches that in the general good, the general happiness of the whole community; Kant finds it in an organization of rational human beings, who apply rationality to the form of their acts. Neither of them is able to state the end in terms of the object of desire of the individual.[10]

What Mead is trying to demonstrate in this way is that it becomes apparent that there are ends of action which have value in themselves, and that as regards these ends it is a matter of integrating individual action into the 'universalization' of social structures. Now what does this mean more precisely?

From the standpoint of present-day philosophical discussion it is not easy to find access to Mead's ethics. Within the framewordof this discussion, both Mead and Dewey are exposed to the most serious objections because of their categorical claim that moral questions can be treated in accordance with criteria of rationality and truth, in a way comparable to the scientific solution of factual problems. It is no accident that Dewey's ethics, which in the United States was regarded as representative until well into the 1930s, has been forgotten or else is considered a naive or 'rhetorical' mixture of substantial questions, such as that of the ethical value of 'democracy', with the meta-ethical tasks of a scientific philosophy.[11] Since the publication in 1936 of A. J. Ayer's famous book, this discussion has been defined by the return, within the framework of analytical philosophy, to classical philosophy's chasm between 'is' and 'ought'. The thesis that values cannot be grounded, one of the pillars of positivism, was now advanced in the form of the assertion that moral judgements do not have the character of statements of fact, a character proper only to the propositional content of such expressions. What is specifically moral in such judgements is only the expression of subjective emotions or of intentions to influence a partner in an action. This strict distinction between evaluative and descriptive statements was shaken, it is true, when in the wake of the later Wittgenstein attention was directed, primarily by Austin, to the action-related and not merely descriptive character of all utterances.[12] Thus an initial re-approximation of the pragmatists' position was accomplished, in so far as they had – without having at their disposal the instruments of linguistic analysis – placed at the centre of their reflections the relation to action of both moral judgements and statements of fact.

In Anglo-Saxon philosophy the above-mentioned insight led at first to seeing the task of ethics in a 'meta-ethical' reconstruction – neutral itself with respect to evaluations – of the logic of moral judgement. This was the definition of the function of ethics within the main current of analytical philosophy. The next step in this development was taken when doubt arose about the possibility of such a neutral meta-ethics.[13] The question was, then, whether from that doubt one could conclude to the necessity of a meta-meta-ethics, or whether, on the contrary, the conclusion was unavoidable that no meta-level of ethics can make it possible to escape the pressure to take a position in the debates on social problems which is sedimented, so to speak, in ethics. Answering this question required, certainly, thorough and profound reflection on the definition of the function of ethics as a discipline.

The question is – to put it in other words – whether ethics as a discipline is held to be capable of participating, in the rational founding of norms and values, or whether such a role is incompatible with ethics' claim to have knowledge of reality. If ethics is understood to be value-free description, then that is prejudicial to a distinction between evaluation and description, as precisely that distinction has thereby been called into question. Now for the pragmatist it can be proved through examination of mankind's fundamental characteristics that every description is linked to a reference-frame of values constituted by action; and pragmatist ethics is therefore conceived with logical consequence from the perspective of the actor. Pragmatist ethics presents itself, then, as *reflection on the practical procedure of solving moral problems*.

Pragmatist ethics thereby distinguishes itself from any prescriptive ethics, which presents itself as a merely posited system of values. It is not the purpose of pragmatist ethics to annul the necessity of personal moral decisions through a system of thought that unequivocally lays down morally appropriate conduct, deducing it from transcendentally valid values, or that fabricates an evaluation which necessarily follows from the description of states of affairs. Mead's ethics is characterized by resistance to all fixed systems of values and to the denial of the difference between science and ethics. His article 'Scientific Method and the Moral Sciences'[14] is devoted to this theme. There he takes up Julian Huxley's criticism, made from the standpoint of the natural sciences, of a teleological philosophy of history and of a cosmological foundation of values, and goes to the very heart of the matter with the question: 'Can the world of natural science provide objects for the world of social and moral conduct?'[15]

Mead's response to this question is more subtle than the act of violence which completely separates 'is' from 'ought'. It is true, he says, that science does not prescribe such ends, and to that extent the question has to be answered negatively. Mead goes on to describe very graphically the historical process in which the increasing rationality of means is not accompanied by an increasing rationality of the social setting of ends. For him, science consists of the examination of the relations between ends and means, and ethics in the examination of the relation among the ends themselves. He considers it inconceivable, however, that the domain claimed by reason should remain limited to the rationality of the selection of means:

> But it would be a mistake to assume that scientific method is applicable only in the fashioning and selection of means, and may not be used where the problem involves conflicting social ends or values.[16]

On the other hand, science does not establish values:

We do not turn to scientific method to determine what is a common good, though we have learned to avail ourselves of it in some of our common efforts and practices in pursuit of the good. However, scientific method is not an agent foreign to the mind, that may be called in and dismissed at will. It is an integral part of human intelligence, and when it has once been set at work it can only be dismissed by dismissing the intelligence itself.[17]

From this trust in the indivisibility of reason, Mead gains the courage to state anew at the end of the article that there is a relation between morality and the cosmological order. Now, however, this claim is not founded upon a rootedness of a value system in the consummately meaningful cosmic order, but rather on the transformation of the universe through the moral praxis of human beings.

The order of the universe that we live in *is* the moral order. It has become the moral order by becoming the self-conscious method of the members of a human society. We are not pilgrims and strangers. We are at home in our world, but it is not ours by inheritance but by conquest. The world that comes to us from the past possesses and controls us. We possess and control the world that we discover and invent. And this is the world of the moral order.[18]

Mead maintains, then, with great pathos that science and ethics, as partial forms of the one reason, are neither identical nor completely different. Just exactly what their relation to one another is, is left quite unclear however. Mead therefore finds it necessary to turn his attention back to the determination of the practical function of pragmatist ethics. This ethics places itself in the situation of the human actor who has the task of mediating between values and the givens of a particular situation. Reflection on the always risky path to the practical mastering of problem-situations, a path that is open to the future, shows that it is impossible to maintain that values can be simply deduced from other values, regarded as the highest, or from the givens of experience themselves. The belief that science is such a complete system of deduction, completely free of gaps, is destroyed also by the insight into the practical basis of science. But having made ourselves aware of the procedure of both moral action and science, of what Mead calls *the experimental method*, we are able to perceive a completely new dimension of the matter we are examining.

Ethics is to be understood, then, as the clarification and systematization of the attempts to proceed according to this experimental method which occur in individual reflection on problems encountered in action. Thus science and ethics are as much intertwined with one another as are the search for the appropriate means to attain ends and reflection on the suitableness of the ends themselves in practical situations. The separation of the setting of ends from the differing proposals of the partners in an action, or from the means offered by the situation, is artificial and has no basis in practical experience. Here, for the first time, there becomes apparent the possibility of reconstructing, in the analysis of how situations requiring moral decisions are mastered, a procedure that could also be recognized as a value which is legitimated in and of itself. This happens again when Mead considers the second characteristic of ethics as a discipline, namely that it subjects the naive and immediate evaluations and decisions of individual subjects to a public, and that means a comprehensively social, scrutiny. But can sociality and experimentalism[19] be looked upon as empirically given features of a method that provides a non-arbitrary criterion for passing judgement on moral values?

Solving moral problems requires, according to Mead, creative intellectual effort and consideration of all values relevant to the given situation. When the paths to a solution are irremediably risky, then morality is impossible without pertinent factual knowledge; when one has gone beyond an ethics of conviction, then experimental reflection on the consequences of one's alternatives in acting belongs to the innermost core of morality. Mere good will, without striving for the required ability to act, is futile and without moral value. Mead's demand that all values be taken into consideration, which he explicitly places in parallel with the demand that the scientist take all facts into consideration, is directed beyond the sphere of action to the sphere of intersubjectivity. The manner in which Mead ethically utilizes his conception of intersubjectivity still remains to be discussed. At this point, however, it is necessary to prevent the misunderstanding of Mead's ethics, which sees it as essentially nothing more than the making of empty compromises, the indiscriminate acceptance of stated interests. Consideration does not mean acceptance, but what it does mean is rational examination. Mead goes so far as to say:

> The only rule that an ethics can present is that an individual should rationally deal with all the values that are found in a specific problem.

That does not mean that one has to spread before him all the social values when he approaches a problem. The problem itself defines the values. It is a specific problem and there are certain interests that are definitely involved; the individual should take into account all of those interests and then make out a plan of action which will rationally deal with those interests. That is the only method that ethics can bring to the individual.[20]

This passage is noteworthy in two regards. First, Mead links here the sphere of moral reflection or moral discourse to the specific problem encountered in action which gave rise to the reflection or discourse. In Mead's view, there is not a yawning chasm between discourse and action.[21] The discourse remains functionally related to the action-situation; in the discourse only those validity-claims can be considered as problematical which are in fact called into question by the conflict of values. The discourse, too, is subjected to the pragmatist criticism of the Cartesian concept of doubt, which was conceived of as being exercised freely and arbitrarily. Yet, for the pragmatist Mead, this rigorous correlation of reflection and discourse to action is no reason to forgo arguing that here an ethical rule becomes apparent in the very method of ethics. This is the second remarkable feature of the passage quoted above. For Mead it is the essence of science not to maintain the definitive validity of any proposition, but instead to subject all knowledge to re-examination, so that ultimately only this core of science's method of proceeding remains as the stable centre of science. In the same way Mead holds that ethics is to be limited to a method of rational examination of validity claims and of the rational solution of moral conflicts and problems, and that an Archimedean fixed point can be found precisely in this method. It will be necessary to ask, though, in what relationship this insight stands to the question, whether from a historical perspective only adherence to the 'critical method' is thereby grounded, or whether substantive values of social organization also can be grounded with this method. On these matters Mead is not unequivocally clear. But before we look for the causes of this lack of clarity, we must understand still more clearly what Mead really means when he calls for rational examination of and reflection on values. Just what is a value, and in what does critical examination of and reflection on values consist?

Mead's concept of value is a result of the fundamental framework of his theory of action. He rejects both an objectivist and a subjectivist concept of value. Values are not simply objective givens, which are independent of human existence. They are, however, also not merely the product of the subjective evaluation of objects which are essentially neutral with regard to this evaluation.[22] Rather, says Mead, the evaluation is the result of an 'interaction' of subject and object, organism and environment. Mead explains this practical relation of the human organism and its environment with his model of action, containing the different stages of the impulse to action, perception, manipulation, and the consummation of the act, in which the actor's needs and desires are satisfied.[23] The value of an object results, then, from its relation to the 'consummatory phase'. The value of an object is thus constituted in the practical interaction of subject and object, but the subject necessarily experiences values as objective qualities of objects that can be sensuously experienced.

For Mead, therefore, the value-relation is indeed an objectively existing relation between subject and object, but he does not equate it with a cognitive relation. Value-relations and cognitive relations are definitely distinct for Mead. Their difference does not lie, however, in a merely subjective character of evaluation as opposed to the ascription of objectivity to cognition, but rather in their correlation to different 'phases' of an act. Cognition of the so-called primary qualities, such as mass, is constituted by the manipulation phase, whereas cognition of 'secondary qualities', such as colours and sounds, is constituted by the phase of perception from a distance. From primary qualities to secondary qualities, and then to evaluations, there can, admittedly, be a diminution of objectivity, in the sense that in manipulation the pre-structuring of sensuous experience by the universal characteristics of human beings is the greatest, while distance-perception is more susceptible to cultural influence, and the entire spectrum of historically, culturally, and individually different needs and desires is determinative for evaluations. Nevertheless, Mead maintains, this diminution of objectivity is to be distinguished from an essentially necessary gulf, making values (or even the secondary qualities) irremediably subjective. It is clear that Mead's interpretation of the concept of value from the standpoint of his theory of action requires fundamental opposition to a mechanistic world-view shaped by the natural sciences.[24] In order to establish that ethical propositions can be true or false, Mead had to provide a critique of the world-view that attributes objective reality only to primary qualities. That, however, is a topic which must be treated separately.

Mead thus preserves the claim that evaluative predicates can be objectively valid, without reducing them to empirical predicates. Within an action, therefore, it is in Mead's view impossible to 'deduce' the one kind of predicate from the other, to deduce 'ought' from 'is'. All empirical predicates, though, must be constituted within a framework of action which is related to values. Mead expressly refuses simply to equate morality with cognition and emotional expression and to assume an unresolvable conflict of the different spheres of value.[25] Only morality, moral consciousness, is a property of action in its entirety; in contrast, the other types of consciousness must each be regarded as abstractions from particular phases of an action.

It seems to me that with these assertions Mead, without having the tools of linguistic analysis, anticipates the thesis that the semantic demonstration of the difference between 'is' and 'ought' does not refute the contention that the determination of being is referred pragmatically to an 'ought'.

In the same article, 'The Philosophical Basis of Ethics', Mead presents an idea that points to an important problem, which he did not think through completely in his fragmentary theoretical position regarding value. There he attacks a subjectivist theory of the constitution of the ends of action with the argument that from the standpoint of this theory morality must remain external to an action, because the social character both of morality and of the individual capacity for action is not grasped. If the individual acts only for subjective ends, whether these ends are conceived of as set by the individual himself,[26] or as naturally determined, then it cannot be maintained that moral obligation means to attain common ends through individual action.

> Moral necessity in conduct from this point of view is quite independent of the activity itself. So far from being the most fundamental reality it is a derivative by which, through what it is hard not to call a hocus-pocus, the individual acts, for what is only indirectly his own – a distant end, through a social *Dressur*. It is, of course, natural that this point of view should mediate the process of training by which men are to be led unwittingly to socially worthy action, rather than the immediate conduct of the individual who finds himself face to face with a moral problem.[27]

Apt remarks, but ones which raise the question of whether Mead himself really oriented his concept of value in a logically consequent fashion to the concept of the 'social act', understood as the co-ordinated activity of a group of organisms, or whether his model of the stages of an action does not after all contain an individualistic component: action as the satisfaction of needs and wants. In my opinion, in this theoretical model of action, as in 'The Definition of the Psychical', Mead does not take into account in a completely consequent manner the implications of a theory of intersubjectivity.[28]

This question becomes critical if we ask when in fact are values called into question, and what rational questioning and examination of values means in this case. It is clear that for Mead not only is there no enduring system of values guaranteed by religion or by anything else, but in addition moral conduct has no biological roots, for example, in an instinct for parental care. Biologically or normatively determined behaviour is prior to the moral situation proper. This situation arises when the values of different actors enter into conflict with one another. Ethical problems are thus of a social character through and through; they are social problems, the solution of which is left directly to the individual actors.

> Ethical ideas, within any given human society, arise in the conscious-ness of the individual members of that society from the fact of the common social dependence of all these individuals upon one another. . . . and from their awareness or sensing or conscious realization of this fact. But ethical problems arise for individual members of any given human society whenever they are individually confronted with a social situation to which they cannot readily adjust and adapt themselves, or in which they cannot easily realize themselves, or with which they cannot immediately integrate their own behaviour . . .[29]

The investigation of this moral problem-situation is at the heart of Mead's ethical analyses.

According to Mead, the moral situation is – to use an epigram-matic formulation – a crisis of the entire personality. In the moral situation the individual experiences a conflict between certain of his own values and others, or between his values and those of partners in the situation, or the values embodied in the 'generalized other'. Mead thinks of such a conflict in terms of the model of a discussion or a court proceeding. Every value is physically represented by an advocate demanding recognition of it. In 'The Social Self', an article in which the social-psychological discussion passes over smoothly into the discussion of ethics, Mead writes:

> Assuming as I do the essentially social character of the ethical end, we find in moral reflection a conflict in which certain values find a spokesman in the old self or a dominant part of the old self, while other values answering to other tendencies and impulses arise in opposition and find other spokesmen to present their cases.[30]

Now, the conflict of these claims of different values paralyzes the actor, and tends to lead to the disintegration of his old self. This disintegration can be overcome only by the individual himself, acting in a creative way. Mead, of course, knows that the old self can try to avoid dealing with the problem through strategies for warding it off or for evading it. But the self finds itself thrown back on this problem again and again. By stubbornly adhering to the old self, without at least broadening it through argumentative engagement with the new demands, the individual loses the opportunity for his own development. Mead therefore regards egotistical behaviour as a constriction, a ligation of the self, which attempts to forget its social character.[31]

In order truly to resolve a problem-situation, the individual must examine the values, expectations, and impulses he has brought to the situation, and should he become convinced of the necessity for changing them, he must then re-structure them. Only through the elaboration of a practicable moral strategy which is suited to a given situation is a resolution of a conflict of values and a re-integration of the self possible. However, in contrast to what is required by the scientific problem-situation, this strategy must be elaborated under conditions of situational pressure to make a decision and of the involvement of the whole person in the situation and its resolution. From the solution of the moral problem neither the actor's self nor the social complex of values emerges unchanged.

The actor's self develops through consideration of the values and interests of others, and only through such consideration. In order to realize his self, the actor must therefore take part in the central conflicts and discussions about values in his society. Thus Mead situates the formation of the self within social and political praxis. He attempts to describe the stages in the formation of the self as stages in moral development, and also as stages in the development of society to freedom from domination.[32] Orientation to a concrete particular other is followed by the orientation to organized others, to a group. Going beyond the group, and beyond conflicts among different generalized others, the individual's orientation proceeds to ever more comprehensive and at the same time more perfect social units and finally to a universalist perspective, the ideal of the comprehensive development of the human species. This perspective lifts us out of any concrete community and leads us to question ruthlessly the legitimacy of all socially recognized standards.

Mead did not complete this theory of the stages of moral consciousness, nor did he give it a form that could be empirically verified. It is of interest, though, to call attention to the fact that his ideas have had direct influence on what is today the most important and highly differentiated theory of moral socialization, that of Lawrence Kohlberg.[33] Incomplete though Mead's theory is, the manner of his approach makes it clear that the understanding of morality as sociality does not come down to a morality of conformity. Rather, the individual can be morally required to oppose certain socially recognized values. A universalizable principle is to be obtained not from adaptation to a given society, but from the furthering of a principle that is inherent in the sociality of the human being.

Ethical universality, therefore, can only be grounded in sociality, since only by sociality is it made possible:

Sociality gives the universality of ethical judgements . . .[34]

Ethical universality, according to Mead, is possible only through the universality of the human capacity of role-taking. Thus a universalist orientation is in his view not orientation to an activity identical with that of the others; it is, rather, acting as a participant in an ideal process of cooperation.[35] Mead recognizes that human communication itself and the elementary capacity of role-taking which underlies human communication contain a 'formal ideal':

Universal discourse is then the formal ideal of communication.[36]

At the conclusion of his essay on Cooley, Mead asserts that communication is at the heart of human rationality, and that it is for that reason the logical basis of a consistent critique of society:

If symbolization can be stated in terms of the behaviour of primitive communication, then every distinctively human being belongs to a possibly larger society than that within which he actually finds himself. It is this, indeed, which is implied in the rational character of the human animal. And these larger patterns afford a basis for the criticism of existing conditions and in an even unconscious way tend to realize themselves in social conduct.[37]

By means of a concept of sociality, according to which it is an intrinsic human property, Mead introduces a notion of ideal social integration, to which alone he ascribes non-arbitrary value and a force working – in a manner not further explained in this article – towards its own realization. This is an extraordinarily significant line of thought, which, I believe, appears again only with what has been called 'the linguistic turn' taken by Critical Theory.[38] Because of its importance I shall reproduce here, in spite of its length, a passage from Mead's article 'Philanthropy from the Point of View of Ethics', which founds, in densely packed brevity, Mead's notion of ideal sociality through analysis of the moral situation.

It is this feel for a social structure which is implicit in what is present that haunts the generous nature, and carries a sense of obligation which transcends any claim that his actual social order fastens upon him. It is an ideal world that lays the claim upon him, but it is an ideal world which grows out of this world and its undeniable implications.

It is possible to specify the claims of this ideal world in certain respects. A human being is a member of a community and is thereby an expression of its customs and the carrier of its values. These customs appear in the individual as habits, and the values appear as his goods, and these habits and goods come into conflict with each other. Out of the conflict arise in human social experience the meanings of things and the rational solution of the conflicts. The rational solution of the conflicts, however, calls for the reconstruction of both habits and values, and this involves transcending the order of the community. A hypothetically different order suggests itself and becomes the end in conduct. It is a social end and must appeal to others in the community. In logical terms there is established a universe of discourse which transcends the specific order within which the members of the community may, in a specific conflict, place themselves outside of the community order as it exists, and agree upon changed habits of action and a restatement of values. Rational procedure, therefore, sets up an order within which thought operates;

that abstracts in varying degrees from the actual structure of society. It is a social order, for its function is a common action on the basis of commonly recognized conditions of conduct and common ends. Its claims are the claims of reason. It is a social order that includes any rational being who is or may be in any way implicated in the situation with which thought deals. It sets up an ideal world, not of substantive things but of proper method. Its claim is that all the conditions of conduct and all the values which are involved in the conflict must be taken into account in abstraction from the fixed forms of habits and goods which have clashed with each other. It is evident that a man cannot act as a rational member of society, except as he constitutes himself a member of this wider commonwealth of rational beings. But the ethical problem is always a specific one, and belongs only to those habits and values which have come into conflict with each other. About this problem lies the ordered community with its other standards and customs unimpaired, and the duties it prescribes unquestioned.

The claims of the ideal world are that the individual shall take into account all of the values which have been abstracted from their customary settings by the conflict and fashion his reconstruction in recognition of them all.[39]

We can now summarize what Mead understands by rational resolution of moral problem-situations. It consists in taking into account and understanding all values which appear in a situation. This does not mean that one merely juxtaposes these values in a relativistic fashion; rather, it means questioning the claim to validity of each of these values, from the standpoint of bringing about a universal community based on communication and cooperation among its members. Comprehensive communication with one's partners in a moral situation and orientation to the realization of this ideal society are, then, two rules for the solution of moral problems.

Here we have come to a critical point: the politicization of universalist morality. There is no doubt that Mead is taking this path. He speaks not only of the right, but also of the moral obligation to contribute to social change:

The process of conversation is one in which the individual has not only the right but the duty of talking to the community of which he is a part, and bringing about those changes which take place through the interaction of individuals. That is the way, of course, in which society gets ahead, by just such interactions as those in which a person thinks a thing out. We are continually changing our social system in some respects, and we are able to do that intelligently because we can think.[40]

In his impressive essay on philanthropy, Mead establishes, in a subtle analysis of the ethical implications of reciprocity, that individual charity, mere *caritas*, represents the lowest level of ethical development after the biologically determined impulse to help or to care for another. Organized charity and social work, says Mead, is superior to mere *caritas* in virtue of its carefully considered and methodical use of the resources at its disposal, but does not yet attain the level to which the term 'justice' can be applied. Only on this plane is the suffering of the other recognized as exercising a binding claim on us. The highest level is reached when the suffering others are no longer regarded as the object of any kind of love or help, but as subjects who through the organization of their behaviour achieve a political remedy for their suffering. In this essay Mead goes so far as to ponder a de-professionalization of science, its re-insertion into the ordinary communication of the members of society:

> It is not until science has become a discipline to which the research ability of any mind from any class in society can be attracted that it can become rigorously scientific, and it is not until its results can be so formulated that they must appeal to any enlightened mind that they can have universal value.[41]

Here we can see quite clearly the radical way in which Mead drew the conclusions implicit in his ethical position: what is important for him is, first, the establishing of those social conditions in which the formation of the self, rising to the highest levels of capacity for moral decision, will first become possible for all human beings, and second, the continuous change of all social institutions in order to eliminate all injustices and disadvantages.

The moral worth of a society is determined, then, by the degree to which a rational procedure for reaching agreement among its members and an openness of all institutions to change through communication are to be found in the society. Mead calls a society having these features democratic. *Democracy, in his words, is 'institutionalized revolution'.*[42] What this means is expressed most clearly in his paper on natural rights,[43] in which he asserts that the essence of democracy consists in not declaring that there is any social structure that must not be abandoned or altered, and in instead making all social institutions subject to the collective and unconstrained decisions of the society's members. In interpretations of Hobbes, Locke, and Rousseau, Mead shows in this paper that it is impossible to establish once and for all a catalogue of social 'goods' and reveals what real historical targets the definitions of natural rights, which were formulated negatively, that is, with reference to restrictions to be overcome, were directed against. In his discussion of these theories of natural rights, the thrust of Mead's criticism also quickly becomes evident. He calls for the suspension of the allegedly natural right to property,[44] when this right prevents the establishment of the social conditions which are ostensibly supposed to be made possible by it, namely the freedom and independence of the individual.

Many of Mead's scattered articles and theses can be grouped around this politicization of universalist morality. His analysis of the functions of punitive justice,[45] which in his judgement is not therapeutic but does serve to stabilize the structure of domination in a society, belongs just as much in this thematic complex as do his articles on patriotism as an ethical and psychological problem.[46] He recognizes both as functionally necessary in a society in which not all its members can publicly defend their needs and wants and evaluations and which therefore requires an artificial unity: in the solidarity of its members against the criminal as their internal enemy and against other societies as their external enemies. In this connection he clearly stresses that national patriotism can have a progressive function in the overcoming of particularist group-orientations; this shows that he does not understand the creation of a universal community merely as a moral imperative, but situates it in a concrete historical context. He says that real universalization, of which the universal religions represent only an anticipation, can be realized only when an actual action-nexus of all human beings exists, and this action-nexus he identifies as the world market! He mentions the internationalist labour movement as the most impressive example of a social movement that is consciously acknowledging this emerging universal action-nexus. These remarks call to mind some of Marx's ideas, and Mead's ethical founding of democracy is in general agreement with the conceptions of communism as perfected democracy held by the left wing of the Young Hegelians and expressed by Marx in his early writings.

Although Mead does go this far, in most of his political writings and statements he turns aside from this path into vague hopes for a compromise between the capitalist class and the workers, for a strengthening of the general public's and the state's willingness to undertake reform, and for a readiness on everyone's part to achieve reconciliation. While voicing these hopes, he does not ask whether a compromise is appropriate when two opposed positions, both demanding recognition without being equally capable of being universalized, enter into collision with one another.[47] He does not ask whether it can become necessary to break off discussion, when discussion is only intended to be a means of offering dilatory resistance to changing the existing circumstances. Nor does Mead ask if the basis of common interests in social reconstruction, which he holds must be presupposed between the partners in such an undertaking,[48] exists at all. However, this is not the place for a political critique of Mead, but for raising the question whether the significance of Mead's ethics is restricted by the consequences of these criticisms.

The limits of Mead's ethics are not delineated by describing it as an 'ethics of reconciliation', as I have done elsewhere.[49] This criticism proves to be groundless when it has become clear that Mead understands by the taking into account of interests and values their rational examination, subjecting them to a rational procedure of justification. His argument is therefore without doubt consistent when it ultimately leads to the grounding of this rational or 'democratic' method of resolving moral conflicts as the only way of doing so that is legitimated in and of itself, and whose legitimation is free of contradiction. And yet this conclusion of his reasoning only shifts the problem to a different terrain.

The concepts of 'rationality' and 'democracy' are clearly broad enough to permit their being used in very different connections. They alone do not prevent ethics from becoming a superficial, ideological counter-argument against social movements. They leave it open whether one ascribes to social movements the creative ability and the prospect of bringing forth social forms which make a higher degree of self-expression and participation possible for all their members. It is not a matter of sparing social movements from moral criticism; I give no credence to the thesis that understanding the laws of societal development makes ethics superfluous. Indeed, this thesis leads only to a primitive utilitarianism based on individual, national, or class interests. Marx, too, did not consider the interests of the proletariat justified because they were the interests of the class which he had resolved, *per decisionem*, to represent, but because in their particularity these interests represent the universal interest of humanity in the higher development of the species. Marxism could forgo ethics only if it could forgo the activity of individual human beings. It is, then, not a matter of abandoning ethical judgements of value, but rather of making these with awareness of their proper social status, and so of bringing them to the same level of concreteness as that of the social movements themselves.

It now appears that a pertinent critique of Mead's ethics should begin not with a fallacious supposition of a *social harmony of interests*, but with the *formalism* of the democratic-experimental method of that ethics. For Mead emphasizes again and again, in many different contexts, and especially in those having to do with the philosophy of history, that we have no other guarantee of progress than this very method, no ultimate ends or original first principles. However, the error of a critique that took the formalism of Mead's method as its starting point would be that it identifies too hastily Mead's understanding of his work with that work itself.[50] For Mead himself shows repeatedly that for him, too, the method not only is an ideal, but also implies a substantive ideal. Wherever he sees the danger that the attempt to reach this substantive ideal of a society free of domination will be made with other means than those of the democratic 'method' as he understands it, there he draws back into a formalism of method. The effect of his withdrawal to this position, however, is to make inoperative the dialectic of the historical goal and the historically available paths to that goal. Against Kant, Mead argued that in his 'formalism' itself was contained a quite determinate ideal of a rational society, and that this was true not in an external manner, not as a theme that Kant was concerned with, but with logical necessity. This argument can also be turned against Mead. In Peirce's pragmatism this dialectic had been preserved, as when, for example, he wrote:

The only moral evil is not to have an ultimate aim . . . In order to understand pragmatism, therefore, well enough to subject it to intelligent criticism, it is incumbent upon us to inquire what an ultimate aim, capable of being pursued in an indefinitely prolonged course of action, can be.[51]

But Peirce preserved the dialectic of historical end and historical means at the price of remoteness from the question of political action in general. In the reflections of Dewey[52] and Mead, though, both of whom were concerned with social science as well as social reform, there appears the internal contradiction that having an ultimate end is judged to be justified in one context whereas it is deemed to be arbitrarily proposed in another. As a consequence of this contradiction, in the thought of both philosophers, ethics remains to some degree alien to politics, and the concept of method remains extrinsic to social praxis.

What this means can be succinctly illustrated by a controversy between pragmatist philosophy and an important theoretician and practitioner of Marxism, which took place a few years after Mead's death. In 1938 John Dewey replied, in a very interesting little article, to Leon Trotsky's brochure *Their Morals and Ours*, in which the latter responded to the criticism frequently made of him that he was only a 'failed Stalin'.[53] Trotsky defends himself against being placed on the same moral level as Stalin, and in so doing he arrives at an illuminating reflection on the maxim that was attributed to him, and for which he was attacked, namely that the end justifies the means. In his essay Trotsky offers a formulation of his thoughts on this point, one that is to be found only rarely in Marxist literature because of most Marxists' horror of utopian or normative determination of goals:

> A means can be justified only by its end. But the end in its turn needs to be justified. From the Marxist point of view, which expresses the historical interests of the proletariat, the end is justified if it leads to increasing the power of humanity over nature and to the abolition of the power of one person over another.[54]

What this end precisely does not do, is to justify any and every means; rather, it justifies only those that can really lead to it. Trotsky refuses to admit as true that base means and ways can serve this lofty end in any fashion. Just as he refuses to separate ethics and politics and argues polemically against a democratic ethics, which seems to him a 'flight from the class struggle', so too does he steadfastly insist on the ethical value of his (and that means of Marxist) political goals and the ways to those goals in the people's self-confidence and activity on their own behalf.

Dewey's reply to Trotsky's arguments is at first surprising, inasmuch as he agrees with much of what his opponent says, and allies himself with Trotsky in opposition to 'absolutist ethics', which remains extrinsic to historical processes. But he also recognizes, with great acumen, the weak point in Trotsky's reasoning. He contests Trotsky's claim that by means of Marxism one can deduce from the laws of history the ends which need to be accomplished at a particular time. With this 'super-scientific' claim,[55] a scientistically understood Marxism robs the tasks set for human action of their – normative as well as instrumental – riskiness. Dewey, however, can only abstractly counterpose to Trotsky's claim the openness and uncertainty of the historical future, and is unable to offer an alternative theory of historical tendencies of development and effective reform strategies. Thus he is correct when he writes:

> To be scientific about ends does not mean to read them out of laws, whether the laws are natural or social.[56]

But when he continues with the next sentence:

> Orthodox Marxism shares with orthodox religionism and with traditional idealism the belief that human ends are interwoven into the very texture and structure of existence – a conception inherited presumably from its Hegelian origin[57]

then it is unclear how he intends to argue against Trotsky's position. Are not the human being's ends – for Dewey himself as well as for Mead and other pragmatists – rooted in the profoundest depths of the nature of human beings and of the world? In order to keep the relationship between ends and social science open, Dewey leaves it completely undetermined.

The same criticism holds for Mead as for Dewey, in spite of the former's intense study of the problems of intersubjectivity and its ethical implications. Between a scientistic Marxism and a liberal ethos of democratic procedure, which remains without consequences for social science, there is an empty place. This place should be occupied by a democratic socialism. Especially pragmatist ethics, which so emphatically regards the procedure for the resolution of moral conflict as applicable to social problems arising from action, cannot orient itself to the sciences without basing its reflections on a maximum of scientific information; it cannot suppress the gulf between its intentions and the historical processes of its time. Mead's ethics, therefore, would be completed in a consistent manner only if it incorporated into itself its relationship to the problems of political action encountered by a movement to democratize society.

7

Constitution of the Physical Object and Role-Taking

The key to an understanding of Mead's work, in its coherence and in its significance, is provided by the concept of practical intersubjectivity. Up to now I have attempted to make clear the social-historical horizon of this approach and the scientific and philosophical matrix in which it originated, and then, on that foundation, to show that an adequate concept of the psychical cannot be developed without reference to subjectivity. This has to be thought of as the capacity for intentional action, and for Mead that means as self-reflectivity; this self-reflectivity and intentionality are necessarily formed in the structures of intersubjective praxis. The last point up to now was that all action is embedded in a matrix of values. However, if we follow this line of argument, we appear to encounter a boundary when we leave the sphere of intersubjective praxis, of social action, and turn our attention to action directed to the inanimate objects of our environment.

Emphasis of the specifically human structure of intersubjectivity does indeed mark a boundary between the spheres of action regarding other subjects and regarding inanimate objects. But is it sufficient merely to mark this boundary, to stress the difference between these spheres? Does not the question immediately arise, in any analysis of social processes, of the way in which these two kinds of action are intertwined when, instead of isolated individuals, collectivities actively engage themselves with objects, with nature? But even in the case of the individual who acts in an instrumental fashion without any manifest cooperative relations with others, can one at all assume that it is a matter of a kind of action that the intersubjective matrix in which the capacity for action originated does not constitutively enter into? Should it not be assumed, if the

145

capacity for intentional action is supposed to be rooted in the very structures of intersubjectivity, that instrumental action, too, is formed in important respects from intersubjective action? Finally, admitting the necessity of investigating the constitutive importance of intersubjective action also for the manner of human engagement with nature, can this investigation be restricted to the familiar question of the significance of language for perception, or is 'language' itself already a particular and developed form of intersubjectivity, which even in its more elementary manifestations imposes form on instrumental action?

With his theory of the constitution of the physical object, Mead gives clear answers to these questions. Chronological study of Mead's work quickly makes clear how little the development of his theory of intersubjectivity owes to efforts to fight against the threat of predominance of a concept of social praxis that is reduced to instrumental action. Mead was not motivated by a sharp distinction between the human and the natural sciences, nor by scepticism towards progress in technology and the natural sciences, nor yet by criticism of technocratic ideology; rather, he had implicit confidence in the emancipatory prospects offered by technical and scientific progress, and in his research themes and his orientation he continued to be guided by the model of the natural sciences. It must be pointed out, though, that he defended a different understanding of natural science, technology, and social praxis, from the one which was generally held. For Mead was attempting to lay bare the foundational significance of social praxis also, and especially, for the natural sciences and for the sphere of instrumental action. These efforts can be found in all the phases of Mead's life's work, but in the last ten years of his life they occupied a very great part of his attention. In this period, the products of which I often refer to as Mead's 'later work', Mead undertook to relate his developed theory of intersubjectivity to the constitution of natural science. This enterprise was concerned in particular with the elementary categories of action directed to nature: the physical thing, space, and time. Only when he was able to show how these elementary categories are also genetically formed in the matrix of the development of the capacity for communication, had he truly combined in a logically consistent manner the fundamental premises of pragmatism with his orientation towards a theory of intersubjectivity. This chapter will present an examination of Mead's theory of the constitution of the physical object; then, in the next chapter, his theory of 'time' will be discussed.

The treatment in Mead's writings of the problem of the constitution of the physical object enables us to document particularly clearly that for a long time Mead was a proponent of the arguments of both 'pragmatism' and the 'theory of intersubjectivity' concurrently, without succeeding in integrating them. The one argument consisted in pragmatism's central thesis that perception of things cannot be understood simply as a copy in consciousness of pregiven real objects in the external world, nor can it be thought of as a mere assumption, in contrast to sensory data or sensations which are actually given, but that all perception is instead constituted in action, whatever that might mean more precisely. The other thesis consisted in the assertion that social consciousness precedes consciousness of physical objects.

Traces of the first thesis can be found in Mead's work as early as in his plans to write a doctoral dissertation on the constitution of space; the early review of Lasswitz's book already introduces the 'act' as the point of reference for perception, a position Mead then retains in all his early writings. The first fully developed account of how the physical object and space are constituted in action is contained in an article on animal perception, published in 1907.[1] With this explanation Mead associates himself entirely with the themes of pragmatism in its original form, but pursues them in the domain of psychology.

The second thesis appears in the series of articles in which Mead developed the concept of symbolic interaction, admittedly without substantiating explanations most of the time. It appears to be descended from idealist forerunners of the philosophy of reflection, for this thesis can already be found in works by Royce dating from 1894–95.[2] Royce took it over from Fichte, who conceived of the self-realization of the ego as taking place by means of the resistance of the object, a resistance which was, for its part, 'posited' by the ego itself. If physical objects could only be given to a self-reflective ego, then self-reflectivity was prior to the structure of commerce with physical objects. For the time being this second thesis can only be kept in mind as a theme from which the solution to the problem of the thing's constitution eventually resulted that is properly characteristic of Mead's approach. The first thesis, however, can be explained somewhat more precisely. It is this thesis which allows us to achieve any understanding whatsoever of Mead's original approach in the field of the psychology of perception.

Perception is a part of action and is functionally concomitant of it –

this is one of the central propositions of Mead's and of any other pragmatism. Mead stresses that perception is embedded in action-nexuses, but also points out that it is precisely the interruption of the action that 'liberates' perception.

> There are two characteristics of perceptual experience which I have already indicated, but which I wish to again emphasize. The first of these is that perception of physical things presupposes an act that is already going on in advance of perception and is a process within which perception lies; that perception implies an inhibition of this process of movement toward or away from a distant stimulus, an inhibition that arises from the presence in the organism of alternative completions of the act; . . .[3]

Mead is only being consistent when to this intimate linking of perception to action he joins a sharp attack on the conception of perception as the mere mental presentation of objects. In defence of his position he adduces the active character of perception itself:

> The process of sensing is itself an activity. In the case of vision this is most evidently the case. Here the movement of the eyes, the focusing of the lens, and the adjustment of the lines of vision require a complicated activity which is further complicated by the movements of the eyes which will bring the rays of light coming from all parts of the object upon the centre of clearest vision.[4]

Mead shows that this active character is proper not to visual perception alone, but is possessed also by feeling, hearing, smelling, and tasting. Now, if perception is part of an action, and also possesses itself the character of an activity, then it is but a small step, and one that seems called for, to conceive of perception as a *stage* of the action-process.

In his argument Mead employs a four-phased model of action.[5] According to this model, action consists of the stages of the impulse to action, perception, manipulation, and consummation, that is, the completion of the action in which needs and wants are satisfied. The first stage forms the motivational groundwork for the entire action-process. A feature of this process that is characteristic for the human being, and that must be stressed, is the fact that between the impulses and the need-satisfying action there is inter-posed not simply the effect on the sense organs of a possible object of an impulse, but the two separated phases of perception and manipulation. In the emergence of a distinct manipulatory phase and the modification of the perceptual phase that is thereby made possible, as well as in the systematic significance for humans of the inhibition of action, Mead sees fundamental conditions for the uniqueness of the human being in comparison with animal organisms.

The 'systematic significance of the inhibition of action' refers precisely to the notion that since Gehlen has gained currency in Germany as the 'instinct reduction' which is proper to human beings. Only through instinct reduction are physical objects freed from instinctually compulsive incorporation into need-satisfying actions.

It is the fact that the individual abides with the physical object, i.e., that he neither passes on to the completion of a physiological process which contact implies nor finds in the physical object an immediate step to a later act, which provides the situation for the development of the thing.[6]

In contrast, for animals manipulative commerce with things is completely integrated into their need-satisfying activities.[7] Even in the case of monkeys, as Mead observes,[8] the function of their paws lies more in the area of locomotion than in that of feeling. Only with the human being does an organ – the hand – become specialized in manipulative actions not linked to direct pressure from needs. The liberation of the hand from other functions progressively makes possible an extraordinary differentiation and storing of experiences from manipulation of objects.

As the next step toward his theory of perception, Mead proposes his thesis of the primacy of contact perception over the other forms of perception. In support of this claim can be adduced not only arguments from biology and the history of evolution, which indicate that distance receptors evolved later than contact receptors and that the retina, for instance, evolved from the skin. In addition, there are also functionalist arguments for it. Mead repeatedly stresses the greater reliability of information given by contact perception in comparison with that provided by the distance senses, as the latter information is more likely to be erroneous or illusory, and must prove its accuracy in subsequent commerce with the perceived objects.[9] Mead regards recognition of the primacy of contact perception as crucially important for linking perception to action and refuting any form of the copy theory of perception.[10] If one accepts the primacy of contact perception, then one is immediately confronted with the question of the relationship of the other forms of perception to contact perception. In what relation to each other do the hand and the eye, contact perception and distance perception, stand?

Mead's article 'Concerning Animal Perception' propounds the thesis that the contact of the human hand with objects provides the identical core to which the fugitive and various stimuli of the other senses are 'adjectively' referred.[11] Mead asks here whether there is a qualitative difference between human 'isolating' perception and non-rational, though intelligent, cognitive processes occurring in animal adjustment to an environment. He knows that this question is of critical importance for a theory of learning, and for that reason discusses contemporary attempts to separate human and animal learning and 'perception' from one another or to ascertain how and to what degree they resemble each other.

In rejecting the views of those who would like to conclude from the irrefutable existence of animal learning to animal perception, he is led to formulate a concept of 'imprinting' (as was subsequently developed by biological ethology), which stands in direct opposition to human learning. It is true, Mead grants, that in animal learning a new stimulus is acquired by means of the new reaction, but this happens not because of the connection of old and new sensory experiences, but because of the super-imposition of the ones on the others. For such a connection a stable core is necessary, to which all perceptions can be referred. Such a core, however, is to be found only in contact perceptions. A permanent space, says Mead, is constituted through the referral of all distance experiences to contact experience.

> It is this contact experience which gives the identical core to which the contents coming from the distance senses are referred in the so-called process of complication. It is this core which answers to varying experiences while it remains the same. It is this core which is a condition sine qua non of our perception of physical objects.[12]

The physical object is constituted, then, when the hands and the eyes cooperate; when the eyes regard that which the hands are seizing, and when the hands can reach for what the eyes have caught sight of.

If the object is thought of as constituted in this manner, then its function as a means is not extrinsic to it: 'Every perceived thing is in so far as perceived a recognized means to possible ends . . .'[13] The object is given only as a means, but as such only when we free it from instinctually automatic subsumption under our ends.[14] Our perception does not mirror the object-structure of the world; rather, in action the opportunity emerges reconstructively to apprehend this object-structure for the purpose of solving problems encountered in action. It is extremely illuminating to see how Mead makes use of the emphasis on the qualitative difference between animal and human 'perception' to efface the difference in the human being between perception and interpretation, sensuousness and concept. If human perception has the structure he has found in his analysis, then – continuing the sentence last quoted –

> . . . there can be no hard and fast line drawn between such perceptual consciousness and the more abstracted processes of so-called reasoning.

If human perception, one could say, already has itself the *per se* reflective character which is required for the identification of things as things – and this is what Mead maintains in his article – then there is no separating gap between reflection and perception. However, Mead does not yet know how he can ground this reflective character of perception.

Mead's venture into the psychology of perception carries him, of course – as any psychology of perception does – into the middle of the shoreless sea of epistemological controversies. In spite of the importance Mead himself ascribed to the justification of his position and to situating it in the history of epistemology, these topics will be dealt with here only in passing. Mead's theory of the constitution of the physical object in perception rests upon the idea that an action of the organism in an environment, which is immediate and not reflected on, must be assumed as the basis for the constitution of all forms which are products of reflection. Inasmuch as he subscribes to this notion, Mead stands close to the various attempts of his time to begin epistemology from a point where the object and consciousness are not yet separated. In this respect the contemporary versions of positivism, that of Mach, for instance, and the thought of Dilthey and Husserl resemble one another. In the case of positivism, elements, of which both the sensations and the world are composed, are taken as the point of departure: in Dilthey's reflections the structural unit of the mentally lived experience *(das Erlebnis)*, in those of Husserl the structural unit of the phenomenon stands at the beginning. All of these approaches are attempts to escape from the classical dualism of consciousness and object, which had arisen as soon as naive belief in the objective existence of all features of the external world independent of human beings had yielded before the attacks upon it. The form in which subjectivity first recognized itself was encumbered, though, with the unanswerable question of how, from the self-certainty of the thinking subject, proof of the reality of the external world and of other human beings could be obtained. For Mead, the history of philosophy since Descartes is a history of the attempts to escape from the dilemma created by Cartesianism's erroneous enquiry.

To Mead's way of thinking, a large role in this collective philosophical effort is played by the stages of British empiricism leading from Locke to Berkeley and then to Hume: from the separation of the primary and the secondary qualities, of contact and distance perception in the thought of Locke, who assigned the former qualities to the objective world and the latter to the subject; to the subjectifying of both in the theories of Berkeley, who accorded objectivity only to causation and made it the basis of religion; and then to the analyses of Hume, who referred causation, too, to the subject and so arrived at complete scepticism. Mead sees Kant's philosophy as the continuation of these attempts arising from the Cartesian dilemma. Kant recognized the constitution of the object as the transcendental unity *a priori* of apperception through the 'I think' which accompanies all experience; but he cannot account for the emergence of this 'I think' itself, and comes to philosophical grief on the phenomenalism of the 'thing in itself'. However, Mead attaches no importance to the continuations of empiricism, which avoid posing the pertinent questions with Kant's rigour, or to a simple rehabilitation of realism. Rather, from his point of view it is critical to attempt to transform epistemology's transcendental line of enquiry *by making it genetic and by referring it to the human body, to human praxis, and to intersubjectivity*. He finds the possibility of such a transformation in taking as the point of departure for his investigation the model of an organism securing its survival in an environment. By using this model the deficiencies of the other non-Cartesian attempts to account for the constitution of objects could be eliminated.

Mead's epistemological position must prove its superiority by providing a convincing analysis of the constitution of the physical object. Up to this point all that had been established is that the 'thing' presupposes the 'reciprocal assimilation of the schemata of assimilation', hand and eye, to borrow an expression from Piaget. If this genetic thesis is correct, then that is enough to cause the collapse of the empiricist, realist, and transcendentalist explanations. But on the other hand this genetic explanation does not yet suffice as an explanation of the origin of the unifying power of the self, or as a solution to the problem which Mead has posed for himself, namely to account for the *per se* reflective character of the perception of 'things'.

This problem became solvable when Mead had evolved his theory of the development of the self and of self-reflectivity from the 'conversation of gestures'. He had discovered in the latter an action-situation in which the actor's attending to himself, his making mentally present to himself the consequences of the action which he had begun and the reaction to be expected from the other, was functional. By examining this situation he had shown how a structure could function that was founded on the reciprocal anticipation of behavioural expectations. The breakthrough for Mead's theory of the constitution of the object came, then, when he recognized *that the cooperation of the hand and the eye creates 'things', permanent objects, only when the capacity for role-taking, which has been developed in social intercourse, is also utilized in the individual's dealings with non-social objects*. Now, what does that mean?

The critical defect of all previous analyses of the constitution of objects was that they could give only a necessary, but not a sufficient reason for it. The cooperation of hand and eye does not at all have to lead to the constitution of permanent objects; rather, it could, just as the cooperation or coordination of two senses generally, bring into being a 'polysensory complex', an intermingling of sensory experiences, that is definitely to be distinguished from the combination or linking of two kinds of perception despite their difference. What distinguishes such a polysensory complex from permanent objects is, then, still not clarified. According to Mead, the source of the distinction lies in the fact that we attribute to the object a substantial interior, an inside, from which the pressure emanates that we experience in our dealings with the world as the resistance of the physical object.

But what now has to be explained is how this inside, this substance, this pressure, is constituted. This inside can never be reached through dissection of the object, for that would only give us new surfaces. Clearly, we mean by 'inside' not something that is located within, but rather something representing an active, resistant character and the centre of this character's effectiveness. Although we can never feel or see this inside, we nevertheless constantly assume it. This inside is nothing other than the expression in the perceptual object of the active character of our perception.[15] We attribute an inside to the object when we locate within it the resistance of the object which we experience in our active commerce with our environment. Contact experience is the experience of resistance.

> The contact, however, is not simply a pressure, not simply a hardness or roughness. It is primarily a resistance.[16]

Thus Mead stresses that the real peculiarity of contact experience does not lie in the fact that it provides us with very special sensory information about the surface of objects, but, on the contrary, that it offers us the 'inside' of things. This inside, though, appears only in activity.[17]

Thus, in our immediate and practical dealings with the world we impute to objects an inside, and that means, a resistance originating with the objects and independent of us. But how do we come to make this imputation? Mead founds it in the individual's experience of his body parts, for instance, of his two hands, in which the subject and the object characters occur together. In the play of my two hands I sense a pressure exerted by myself on myself. Now, observes Mead, the child continually incorporates into such play other objects that are not parts of his body. These things are then found to have the very same active, pressure-exerting character as the child's body parts. The organism, which is itself a material object in the world of objects, 'transfers' to the objects its perception of the pressure experienced by its body parts.

At this point there is danger of a profound misunderstanding of Mead's conception of how human beings constitute physical objects. One might think that the constitution of the object results from a projection of the subject's kinaesthetic sensations into the object. And that explanation was in fact advanced prior to Mead.[18] Its error, though, is that for such a projection the subject's identification of these sensations as belonging to himself would have to be presupposed. Now it is the goal of Mead's theory of intersubjectivity to refute the possibility of an originarily given self-perception of the subject. Therefore Mead has to explain the transferral of the subject's experience of the pressure he himself exerts to the thing as an 'action-centre' in such a way that his explanation does not contradict the analysis of the origination of self-consciousness given by his theory of intersubjectivity. Accordingly, Mead rejects the 'projection theory', arguing that at first the human organism is only a perceptual object for itself among other such objects. Nevertheless, this organism, which is still completely unaware that it is delimited from the world around it, is already tied into the structure of social interaction. It has already begun to react to the gestures of partners in interaction and to express itself gesturally. But these gestures, too, which come from the organism itself, cannot yet presuppose a boundary between the organism and the other. However, there does exist a form of communication through gestures which specifically does not pre-suppose a separation of the identities of the organisms participating in the communication, namely identification of the one with the other. It is on this model that Mead conceives of the transferral of the experience of pressure to the object. On the basis of the similarity of organism and object as material bodies, the organism identifies the movement of the thing with its own reactive effort. The organism takes the 'role' of the object, as Mead describes the subject's activity in conscious analogy to the analysis of role-taking in social interaction.

To verify the accuracy of this interpretation[19] and as preparation for following Mead's analysis further, let us read a summary in Mead's own words of what has been said so far about the constitution of physical objects.

The necessary condition of this physical but cooperative 'other' getting into experience, so that the inside of things, their efficacy and force, is an actual part of the world, is that the individual in a premonitory fashion should take the attitude of acting as the physical thing will act, in getting the proper adjustment for his own ultimate response. I do not mean that the presence of this cooperative physical other is necessary to a successful adjustment to a limited physical environment. There is a very wide field of physical adjustment, such as that acquired in learning to ride a bicycle, which can be won without the inner efficacy of the things that cooperate with us in our conduct appearing as isolable elements in experience. Presumably this latter is the type of adjustment which is acquired by all animals except man. It is only man who has entered into a social relation with his environment, and then has abstracted and generalized it into a physical theory. What is essential to this social relation to the environment is not that the physical thing is endowed with a personality, although in the experience of little children and primitive man there is an approach to this. The essential thing is that the individual, in preparing to grasp the distant object, himself takes the attitude of resisting his own effort in grasping, and that the attained preparation for the manipulation is the result of this cooperation or conversation of attitudes. The mechanism for it presumably arises out of the interplay of different parts of the body against one another in adjusted stresses, primarily of the hands. If this were elaborated into its implied details, it amounts to a social hypothesis of what will happen when one comes into manipulative contact with the distant thing. I am prepared to seize the object, and then in the role of the thing I resist this grasp, pushing, we will say, the protuberances of the thing into the hand and arousing more effort in the hand by the leverage which the extended portion of the object will exercise, and through these responses of the thing I reach not only the final attitude of prepared manipulation but also a physical object with an inside and an inherent nature. About this fundamental core can gather the other things that an object can do to us, its efficacies, its active properties.[20]

Beyond what has already been analysed, this passage contains references to several other matters. First, Mead makes it clear that by no means does all human commerce with nature proceed by way of the self-reflective concentration of the events on permanent objects, but that in the case of the human beings, too, there are processes of adjustment which are immediate physiological reflexes. With regard to the constitution of objects, however, Mead does not tire of applying to our dealings with things the expressions and categories of the sphere of interaction. He speaks of taking the role of the thing, of empathy with the object, indeed, of the object's gestures.[21] Further, it is important that of course commerce with things, too, like social intercourse is dependent on *anticipatory* role-taking. Anticipatory role-taking enables us to adjust in advance our own behaviour to the expected behaviour of whatever is confronting us, and so to deal with things in a considered and planned manner. This anticipation is contained in the very fact that distance perceptions by their nature allow only a later fulfilment of the contact expectations which they call forth. But precisely because contact experiences are transferred to distance perceptions, and because things that are, say, visually perceived already trigger in the perceiver the beginning of contact attitudes which can attain their object only after some delay, on account of the object's distance, anticipation is necessarily built into the interplay of hand and eye.

> Within the field of matter, the resistance which the volume of a body offers to the hand, or to any surface of the body, and the tendencies to manipulate it when seen at a distance, are organized in various ways. There is, for example, the tendency to pick up a book on a distant table. The form and resistance of the book are present in some sense in the adjustment already present in the organism when the book is seen. My thesis is that the inhibited contact responses in the distance experience constitute the meaning of the resistance of the physical object.[22]

The significance of this thesis for the problem of the constitution of time will not be treated until we turn our attention to Mead's theory of time.[23] However, it should be mentioned here that in his writings on the 'physical thing', Mead set himself the task of solving the problem of what becomes of all of the contents which are conveyed by distance perception, but which are not able to direct the manipulatory action. Mead assumes that these must be inhibited, but that this does not at all mean that they are completely inefficacious. Rather, they retroact on the dominant attitude of response, influence the more precise definition of the object, and are indispensable for dealing with objects in a completely appropriate fashion.[24]

There are two other problems which still require further elucidation in this context: the problems of 'personalization' of objects and of 'perspective'. Mead attaches importance to making a distinction between the child's commerce with things in accordance with the schema of gestural communication and a personalization of inanimate objects, which is itself reflective in character.

> The child gets his solutions of what from our standpoint are entirely physical problems, such as those of transportation, movement of things, and the like, through his social reaction to those about him. This is not simply because he is dependent, and must look to those

about him for assistance during the early period of infancy, but, more important still, because his primitive process of reflection is one of mediation through vocal gestures of a cooperative social process. The human individual thinks first of all entirely in social terms. This means, as I have emphasized above, not that nature and natural objects are personalized, but that the child's reactions to nature and its objects are social reactions, and that his responses imply that the actions of natural objects are social reactions . . . The distinction between this attitude and that of personification is that between the primitive cult attitude and the later attitude of the myth, between the period of the Mana, of magic in its primitive form, and the period of the gods.[25]

It is clear that the personalization of inanimate objects is suggested by the original 'social' commerce with things. But to interpret the child's dealings with objects in this way would be to commit the very mistake that must be avoided in a theory of intersubjectivity, that is, placing the formation of the schema of the person at the beginning of the history of the development of social behaviour. What separates Mead's position from both the projection theory and the personalization theory is, then, the insight that the child's social forms of behaviour must be considered not the result but the presupposition of the self and self-reflection.

In many of his later writings, Mead treats the problem of the constitution of the physical object as it relates to the problem of the perspectival character of perception. There Mead asks how the human being is able not to be confined to his own body-centric perspective, but instead is capable of taking several different perceptual standpoints simultaneously and ultimately of attaining universality in the apprehension of the object. Mead grounds the human capacity for changing in consciousness, from one perceptual perspective to another in the capacity for taking roles. When I take the role of another, two different perceptual perspectives are represented in me simultaneously, which I must integrate into a many-sided image of the object, in a manner similar to the way different 'me's' can and must be synthesized into a unitary 'self'. By putting myself in the place of others, and finally of the generalized other, I achieve a comprehensive view of the object and ultimately a reconstruction of the structural nexus which, in addition to others, contains me and my perspective. Mead thereby links dealing with things in the appropriate way with the development of the self; damage to the self threatens, then, not only an individual's communicative behaviour vis-à-vis partners, but also the free manipulatory engagement with the objects of his environment.

I have said elsewhere[26] that Mead's account of this matter was another version of the position he took in his analysis of the cooperation of hand and eye. But in making that assertion I was being imprecise, since in the two instances it is a matter of two quite different 'decenterings' – borrowing from Piaget – which should be distinguished. In one case there is an elementary decentering of two kinds of perception, differing with respect to the sense organ used for each; in the other case, however, there is a decentering of the individual's whole body-centric perspective with regard to the perspectives of his partners in interaction. Whereas the first decentering is prior to formation of an elementary self-identification, the second is to be identified precisely with the formation of a self that can be maintained in the face of changing partners. The first decentering is dependent on the formation of the elementary 'identificatory' form of role-taking in immediate communication with gestures; in contrast, the second is referred to the stabilization of patterns of behavioural expectations in significant symbols and their availability in thought. It is a matter, then, of two different processes of development, one of which concerns the constitution of the physical objects, while the other pertains to the supersession of 'sensory-motor egocentrism'. *Mead established, however, that developments in the sphere of social behaviour are the precondition for both.*

Mead drives his intersubjectivist analysis even deeper into the processes of primary socialization by connecting the constitution of the object with the constitution of the individual's own body. In the published portions of Mead's literary remains the reader comes repeatedly upon allusions to this connection. While some of the unpublished manuscripts treat this topic in more detail, they, too, cannot by any means be considered a completely adequate exposition of this line of analysis.[27] However, the following is clear: when Mead refuses to accord primacy to self-perception, that means he rejects the possibility of originally identifying perception of one's own body as experience of one's own body: 'A pleased palate or an aching tooth is an object in experience just as a tree or mountain is an object.'[28] A perception can be identified as an experience of one's own body only when one is already conscious in an elementary fashion of the unitary nature of one's own body.

But how can the body ever be experienced as unitary, if in fact every perception presents it only in part?

> The body of the percipient individual is not an object as a whole. Different parts of the individual are seen and felt, or are both seen and felt, but there is no experience in which the entire individual appears as an object. That there are peculiar characters that are common to these parts of the body of the individual does not constitute them a single object, for that arises only in so far as the individual acts with reference to it as a whole. It is only as the objects are fixed in a field of contemporaneity that the individual can be fixed as a persistent whole within such a field, and only as the hypothetical content of the physical object is so identified with the attitudes of the individual that the individual presses against the body's resistance to the object, can the percipient individual become an object in the field of physical objects.[29]

Here Mead makes it quite clear that the individual's identification of his body as his own is not pregiven, nor can it be additively built up out of separate perceptions. Rather, it requires the very same process of identification that was presupposed for the constitution of the object. We arrive at the unity of the body only by way of the *per se* social path of self-identification. The separation of body and mind, which takes on the appearance of being self-evident, is, then, the result of a process in which inanimate objects are gradually recognized as such, and their original 'naive' incorporation into social behaviour is on the one hand habitualized, but on the other accompanied by awareness of their non-sociality. Mead calls this a 'process of de-socialization' and maintains that the distinction between one's own body and mind, or consciousness, must arise hand in hand with this de-socialization of physical objects.

> It was not until the desocializing of physical objects has taken place or was taking place that the distinction between the active self as a social being, and of the body as a non-social, i.e., purely physical being, was made.[30]

Thus Mead obtains the following logical sequence of developmental stages: The elementary incorporation of the child into social intercourse and the resulting capacity for identificatory role-taking makes possible the critically important step in the sensory-motor phase of cognitive development: the constitution of the physical thing. This, in turn, permits the crucial next step in the formation of the self: the individual's elementary identification of his own body. Together with the de-socialization of the individual's dealings with objects, there occurs a progressive separation of his own corporeality from his capacity for self-reflective, intentional action, which is understood as 'mind'. Clearly, for Mead the paths of development of cognitive and communicative abilities are much more intimately linked than in those theories in which only the communicative genesis of linguistic symbols is considered relevant for cognitive development. With his theory of the social genesis of the individual's identification of his own body, Mead put forward an approach which makes it possible to elucidate from an intersubjectivist standpoint what is currently being discussed under the opalescent term 'body image'.[31] Such an elucidation would have, as Mead knew, immediate ethical and practical implications. When Mead argues at length against the possibility of grasping the unity of one's own body through self-perception in the experience of seeing one's reflected image in a mirror,[32] then he is – to put it briefly – contributing to the refutation, founded on the human being's fundamental characteristics, of a narcissistic notion of self-experience. Neither the experience of his own body nor the sense of his own life-history can be experientially grasped, if the subject acts alone and attempts to relate himself back to himself in a mirroring fashion, but only if an individual actively participates in practical intersubjectivity as a part of the world and apprehends himself in that practical intersubjectivity. Only the objectification of our activity and social intercourse make it clear to us who we are.

Such far-reaching conclusions, must, of course, be preceded by improvement in the empirical foundation of Mead's theses. In the meantime, however, we can ask about the relationship of Mead's theory of object-constitution to competing approaches in psychology.

The dominant psychology of the period since Mead, behaviourism, does not even recognize the problem of the constitution of the object. For behaviourism the object-structure of the world is, certainly, beyond doubt; its theory of learning offers an account only of the processes of discrimination between objects and between the qualities and features of objects. However, in those currents of psychology and anthropology in which there has been any awareness at all of the problem of object-constitution, and in which a development from an 'objectless' phase was postulated, this problem was confined to the functional sphere of instrumental action. This is true of the important works written by the members of the Soviet-Marxist school which has endeavoured to pass beyond behaviourism and Pavlovism,[33] as well as of the Philosophical Anthropology of Arnold Gehlen in Germany and Piaget's constructionist psychology of development.

Leontjew reinterprets the functional primacy of material reproduction, transforming it into the genetic priority of work – vis-à-vis language – and his psychology of perception generally suffers from an inadequate concept of language and interaction. Gehlen's theories, it is true, cover linguistic and gestural elements, but in an instrumentalistically and solipsistically reduced form which is consonant with the political orientation of his anthropology.[34] As for Piaget's studies, there can be no doubt that they are the theoretically and empirically most important of all the investigations in the field of object-constitution and the 'construction of reality in the child'.[35] Piaget, however, very clearly vacillates in his statements on the relationship between cognitive and communicative development. He asserts repeatedly that cognitive development does not condition social development, but that instead a relationship exists between them in which both are equally important. Yet it is difficult to imagine in concrete detail what this means. Not only does Piaget, after studying moral judgement in the child, hardly discuss any more the development in the child of the capacity for interaction and communication; he is also tending more and more to interpret cognitive development as a self-regulating process with an inner logic of its own. In its presuppositions and its consequences, this thesis has recently become the target of penetrating criticisms.[36]

We can use the problem of the construction of the object to present the critique of Piaget *in nuce*. Piaget distinguishes convincingly six stages of sensory-motor development on the way to the 'thing'.

During the first two stages (those of reflexes and earliest habits), the infantile universe is formed of pictures that can be recognized but that have no substantial permanence or spatial organization. During the third stage (secondary circular reactions), a beginning of permanence is conferred on things by prolongation of the movements of accommodation (grasping, etc.) but no systematic search for absent objects is yet observable. During the fourth stage ('application of known means to new situations') there is searching for objects that have disappeared but no regard for their displacements. During a fifth stage (about 12 to 18 months old) the object is constituted to the extent that it is permanent individual substance and inserted in the groups of displacements, but the child still cannot take account of changes of position brought about outside the field of direct perception. In a sixth stage (beginning at the age of 16 to 18 months) there is an image of absent objects and their displacements.[37]

Mead would certainly not have found fault with this distinction of various phases. The controversy would begin only with the explanation of the conditions of this development. Piaget, too, persuasively rebuts the explanations according to which the constitution of the object emerges from the combining of visual and tactile perception as such, or can be derived from the mere experience of resistance.[38] Rather, says Piaget, it is necessary that the individual child apprehend its body as an extensional entity among other bodies, and he also does not conceive of the 'body image' as an *a priori* given, nor as the product of 'training by purely empirical associations', but as a construction.[39] And yet his own explanation does not satisfy the requirements that he himself erected. In his opinion, the constitution of the object can be explained by the reciprocal assimilation of secondary schemata.

This is disappointing. Since his explanations of the other nodal points of cognitive development also proceed according to a similar logic, this manner of explanation offered a purchase for a critique of Piaget, one that is significant for his entire system of thought, and that carries the analysis further. On the one hand this critique comes from the Piagetian school itself. Following a study by Smedslund,[40] the series of works written by the team of Doise/Mugny/Perret-Clermont, in particular, made important advances in providing a basis of empirical research for correcting Piaget's findings from the intersubjectivist standpoint.[41] In a number of investigations these authors have shown that as a matter of principle groups can solve cognitive problems better than individuals, and that this is also true when the problems in question go beyond the performance limits determined by the stage of cognitive development reached by the participating children. The reason for this is that the overcoming of contradictions in perception, which is necessary for continuation of cognitive development, can be achieved more easily by a collective, since the individual child, precisely because of its 'egocentrism', can endure contradictions without recognizing them as such. However, when the contradictory perceptions are each advanced by different members of the cooperative group, then they cannot be ignored or dismissed, and compel the members of the group to attempt to resolve them. The advancements of performance which are acquired in cooperation can demonstrably be stabilized and reactualized in the individual group member. These authors do not understand learning as the mere internalization of coordinations, but as the internalization of collective-intersubjective coordinations. Therefore, they do not abandon Piaget's constructionist standpoint, but relate it to the social character of learning with greater consequence than he did. Their central thesis is, then, the very one which Mead held to, namely that social interaction 'intervenes' in the individual's cognitive development.[42]

Now, as regards our enquiry, the deficiency of these investigations is that they examine exclusively the sphere of 'representative' egocentrism, and do not deal at all with sensory-motor egocentrism. The critique of Piaget from the standpoint of the theory of intersubjectivity is developed with philological precision and in detail by van de Voort in an important study.[43] Van de Voort's work was prompted by observations made by Oevermann about Habermas's efforts to elaborate a theory of communicative action, but goes further than those observations. He is not content to refer cognitive and communicative development to each other with regard to the formation of linguistic symbols.[44] Instead, he pushes the linking of these two developments forward in a manner that can be understood as genuine convergence with the theses yielded by Mead's interpretation of these matters.

Thus, it has at least been shown that Mead's theory of object-constitution is not only logically consistent, but also that it has not been disproved by the most important empirical studies on this topic. Additional confirmation is provided by two other areas of research, which can only be touched on briefly here. Psychoanalytic psychology of development can be a significant complement to the above-mentioned studies when it concerns itself directly with the empirical reality of the young child's development, rather than seeking to reconstruct it out of the pathology of adult personalities, and when it does not confine its concept of the object to the object of libidinous impulses in the narrower sense. This is true, for instance, of the researches of René Spitz, who empirically ascertains both the existence of an objectless early stage of development and the temporal priority of social objects.[45] A study by Silvia Bell, in which she tries to combine a psychoanalytical approach with that of behaviouristic learning theory, shows – despite some defects in her theory and in her use of it – the constitutive importance of the child's interpersonal relations and capacities for the development of its commerce with things.[46] Finally, let me remind the reader that correction of Piaget's findings and recognition of the importance of early social development have come also from experimental psychologists' reflection on their discipline, which made clear the social character of the experimental situation and brought out the importance of the relationship between the experimenter and the child, of the affective charge for the child of the task set it, and of the tasks's approximation to the child's life-world.[47] Even if the theories of human sociality predominant in experimental psychology, which are in part behaviouristic and in part ethological,[48] differ from those of Mead, there is a convergence in the direction of a theory maintaining that the individual's social and cognitive development are intrinsically interwoven from birth.

If such a theory in general and Mead's theory of object-constitution in particular prove convincing, then important consequences result from them. For then theories of development are precluded that consider the development of social capacities to be determined by the stages of cognitive development. This position is only an implicit possibility in Piaget's work, but finds full expression in the American continuation of the psychology of cognitive development.[49] Selman's studies on the development of the capacity for role-taking, for example, assert the determinative character of cognitive development. Kohlberg posits a simple parallelism of the development of the perception of the personal and of the physical object,[50] but then in another passage he supplies a self-critical addendum to this proposition: the one development cannot be considered as the condition for the other; rather, both come out of a common structural foundation.[51] Just what this means, however, remains unclear. Nevertheless, only through the introduction of the intersubjective dimension also into the elementary stages of cognitive development – for which Mead prepared the way – is this field opened up to truly sociological research on socialization. In the other direction, this anchoring of object-constitution and the concomitant development of a concept of objectual meaning which is founded in intersubjective praxis are a remedy for the conception of meaning which restricts it to language and for a confusion of the constitution of meaning with verbally reached agreement, such as characterizes Blumer's account of the basis of symbolic interactionism.[52]

In summary, we can say that Mead roots perception and meaning in a common praxis of subjects, not – as Blumer does – in a merely verbal communication about definitions that is unrelated to praxis, nor – as Kohlberg – in a presocial cognitive dimension of the individual's development, and, lastly, not – as Habermas – in a communication that is severed from active engagement with nature[53] and only subsequently, in the framework of a theory of evolution, refers normative problems to the problems of economic systems.[54]

8

Temporality and Intersubjectivity

Mead's philosophy of time is certainly the least intelligible and least well elucidated part of his work. Its best-known expression is to be found in the book *The Philosophy of the Present*, which was prepared from his manuscript for the Carus Lectures one year after Mead's death. Thus this text, too, was not completed for publication by Mead himself and presents the reader with considerable difficulties. The argumentation is disconnected, leaping from one theme to the next, while the wealth of ideas and references threatens to overflow the confines of the book. This is surely attributable to the fact that the manuscript was intended primarily as an aid to the speaker's memory when he delivered his lectures. Nevertheless, the manuscript provides a more reliable source for Mead's thoughts in this area than students' notes. But the slender volume that was prepared from the manuscript does not give the correct impression of the extent to which Mead occupied himself with the problems treated in it. For on these topics Mead left a veritable mountain of fragments and writings, which I cannot claim to interpret and systematize here definitively. These essays and fragments are in part contained in *The Philosophy of the Act* – I refer in particular to the large manuscript entitled 'The Experiential Basis of Natural Science'. Others, though, have only recently come to light again, as, for example, a 130-page-long manuscript bearing the title 'The Creative Character of Human Intelligence'. From no other phase of Mead's work can his relentless circling around a problem be better documented. However, in order to avoid excessive length and to facilitate verification, the following exposition of Mead's thoughts on temporality draws principally on *The Philosophy of the Present* and includes the other relevant material only in those instances when it serves to clarify or confirm the interpretation given of Mead's theory of time.

167

The Philosophy of the Present is a deliberately ambiguous title. [1] On the one hand, it indicates that Mead is concerned with determining the historical locus of philosophy and its tasks in his time. On the other, he defines the task of contemporary philosophy as taking seriously 'the proposition that reality exists in a present'.[2] How are we supposed to understand this proposition? A first approximation of an understanding of the notion 'philosophy of the present' can be obtained if one understands that it is intended to be a counter-notion to a philosophy of the past or a philosophy of the future. In Mead's view, a philosophy of the past regards the present and the future as mere concatenations of effects, resulting from causes which are effective now and for all time. What he has in mind is the world-view of mechanistic determinism. In contrast, a philosophy of the future turns such mechanistic determinism on its head and sees the present as merely a stage in a process, the final goal of which was fixed prior to all history. Here Mead is thinking of the philosophy of history of a teleological determinism.

The 'philosophy of the present' thus finds itself embattled on two fronts. Since mechanistic determinism chiefly employs arguments taken from natural science, the philosophy of the present is compelled by its combat against that opponent to discuss questions concerning the philosophy of nature or the theory of natural science. On the other battle front, however, rejection of the philosophy of history on the model of a world-historical plan of salvation forces it into debate on ethics and politics and on the theory of the science of history. Further, its arguments against both adversaries must be consistent with each other and compatible with the factual results of scientific research. Mead is therefore led to undertake an exegesis of the research practices of both natural science and the science of history from a unitary standpoint. Perhaps this very brief sketch of the problem-field within which a philosophy of the present must be elaborated will make understandable the definition Mead gave in 1930 of the present task of philosophy.

> It is the task of the philosophy of today to bring into congruence with each other this universality of determination which is the text of modern science, and the emergence of the novel which belongs not only to the experience of human social organisms, but is found also in a nature which science and the philosophy that has followed it have separated from human nature.[3]

This problem was an urgent and serious matter for Mead because it seemed to him that an era had come to an end, one that had not only brought palpable social progress, but had also been shaped by the possibility, appearing in the heart of natural science itself, of drawing from that science other than mechanically deterministic implications. That possibility had been Darwin's theory of evolution. This theory was an important formative experience for Mead and his generation,[4] and meant for them the refutation of the Christian doctrine of salvation through the destruction of belief in the Biblical story of creation and through the proof of unplanned evolution, as well as – and in this regard they were diametrically opposed to the reactionary tenets of Social Darwinism – providing a paradigm of the organism's active engagement with its environment which influenced their entire conception of humanity, of history, and of science. The essential temporality of the world, which Darwinism had expressed conceptually,[5] was threatened by a new revolutionizing of the scientific view of the world: the theory of relativity and those interpretations of it according to which a 'de-temporalization' – as Hermann Weyl put it – could be deduced from that theory.

Mead bases his discussion of relativity on the understanding of Einstein's innovations held by physicists and philosophers, who, working with the concept of a four-dimensional space-time-world, conceived of time in various ways as a subjective phenomenon and not as an inherent feature of the physical world itself. In Weyl's words:

> All that is happening is the successively experienced perception by a subject who is travelling 'along the world-line of its body'. But no temporality can be attributed to the physical world, to the perceptual object; nothing happens in it; it simply *is*.[6]

If this was the demonstrable corollary of the theory of relativity, then the very foundations of Mead's thought were shaken. The extraordinarily stimulating effect of the theory of relativity on Mead was due to his belief that not only were these conclusions unjustified, but that the theory of relativity itself was the best proof of the opposite, if one but understood it correctly. But to achieve this correct understanding it was necessary to bring to bear just those concepts which were central to Mead's social psychology: action and intersubjectivity. When they were so applied, however, these notions did not remain unchanged; they became more subtly differentiated and in return opened new vistas in the psychology of social development.

These remarks indicate the direction my interpretation will take. It is my intent to show that Mead's philosophy of time is not a lapse from his scientific way of thinking back into metaphysical speculation, or worse, an attempt to criticize the theory of relativity from the viewpoint of philosophical presumption. Rather he seeks to demonstrate that the implications of the theory of relativity for a theory of science had been falsely understood even by its proponents, trying to attain a correct understanding by means of his concept of history and natural history, drawing forth, albeit in a sketchy manner, the implications of the correct understanding of the theory of relativity for the theory of socialization and developmental psychology. Here most of the emphasis is given to these implications and their usefulness.

The foregoing is admittedly a systematization which Mead himself did not carry out. His Carus Lectures are organized in the following manner. He begins the first of the four lectures with an initial differentiation of his own position from the predominant interpretation of the theory of relativity, that of Minkowski, and an initial critique of Whitehead's efforts to get beyond that interpretation. In doing this, however, Mead's strategy is primarily to provide a basis for his critique of 'de-temporalization' with a suitable concept of history, gained through interpretation of the procedure of historical science. In a summary at the end of the first lecture Mead states that the outcome of the preceding argument is

> . . . that the estimate and import of all histories lies in the interpretation and control of the present; that as ideational structures they always arise from change, which is as essential a part of reality as the permanent, and from the problems which change entails; and that the metaphysical demand for a set of events which is unalterably there in an irrevocable past, to which these histories seek a constantly approaching agreement, comes back to motives other than those at work in the most exact scientific research.[7]

The first lecture thus introduces the idea of a constitution of the past in the problems of the present. The second lecture then counteracts the 'de-temporalizing' consequences of the theory of relativity through an account of the constitution of all science in the structures of the relation between the organism and its environment. Mead begins by showing that prerelativist Newtonian mechanics can be founded in this way. The third lecture carries this argument further, and is devoted chiefly to developing the general concept of sociality on which the metaphysical interpretations of Mead's work are primarily based. The origin of this concept in the social sciences is not concealed, although it is advanced in the context of the theory of natural science. Later we shall examine it more closely. The fourth lecture presents the ground-plan of a theory of evolution in which distinctions are drawn between the various levels of sociality of animal and human societies, as well as between the levels of the structure of the relation between the organism and its environment in general. This distinguishing of levels of sociality is sufficient in itself to show that the general concept of sociality is not at all intended to efface the stages of evolutionary development.

Even before the formulation of the theory of relativity, the problem of 'time' had been the pivotal point of debates about the validity of empiricism in epistemology and the psychology of perception. Under the influence of Newtonian mechanics, which conceived of all bodies as points of mass that could be unequivocally located in an absolute space, time was thought of as a mere standard, external to physical objects, for the measurement of movement. Newtonian physics' conception of reality led to the conception of time as a 'succession of now-points', as the notion was expressed by Merleau-Ponty. Each particular operative now-point, the present, could, in Mead's words, be thought of only as a 'knife-edge present': as a mere shifting boundary between the extended domains of the past and the future. The present itself could have no temporal extent; and the idea of a constitution of past and future in a present was excluded. The self-certainty of this conception of time, which was also rooted in the general consciousness, was first shaken when, in the late years of the 19th century, emerging empirical psychology conducted studies of psychological 'present-time' (William Stern), which showed that a definite minimal temporal extension was required for perception, and that therefore the punctual present could at best be conceived of as an idealization of this psychical present.

In the Anglo-Saxon arena of discourse on this topic, the term 'specious present' gained acceptance as the designation of this psychical present. The change of meaning that this term has undergone says much about the development of theory in this regard. At first this term, as it was used by Edmund Clay,[8] a proponent of a punctual present, meant a 'pseudo-present' in the sense of an unavoidable deviation of human perception from the exactitude of measurement that was in point of fact truly desirable as the disposition adequate to the proper structure of reality. In contrast, under William James's pen the expression was used to mean the opposite. In his writings, the 'specious present' became the true present, from which the punctual present was only an abstraction, which might be justified for certain purposes of measurement and science, but which could not claim to represent the character of time. This step opened the way for the idea of a non-punctual time that instead flowed; in addition, the insight that physical time was constituted directed attention to the question of the temporality of the constituting dimension itself.

Even more than for James, this became a central theme for Bergson, the true forefather of the modern discussion of time. To physical time Bergson counterposed, in diametrical opposition, 'la durée', the continuously flowing time of introspective experience. Bergson understood physical time as the time which is thought according to the model of space and thereby robbed of just those features which are specific to time as it really is. Viewed from the standpoint of Mead's premises, there was as much truth as error in Bergson's position. It was correct to enquire into the temporality of the constituting dimension itself, as well as to reject the dogmatic presupposition of the physicalist conception of time; but it was wrong to presuppose, as Bergson evidently did, the primacy of introspective experience as such, and hence also of the introspective experience of time, and to hold that an adequate understanding of time could only be gained by passively resonating in sympathy with the flux of the universe, which was beyond rational apprehension. Mead was very clearly aware of this complex of questions, and of the more far-reaching historical aspects of the problem, as proven by his references to Hume's influential denial of the perceptibility of duration, a result of the latter's belief in the atomistic nature of individual events, and to Kant's critique of Hume's position.[9] But for Mead this controversy and his criticism of Bergson only posed the problem of the *constitution* of time, without in any way solving it.

The theory of relativity seemed to Mead an instrument, elaborated by science itself, with which, along with Newtonian mechanics, the vulgar conception of time could be shaken in its very foundation. And this could be done without forcing philosophy to take refuge in an irrationalist and abstract theory of pure passage, of temporal flow. This hope came from the fact that a central consequence of the theory of relativity was the necessity of thoroughly revising the concept of 'simultaneity'. According to Einstein, 'simultaneity' could no longer be understood, as it had been in the Newtonian world-view, as the purely objective coincidence of two movements in one point of time, independent of all observers and their perspectives. The 'point of time' proved to be rather the finite span of time in which perceptible signals from the sites of the events were able to meet in the point defined by the observer. When it was established that the speed of propagation of light was not infinitely great, but instead determinately limited, scientists and philosophers were compelled to recognize that the concept of 'simultaneity' could not be dissociated from the observer's distance from the events in question and from his direction and speed of movement. Now this recognition did more than merely clarify practical questions of measurement. Thenceforth, any scientific statement about the world of moving bodies also had to take into consideration, in an objectivating manner, the corporeality of the observer himself, that is, in such a manner as to make the observer's corporeality part of the objective state of affairs which is being cognized. All scientific measurement rests upon practical activities of cognizing subjects; all scientific cognition must self-reflectively include considerations of the location and the perspective of the cognizing subject.

It soon turned out however that not everyone drew these conclusions from the upheaval in the theoretical foundations of physics brought about by the theory of relativity. Instead, the necessity of objectivating the observer's perspective led to a theory which claimed to achieve definitive independence from the constitution of space and time from a particular perspective. Although the transformation of the concept of simultaneity had resulted in recognition of the fact that it was impossible to determine spatial and temporal indices separately, this did not lead to a theory of the *interpenetration of time- and space-constitution*, but instead to the well-known mathematical concept of a four-dimensional space-time-continuum of events, that is, a continuum including time as well as the three dimensions of space. The debate on the reality-status of this model has not subsided since Minkowski's publications[10] on it appeared, although it has been much more open since the thirties than it was in Mead's day.

It is quite clear that at the beginning of his second Carus Lecture Mead is criticizing Minkowski's model of the four-dimensional space-time-continuum as a renewal of the physicalist misunderstanding of temporality.

> I have spoken of the present as the seat of reality because its character of a present sheds light upon the nature of reality. The past and the future that appear in the present may be regarded as merely the thresholds of a minute bit of an unbounded extension whose metaphysical reality reduces the present to a negligible element that approaches the world at an instant. This view of reality as an infinite scroll unrolling in snatches before our intermittent vision receives another variant in the picture of reality as a four-dimensional continuum of space-time, of events and intervals, forever determined by its own geometry, and into which we venture with our own subjective frames of reference, receiving momentary impressions whose present character is a function of our minds and not of any section of the ordered events in the universe. I have suggested that such an approach to reality does not answer to the scientific technique and method by which we seek for disclosures of the universe. Scientific procedure fastens upon that necessary conditioning of what takes place by what has taken place which follows from passage itself.[11]

We need not concern ourselves here with the details of Mead's argument. It is plain, however, that Mead is interested in the attempts to draw alternative conclusions from the theory of relativity. This interest led him to examine Whitehead's interpretations of that theory, principally those offered in the latter's 'realistic' writings,[12] and not Whitehead's turn toward 'organismic' idealism in *Process and Reality*. Whitehead, says Mead, has '. . . undertaken to preserve motion and change within a relativistic universe'.[13] The way he did this was, on the one hand, to expand the concept of perspective beyond spatial seeing and to refer it also to temporality, in accordance with the inseparability of spatial and temporal measurements of moving bodies, and on the other to ascribe such perspectives not only to human subjects but also – in a way similar to Uexküll's conception of environment[14] – to all living beings and even to inorganic moving bodies. Whitehead thereby, as Mead remarks, keeps 'the different time systems as perspectives in nature',[15] rather than conceiving of them as merely subjective ornamentation on the outside of the closed realm of nature.

But now another problem arises to confront Whitehead, that of a consistent concept of the present in this universe of perspectives. He solves this problem with his concept of the 'event', and in this solution Mead follows Whitehead. However, Whitehead then metaphysically separates the occurrence of events from their substantive reality. The motive for taking this step is probably that another way of preserving universal validity – a problem with which the logician Whitehead was especially familiar – did not appear conceivable to him in a universe of perspectives which seemed to imply relativism. The substantive attributes of events, however, must then be assigned to a world of Platonic 'eternal objects'; they enter into events through 'ingression' into the temporal flow, conceived as pure. Mead considers this the point where the undeniable fruitfulness of Whitehead's interpretation passes over into metaphysical speculation, springing from the metaphysical hypostatization of an abstraction:

> This seems to me to be an improper use of abstraction, since it leads to a metaphysical separation of what is abstracted from the concrete reality from which the abstraction is made, instead of leaving it as a tool in the intellectual control of that reality. Bergson refers, I think, to the same improper use of abstraction, in another context, as the spatialization of time, contrasting the exclusive nature of such temporal moments with the interpenetration of the contents of 'real' duration.[16]

This sketch of Mead's assessment of Whitehead immediately makes two things clear. First, that Mead had to undertake to develop further, in a fruitful way, the notions of the objective reality of perspectives and of the event; second, that according to his rejection of metaphysical abstractions, he could not seek fulfilment of his task in a speculative philosophy of nature. The tissue of concepts that Mead roughed out in his writings on the theory of time in order to demonstrate that the theories of evolution and relativity were compatible with each other is therefore continuously referred to scientific cognition of the world.

The internal coherence of this web of concepts can perhaps be best shown through examination of the concept of the 'event', as it is understood by Mead. In contrast with Whitehead, Mead does not conceive of the event simply as an arbitrarily singled-out part of temporal passages, but rather as a part that thrusts itself forward, so to speak. 'These events always have characters of uniqueness. Time can only arise through the ordering of passage by these unique events'.[17] The event is thus conceived of *not only* as part of an objective temporal passage, but as the origin of all structuring of time. Without the interruption of the passage of time by the event, no experience of time would be possible. Here there is danger of a misunderstanding, with which Mead takes issue again and again. The constitutive role of the event *for the experience of time* can be recognized, and yet experience can be construed as an ever-changing processing of a world which is pregiven and unaffected by the subject's experience. In opposition to this view, Mead contends that it is based on an erroneous understanding of subjective experience and specifically does not take into consideration the objective reality of perspectives.

> For, in the first place human experiences are as much a part of this world as are any of its other characteristics, and the world is a different world because of these experiences. And, in the second place, in any history that we construct we are forced to recognize the shift in relationship between the conditioning passage and emergent event, in that part of the past which belongs to passage, even when this passage is not expanded in ideation.[18]

Mead adduces here several arguments, all of which serve the purpose of proving the objective existence of novelty. Behind all these arguments stands the mighty rock of the theory of evolution. For Mead this theory shows that from causal nexuses effects can emerge which are not reducible to their causes. This makes it possible for him to construe any experience whatsoever as a step of nature: the creative character of human intelligence is not the opposite of nature, but rather the result of nature and a part of it.

The concept in which this conception became crystallized was that of 'emergence'. In the contemporary controversy between the reductionists and the emergentists, Mead sided with the latter, without, however, sharing the religious or speculative tendencies of famous partisans of this position, such as C. Lloyd Morgan or Samuel Alexander.[19] Since in Mead's opinion both physicalist and biologist reductionism were doomed to fail, and since the 'emergentist' view is thus left as the compelling explanation of novelty in the universe, Mead can easily integrate the notion of reconstruction into his tissue of concepts. For Mead's concept of the present, this is the crucially important step in his reflections.

To be sure, the new event is located in an unbroken causal chain lying in the past. But precisely because of its novelty, it could not, *per definitionem*, be deduced from this causal chain, but rather compels the reconstructive interpretation of the causal chain.

> The relation of any event to the conditions under which it occurs is what we term causation. The relation of the event to its preceding conditions at once sets up a history, and the uniqueness of the event makes that history relative to that event. The conditioning passage and the appearance of the unique event then give rise to past and future as they appear in a present. All of the past is in the present as the conditioning nature of passage, and all the future arises out of the present as the unique events that transpire. To unravel this existent past in the present and on the basis of it to previse the future is the task of science. The method is that of ideation.[20]

This quotation makes it clear that it never occurs to Mead to deny the objectivity of time or causality. It is true that the present results from the past, but how the present results from the past is revealed only in reconstruction.

> The long and the short of it is that the past (or the meaningful structure of the past) is as hypothetical as the future ... And the metaphysical assumption that there has been a definite past of events neither adds to nor subtracts from the security of any hypothesis which illuminates our present. It does indeed offer the empty form into which we extend any hypothesis and develop its implications ...[21]

Thus, with regard to historical cognition, matters stand as they do with all cognition: it is directed to an objective reality, which, however, it is impossible to grasp without interpretation. Every testing of an hypothesis requires ascertaining anew whether it is compatible with data, which themselves have already been interpreted by the process of their constitution. An escape from this circle is just as logically impossible as an abandonment of the regulative claim to the truth of the hypothesis.

In this connection Mead develops succinct but finely differentiated ideas about a pragmatist logic of the science of history. The specific characteristic of Mead's thoughts on this topic, in comparison with the German discussion of the problematic of historicism, consists in the fact that he does not consider the problem to be merely one of epistemology or even of cultural history, but, as it were, of natural history. This means several things. For Mead reconstruction of history always means also the reconstruction of prehuman organic and inorganic history; his examples are taken mostly from the sphere of cosmological explanations of the history of the universe. For Mead, then, nature is by no means to be regarded only from a technical and instrumental viewpoint, but also historically. Consequently, Mead understands human knowledge and its practical results as advances in natural history, and locates the problem of 'retrospective determination' prior to the problems of human history and of intentional action. This manner of considering things makes it possible to overcome the rigidly deterministic outlook of the mechanistic world-view in the area of prehuman history also and to construe human history as part and as continuation of the history of nature. These are two very modern ideas.[22] Reconstruction of the past is begun by the new event. New events constitute new pasts. A definitive reconstruction of the past would be possible only if no more new events could occur, in other words, only under the condition that history were concluded, if there were no future. However, according to Mead, this is, as a matter of essential principle, inconceivable.

Now, in any history a reconstruction of the past is necessarily referred to the future. Mead describes how this is done and explains why:

> When these emergents have appeared they become part of the determining conditions that occur in real presents, and we are particularly interested in presenting the past which in the situation before us conditioned the appearance of the emergent, and especially in so presenting it that we can lead up to new appearances of this object. We orient ourselves not with reference to the past which was a present within which the emergent appeared, but in such a restatement of the past as conditioning the future that we may control its reappearance.[23]

This necessary referral to the future of every reconstruction of the past takes place, it is true, in a situation of the present. The reconstruction of the past can only be established by drawing on material existing in the present, can only be related to problems in the present, and can only be tested with the touchstone of present experiences. With these assertions Mead attacks the belief of naive historicism that we can use past events themselves to ascertain the validity of our reconstruction of the past. Mead justifies his position by calling attention,

> . . . *first*, to the evident fact that all the apparatus of the past, memory images, historical monuments, fossil remains and the like are in some present, and, *second*, to that portion of the past which is there in passage in experience as determined by the emergent event. It comes back, *third*, to the necessary test of the formulation of the past in the rising events in experience. The past we are talking about lies with all its characters within that present.[24]

The second of these arguments requires clarification. At first it might sound like a contradiction of the thesis that the past can be ascertained only reconstructively, when Mead speaks here of a part of the past to which one can have immediate access in experience. Mead is quite aware of this apparent contradiction; however, he regards the opinion that change cannot be experienced in the present itself as a vestige of the idea of a punctual present. If, however, change can be experienced, then the embeddedness of perceived things in temporal and causal nexuses can itself be experienced. This perceptible change, is, then, the specific presupposition for the more far-reaching reconstruction of the past.[25]

> The organization of any individual thing carries with it the relation of this thing to processes that occurred before this organization set in. In this sense the past of that thing is 'given' in the passing present of the thing, and our histories of things are elaborations of what is implicit in this situation. This 'given' in passage is there and is the starting point for a cognitive structure of a past.[26]

In a fragment from his literary estate, which was included in *The Philosophy of the Present* by the book's editors, Mead attempts to explain more precisely the relationship of his conception of history to historians' understanding of their science. There he makes it clear that he does not only reject naive historicism, but that this rejection still leaves open what conclusions must be drawn from this position. The conclusion drawn most frequently is that an approximation to the past in its peculiarity, purified of all traces of any present, is an ideal which, although ultimately unattainable, is nevertheless worth striving for. The effect of this position on the philosopher of history is to incline him toward scepticism and relativism; with respect to scientific methodology, it makes compulsory the historian's ethos of detachment from all interests in the present and his taking all facts into consideration. In contrast, Mead does not hold that the unattainableness of a past 'in itself' is a consequence of the deficiencies of our cognitive capacities; rather, he considers it an essentially necessary aspect of the constitution of temporality. Therefore, regarding the science of history as being similar to a mnemotechnical exercise is, in his opinion, essentially incorrect.

> If we could bring back the present that has elapsed in the reality which belonged to it, it would not serve us. It would be that present and would lack just that character which we demand in the past, that is, that construction of the conditioning nature of now present passage which enables us to interpret what is arising in the future that belongs to this present. When one recalls his boyhood days he cannot get into them as he then was, without their relationship to what he has become; and if he could, that is if he could reproduce the experience as it then took place, he could not use it, for this would involve his not being in the present within which that use must take place . . . Another way of saying this is that our pasts are always mental in the same manner in which the futures that lie in our imaginations ahead of us are mental.[27]

Clearly, Mead does not intend to proceed from his thesis of the unattainableness of the past in itself to the assertion that 'objective' knowledge of history is impossible, even though it is still unclear how he will ground the claim that such knowledge is possible. He rejects the sceptical consequences from the critiques of the historicist conception of the possibility of historical knowledge,[28] but not the conclusions drawn on the level of the historian's ethos. These, however, Mead re-interprets, by making the important distinction between complete consideration of all data available at the present time for the reconstruction of a past in a given present, and the complete anticipation of the future, which would be the presupposition for a definitive and conclusive interpretation of history.

Only with regard to the first problem is the ethos of the historian pertinent; through industry, skill, and intense effort, an approximation – but never more than an approximation – to a comprehensive reconstruction of the past is in fact possible.

> We can then conceive of a past which in any one present would be irrefragable. So far as that present was concerned it would be a final past, and if we consider the matter, I think that it is this past to which the reference lies in that which goes beyond the statement which the historian can give, and which we are apt to assume to be a past independent of the present.[29]

But even if the maximum of historical research were achieved in a particular present, the reconstruction of the past 'would be a truth which belongs to this present, and a later present would reconstruct it from the standpoint of its own emergent nature'.[30]

However, these remarks still do not answer the question of what objectivity of historical reconstruction can mean. It is clear that Mead must attack this problem within the framework of his notion of the objective reality of perspectives. History, like the world of the present does not stand in an absolute and proper structure before the cognitive subject, who has only to achieve cognitive adequacy to this structure by drawing back what is left of his subjectivity. Rather, objective knowledge of reality can only be reached by means of a progressive universalization: through the constitution of the world not from every individual perspective separately, but rather in a common praxis as a common world.

Mead's reflections on this theme did not reach a conclusion. Granted, he did develop in great detail the connection between objective knowledge and the universal taking of perspectives, and he also founds the possibility of universal perspective-taking completely in a nexus of effects that is prior to our subjective intervention, and that runs its course 'behind our backs' or traverses us.[31] But I do not see that he went beyond the plane of natural history and thought out the historical origination of the conditions of objective knowledge of history through a process of universalization of praxis taking place in history. The elements necessary for working out this complex of relationships are almost all present in Mead's thought, but he does not link them together. It is difficult not to suspect that the reason for this is the same as for the deficiencies in Mead's ethics that were shown earlier, namely the confusion of a teleological philosophy of history with a conception of history that assures itself of objective historical advances in its present praxis. In the next chapter this point will be taken up again.

Let us, then, first consider, not where the fruitfulness of Mead's approach stops, but rather what it consists in. The foregoing brief remarks have made it clear that for Mead the problem of objectivity of cognition or the universality of the orientation of action is centrally connected with that concept in the tissue of concepts under discussion which has so far not been treated: the concept of sociality. It is this concept which the metaphysical interpretations of Mead's thought regard as the most important of all, and with which, in this view, the relationship of Mead's social psychology and his 'philosophy of the present' can be shown most clearly. And, in fact, those who make this argument can cite many passages in which Mead extends 'sociality' beyond the domain of human and animal social integration and in highly abstract reasoning identifies it with the concept of the 'present'. The meaning of the final phase of Mead's work can only be deciphered if the character of this category is clarified. So, how does Mead define sociality? 'Sociality is the capacity of being several things at once.'[32] This could be understood in the sense of a human ability, an operation of consciousness. However, it is important for Mead that sociality is not to be understood precisely in this way:

> I wish to emphasize the fact that the appearance of mind is only the culmination of that sociality which is found throughout the universe . . .[33]

Thus human sociality is, to be sure, the culmination, but by no means the only form of the structure designated by the term 'sociality'. Instead, every event that is simultaneously of two different kinds can be called 'social'. But what is the meaning of this singular property of being simultaneously of two different kinds? In every referential system any event can only be of a single kind which is identical with itself. To be of two different kinds at the same time means, therefore, belonging simultaneously to two referential systems. Now, an event is in two referential systems only when it is passing from the one into the other. Mead maintains

. . . that there is sociality in nature in so far as the emergence of novelty requires that objects be at once both in the old system and in that which arises with the new.[34]

The simultaneity of this membership, or participation, in two systems is thus a defining characteristic of presents. With the concept 'sociality' Mead emphatically does not mean a general systemic character, but rather the stage of the origination of something new in a present.

> The world has become a different world because of the advent [of the new form (H. J.)], but to identify sociality with this result is to identify it with system merely. It is rather the stage betwixt and between the old system and the new that I am referring to. If emergence is a feature of reality this phase of adjustment, which comes between the ordered universe before the emergent has arisen and that after it has come to terms with the newcomer, must be a feature also of reality.[35]

This passage makes it clear why Mead can say that sociality is the character of the 'present' – understood as a concept of the theory of time – and is the principle of the origination of the new, of emergence as such.

This theory of sociality will certainly perplex all those who mistrust assertions about the fundamental structures of the universe which go beyond the scope of science. However, with this concept of sociality Mead is doubtless following Whitehead to the same level of interpretation as the latter attained with his principles of natural philosophy. In this connection it might also be pointed out that highly elaborated attempts to formulate an ontology grounded in the human being's situation, for example C. A. van Peursen's 'deictic ontology',[36] are situated at a similar level of interpretation and likewise arrive at theses about the 'communicative character of reality'. In order to understand whether this 'principle of sociality' is merely a matter of speculation on Mead's part, or whether, on the contrary, it is the very core of Mead's theories – in my opinion the answer to both questions is no – let us examine the history of the use of the concept 'sociality' throughout Mead's thought, and the meaning of his concept of metaphysics.

The concept of sociality appears again and again in Mead's social-psychological writings from the period during which the concept of symbolic interaction originated. But it is applied there only to human and animal social forms.[37] Even in those writings, of course, Mead stressed strongly that sociality is not the result of conscious actions of pre-social individuals, which are directed to the formation of societies, but rather is an objective intermeshing of individuals; that preconscious sociality is precisely the presupposition for the origination of conscious sociality, indeed of consciousness in general. He says this also in *The Philosophy of the Present*:

> Now what we are accustomed to call social is only a so-called consciousness of such a process, but the process is not identical with the consciousness of it, for that is an awareness of the situation. The social situation must be there if there is to be consciousness of it.[38]

This passage implicitly expresses a concept of sociality that has already been expanded. But when did the expansion of this concept take place in Mead's reflections, and what brought it about? My researches have found two passages from which conclusions can be drawn about the answers to these questions. One is to be found in Mead's 1927 lecture on the 'objective reality of perspectives' and says that

> . . . mind as it appears in the mechanism of social conduct is the organization of perspectives in nature and at least a phase of the creative advance of nature.[39]

The other occurs in the record provided by one of Mead's students of a lecture given in spring of 1928 on 'The Problem of Consciousness'. It runs as follows:

> The parallels overlap inasmuch as the physical field itself is a social situation where the very nature of our organism rests solidly upon cooperation with the environment. Man stands only so long as he keeps himself from falling – a matter of cooperation with the environment and to that extent a social attitude.[40]

From the first of these two passages one can extract a motive for the comprehensive concept of sociality: human social behaviour is construed as a part of natural evolution and is embedded in nature. What Mead clearly intends to accomplish here is the relativization of the opposition between humanity and nature implicit in the human domination of nature. From the second passage quoted one can see how the transition from the narrow to the broad concept of sociality was made possible: through the theory of the social presuppositions of the constitution of physical objects. Since Mead – as was explained in the preceding chapter – extended the application of the concept of sociality beyond the interaction of two human subjects and maintained that the relationship between a human actor and a physical object was also made possible by the capacity for social interaction, he could, in a final step, posit a general sociality also in the domain of the relationships of such physical objects among themselves. More exactly, he found sociality where the origination of something new gave this new something, by virtue of its temporary membership in two referential systems, an objectively double character. The restrictive formula in the second quotation, 'to that extent', makes it clear, however, that in 1928 Mead was still speaking this way only tentatively and metaphorically. By contrast, in 1930 the 'manner of speaking' has become a strongly stated thesis.

This history of the concept of sociality in Mead's thought makes clear that it is wrong to understand his social psychology as a mere field of application of a general theory of emergence or sociality. This is incorrect because alongside this theory in the same work, and in the other writings close to *The Philosophy of the Present*, there are many basically negative and unfavourable remarks about metaphysical interpretations as such. However, unlike the positivists, he does not reproach metaphysics with being inherently meaningless. Rather, from his early philosophical writings onward he saw clearly – witness the place he assigned to metaphysics in his classification of the philosophical disciplines formulated in 1900[41] – that metaphysics was a kind of passing on of fundamental problems, the solution of which could not yet be undertaken scientifically. New scientific advances can make it possible to treat meaningfully new areas of question formerly assigned to metaphysics.[42] Therefore, metaphysics without science is, in point of fact, inadmissible for Mead; in its reflection upon itself, however, science necessarily comes upon problems and areas for which and in which only quasi-metaphysical answers are possible. The alternative would be simply to prohibit thinking about such problems and areas of enquiry, as positivism of all varieties has in fact done again and again.

A synthesis of all these lines of thought yields the conclusion that Mead's theory of sociality is by no means a free-floating, speculative universal theory, which seeks to secure for itself the right to reject the results of scientific research or to interpret them in an arbitrary fashion. It is rather a matter of an enterprise which is continuously referred to science, to its procedure and results, but which must go beyond the limits of science since it undertakes, in advance, to determine the place of scientific progress and of progress in knowledge in a nature that encompasses human beings. There are certain similarities between Mead's undertaking and the attempts of Peirce to construe the natural laws as prehuman 'habits', or with Piaget's general theory of equilibration, which springs from the important accomplishment of a biological grounding of logical functions.[43] Mead considers a cosmology, in the sense of a comprehensive scientific view of the world, possible if it is not conceived of as a theory of a nature which is independent of humanity, but is rather understood from the perspective of a nature which is unfolding itself through the universalization of action and of cognition.

Mead's theory of sociality, or the whole conceptual web of event, novelty, emergence, reconstruction, perspective, sociality, and present, is more than mere trimming on science only if the claim is fulfilled that it does in fact offer a reflection by science on itself. The fruitfulness of Mead's theory must be proved by demonstrating that it is a persuasive interpretation of the constitution of the phenomena conceptualized in the theory of relativity, and that it is, moreover, a theory of the general conditions of human experience of time. I would like to consider the first of these requirements only briefly – to express myself more precisely, only to the extent that conclusions about general features of Mead's concept of science can be drawn from it, as it would severely strain the knowledge and abilities of a social scientist to enter into the details of this matter. In contrast, the second requirement will be gone into more thoroughly by posing the question of the implications of Mead's theory of time for developmental psychology or for the theory of socialization.

As was mentioned at the beginning of this chapter, Mead was motivated critically to examine and take issue with the philosophical interpretations of the theory of relativity by the fact that these interpretations did *not* draw precisely those conclusions suggested by this upheaval of natural science's image of the world. Not recognition of the necessity of taking into consideration the corporeal subjects who measure and perceive, and of their irreducibility, but instead the notion of a structure independent of all subjects and all perception took root in the philosophy of science. Mead attacks these interpretations by returning to relativity theory's point of departure in the problematic of measurement. The question of measurement directs attention to the practical foundation of science:

> But since the scientist can never reach the metaphysical space-time with its events and intervals except by an assumption, and since he can never grasp the entire field of any energy content, he is obliged to test his hypotheses by placing himself both in his own perceptual situation of, say, a system at rest and also in that of the system which moves with reference to his own, and to compare the spatio-temporal structures of the two systems. He proceeds by transformations, but they are transformations which are possible only as the observer grasps that in his own situation which involves his placing himself in the situation of that which he observes. Although this is more complicated, it comes back in its findings to perceptual occasions.[44]

The impossibility of getting rid of the practical foundation of science is for Mead the triumphant proof by the natural sciences themselves that his resistance to the reductionist tendencies in physiological psychology throughout his life's work was justified. The theory of relativity, says Mead in 'The Experiential Basis of Natural Science', has shown that the individual cannot be described in the categories applicable to his environment; the relation between the individual and his environment is thus constitutive of the environment and not an epiphenomenon of the environment.[45] In the same passage, however, an idea is expressed that goes beyond the indication of science's practical foundation: Mead speaks explicitly of *intersubjective* praxis. He founds the possibility of transformational rules, with which one referential system can be converted into another, in the capacity for taking the perspective or role of another. Mead asks: 'what is there in nature that answers to the transformation in the mathematician's mind?' And he responds:

> we can assume that the reference of the constants in these different perspectives is not to entities outside possible experience but to this organized character of the world that appears in what we call mind. To state the matter less cumbrously, the relativist is able to hold on to two or more mutually exclusive systems within which the same object appears, by passing from one to the other. I have already referred to

the experiential form of this passage in which the man in a train passes from the system of the movement of his train to that of the movement of a neighbouring train. His train cannot be both moving and at rest, but the mind of the passenger can occupy in passage both systems, and hold the two attitudes in a comprehensible relationship to each other as representing the same occurrence from two different stand-points which, having a mind or being a mind, he can occupy. If he accepts the two mutually exclusive situations as both legitimate, it is because as a minded organism he can be in both.[46]

Here Mead joins, not only the fundamental approach of prag-matism, but also his conception of intersubjectivity with his reflec-tions on the theory of relativity. The ability to take two points of view simultaneously and to be aware of the relationship between them is, according to Mead, the constitutive origin of the phenomena dealt with by the theory of relativity. Therefore he does not believe it necessary to take recourse to a Minkowskian four-dimensional, unexperienceable world, but rather to introduce a concept of the 'common world', into which the human individuals who are linked with one another through signals have in fact always entered. This is the reason why the theory of relativity can, through conscious reflection on the body-centricity of all perspectives, arrive at a conception in which this body-centricity is not obliterated, but rather preserved in the perspective of a common world. What Mead has shown with respect to the theory of relativity through subtle and extensive arguments, presented here only in very condensed form, permits by inference statements about the constitution of spatial and temporal perspectives in general. *Mead is laying the corner-stone of an intersubjectivist theory of the consciousness of time.* Let us now consider what this means, and how far Mead advances in elaborating this theory. By limiting our interpretation to the themes of Mead's *oeuvre*, these questions can be answered with a concise summary, and a comparison can be made of Mead's theory of the constitution of time-consciousness with other theories, in particular those of Piaget and Heidegger, but as regards the theory of socialization, which is actually our motivating interest, the following can of necessity do no more than provide, as it were, a new vista.

The problem of the constitution of time necessarily arises when naive belief in a time that imposes its objective structure on the individual has been abandoned. In contrast with Bergson, James, and Husserl, the problem is not posed for Mead in the form of the question of how the subjective structuring of time issues forth from a temporal stream of consciousness which is grasped through the individual's perception of psychological time. Rather, Mead asks how the structuration of time is built up in the practical relation of the organism to its environment. A characteristic example of this procedure is given in the manuscript from Mead's literary remains entitled 'The Biologic Individual', which was added as an appendix to his lectures on social psychology. There Mead says:

From the point of view of instinctive behaviour in the lower animals, or of the immediate human response to a perceptual world (in other words, from the standpoint of the unfractured relation between the impulses and the objects which give them expression), past and future are not there; and yet they are represented in the situation. They are represented by facility of adjustment through the selection of certain elements both in the direct sensuous stimulation through the excitement of the end-organs, and in the imagery. What represents past and what represents future are not distinguishable as contents. The surrogate of the past is the actual adjustment of the impulse to the object as stimulus. The surrogate of the future is the control which the changing field of experience during the act maintains over its execution.

The flow of experience is not differentiated into a past and future over against an immediate now until reflection affects certain parts of the experience with these characters, with the perfection of adjustment on the one hand, and with the shifting control on the other. The biologic individual lives in an undifferentiated now; the social reflective individual takes this up into a flow of experience within which stands a fixed past and a more or less uncertain future . . . The immediacy of the now is never lost, and the biologic individual stands as the unquestioned reality in the minds of differently constructed pasts and projected futures.[47]

If one analyses this argument one finds that Mead's concept which is parallel to that of the temporal flow is the 'undifferentiated now'. According to Mead's theory, every organism lives in an objective temporal field which is formed by the precipitation of the past in its response-attitudes, which are determined phylogenetically or else acquired in the organism's own learning processes, as well as by the function of the future in the essentially 'teleological' character of life processes. The organism's past is contained in its attitudes and implicit expectations, the future in the influence of the environment on the organism's acts. Both past and future, however, are not given to the organism as distinct, but rather blur together for it into an 'undifferentiated now'. The existence of a past does not suffice to engender consciousness of the character of the past as past. Mead refers unfavourably several times to Bergson's ideas about human memory, and asserts, in criticism of the latter, that memory is not a crushing ballast of accumulating pasts, but is, on the contrary, essentially reconstructive in character.[48] Quite similar arguments, also directed at Bergson, appear in Merleau-Ponty's and Piaget's reflections on the theory of time.[49] Merleau-Ponty calls attention very graphically to the difference between the mere re-occurrence of a remembrance, which must appear as an irreal perception, and the recognition of a remembrance as such. In Mead's opinion, however, the latter already presupposes the self-reflectiveness which – and this is the central idea of his work – can only originate in social praxis. This makes understandable why Mead states that only the self-reflective individual has a past and a future for itself and nevertheless remains constantly bound to the 'undifferentiated now' as the basis for the constitution of time.

Hopefully, the foregoing discussion has succeeded in clarifying the underlying idea of an intersubjectivist theory of the constitution of time-consciousness. From this idea we can draw forth the fundamental and still very general propositions of such a theory as Mead is advancing. The first of these propositions ought to be that, like all perspectives, time-perspectives exist objectively and also belong to the central possibilities for determining the uniqueness of individuals. These objectively existing time-perspectives are founded in the history of the particular 'self-reflective organism' itself; they do not, certainly, simply originate from this history, but only in conjunction with the social formation of the self in its entirety. Time-perspectives are thus a component of each particular self; each different partner in interaction, each different 'other', also embodies a different time-perspective. Mead conceives of the communication between the partners in an interaction in a manner analogous to the transformation formulas in the theory of relativity, as he understands them. This does not mean, of course, that time-perspectives in the physical sense differ between interacting individuals in any measurable sense, but it does mean that time-perspectives in the cultural-social sense do differ. The emergence of a common time-perspective is, then, bound to the constitution of a common world through common praxis.

A second fundamental proposition of this theory can be joined to the first. The reason why a common time-perspective can be constituted in a common praxis is that time is structured in an action taking place in the present. Mead solves the problem of the early investigations of the experience of time, that is how long the present – which can be regarded as a point only in thought – lasts, not by using the concepts of the behaviourist studies of attention, but by defining the present as the time-span of the actually occurring social action. However, as every action is to be understood as a system of activities nested one in the other, or, vice versa, since every activity is embedded in more comprehensive actions, the concept of the present is also dependent on the particular action in question as regards its compass. Mead explains this point as follows:

The stretch of the present within which this self-consciousness finds itself is delimited by the particular social act in which we are engaged. But since this usually stretches beyond the immediate perceptual horizon we fill it out with memories and imagination. In the whole undertaking these serve in place of perceptual stimulations to call out the appropriate responses. If one is going to meet an appointment, he indicates to himself the streets he must traverse by means of their memory images or the auditory images of their names. And this involves both the past and the future. In a sense his present takes in the whole undertaking, but it can accomplish this only by using symbolic imagery, and since the undertaking is a whole that stretches beyond the immediate specious presents, these slip into each other without any edges. A loud noise behind one's back picks out such a specious present. Its lack of relevance to what is going on leaves it nothing but the moment in which the sound vibrated within our ears. But our functional presents are always wider than the specious present, and may take in long stretches of an undertaking which absorbs unbroken concentrated attention. They have ideational margins of varying depth, and within these we are continually occupied in the testing and organizing process of thought. The functional boundaries of the present are those of its undertaking – of what we are doing. The pasts and futures indicated by such activity belong to the present. They arise out of it and are criticized and tested by it. The undertakings belong, however, with varying degrees of intimacy, within larger activities, so that we seldom have the sense of a set of isolated presents.[50]

Mead attaches great importance to founding all temporal horizons, including even the perspective of a universal history, in a present, in a praxis taking place in a present, more precisely, in *an intersubjective praxis occurring in a present*.

The third fundamental proposition that Mead formulates is that all self-reflective action, and thus the structure of the self-reflective organism itself, that is, the self, are essentially referred to the future. Just as life itself is objectively referred to the future, so too is self-reflection characterized precisely by the fact that it directs itself to the organism's present attitudes which have been formed by the past, becomes aware of their implicit reference to the future, and thereby becomes capable of experimentally testing alternative future possibilities in the present and then deliberately to construct the plan of its own action. Mead formulates this thesis in the following way:

> Now it is by these ideational processes that we get hold of the conditions of future conduct as these are found in the organized responses which we have formed, and so construct our pasts in anticipation of that future. The individual who can thus get hold of them can further organize them through the selection of the stimulations which call them out and can thus build up his plan of action.[51]

Mead recognizes, then, the temporal structure of self-reflection. In self-reflection the actor does not turn back upon himself in a frozen present – as in a mirror – but reflects upon the future possibilities in the present conditions, which issue from the past. Selfhood for Mead does not consist in immobilely remaining identical with oneself; rather, it is the continuously active, reconstructive processing of occurrences and the planning of actions. This insight, which is now clearly grasped in the final phase of Mead's work, was already implicit in the early discussion of the dialectic of 'I' and 'me'.[52] Even then Mead spoke of the fact that the 'I' can never be immediately grasped, and meant this not only in the sense that an individual is dependent in this regard on the responses of his partners in interaction. He also meant that the 'I' can be apprehended only through the execution of the actions it has planned. These are insights that in the German intellectual sphere are commonly considered to be peculiar to the thought of Heidegger and to existentialism.

But these general propositions from Mead's theory of time remain superficial to the extent that they sound more or less like the unfolding of implications already contained in his thoughts on social psychology. Further, they do not go beyond a general concept of action and self, and in particular do not touch upon the domain of instrumental action, in which the constitution of the physical concept of time must certainly be sought. So, I will now undertake to demonstrate that Mead also claims to prove the intersubjectivist constitution of just this 'physical' consciousness of time.

The following exposition presupposes an understanding of Mead's theory of the constitution of the physical thing – the permanent object. As I have set forth,[53] Mead conceives of the constitution of the physical thing as effected through the coordination of distance and contact perceptions (especially of hand and eye), which in turn presupposes elementary operations of intersubjectivity. The capacity for identification, according to Mead, makes possible the transferral to distance perceptions of the experience of pressure in contact perceptions. Up to now the discussion of this transferral has excluded the 'temporality' implicit in it. Our treatment of this topic would be superficial, however, if this state of affairs were allowed to continue.

Strictly speaking, there is immediate simultaneity only in the case of contact experience, for only in that case do two material bodies encounter one another in one and the same point of space. In contrast, the transferral of contact experiences to distance perceptions always has an anticipatory, expectational character. One can remain unaware of this as long as the interplay of expectations and the subsequent perceptions function smoothly, with no problems. When, however, an expectation which is founded in a distance perception is not confirmed in contact experience, then the two spheres are split apart. Thus the situation of the problem arising in the course of action makes it possible to experience that the anticipatory status of distance perceptions grounds a hypothetical and – as Mead does not tire of stressing again and again – futural status of the object of distance perception. The distant object – and, since no thing is exhausted in its contact with a subject's body, everything is such a distant object – is in an immediate sense both spatially and temporally distant. Only the transferral of contact experiences to distance perceptions replaces this undifferentiated spatiotemporal distantness with merely spatial distance. Only

through this transferral are space and time separated in the development of the human individual's consciousness of 'events'. The
charging of distance perceptions with contact experiences brings the
perceived distant object into a simultaneity with the acting organism.
The distance thus no longer appears as spatiotemporal, but merely as
spatial. This spatial distance in a fixed space can be traversed then in
a certain amount of elapsing time. If the steps of action in space
required for traversing the distance are correlated with the time
necessary for them, then there takes place that 'spatialization of time'
in which Bergson saw the essence of the 'physical' understanding of
time. In contrast to Bergson, though, Mead does not present this
spatialization as a deformation of authentic temporality, but as an
essential necessity of instrumental action with reference to things.
Nor is this spatialization the simple transferral of a spatiality, given
in an *a priori* manner, to time, the character of which is of an *a priori*
different kind; rather it is a matter here of the intrinsic interpenetration of the constitution of temporality and spatiality.

Many manuscripts and fragments from the late years of Mead's life
revolve about the line of argument that has been given here in
condensed form. He knows that, if his analyses are not refuted, he
has made an important step in demonstrating that, and how, the
fundamental categories of natural science and of instrumental action
in general are constituted. The demonstration Mead gives has
implications for developmental psychology as well as for 'metaphysics', or a critique of metaphysics; for the temporality-status of
distant objects makes the notion of a world *composed of physical things*
in a punctual present impossible. The constitution of things itself
requires an action-nexus extending beyond the punctual present.[54]

The following exposition of this point in Mead's own words is
taken from the manuscript on the experiential basis of natural
science, published in *The Philosophy of the Act*:

With the abandonment of any fixed set – absolute space and absolute
time – goes the loss of units of space and time which have the same
value from one set to another.

The essential point is found in the simultaneity of moving objects in
a distant field with the perceptual objects of the contact field. The
nonmoving object in the cogredient set, as before stated, has a future
value owing to its distance, which is in some sense abstracted through
the inhibition of the acts which the distance object arouses. Through

identification with the distant object, contemporaneity appears. The distant object as exercising the individual's attitude of pressure is temporally coincident with the individual. It is contemporaneous with the individual at the moment. If the perceptual relation involves a measurable period, the contemporaneity belongs to the moment of the individual's contact experience and antedates the completion of the perceptual process. This becomes appreciable in the case of the sound. Except with reference to stellar bodies, it is not appreciable in the case of light. If one assumes an appreciable time period in the perceptual process of vision, identification with the distant moving object introduces a problem.[55]

And in highly synthetic sentences Mead sums up the relationship to each other of the formation of the self, the constitution of the permanent object, and the constitution of time:

It is evident that it is the formation of the physical object which is responsible for the appearance of the individual as an object, since it brings contemporaneity and also brings the possibility of the distinction between rest and motion, and the separation of space and time, and thus constitutes a new environment answering to the new individual. In other words, contemporaneity can arise only as distant objects which are future in their import can be brought hypothetically into the contact field, and so become physical objects.[56]

From all the various formulations it becomes clear that to a very great extent Mead's theory of the constitution of time originated inferentially from the problems of measurement which led to the theory of relativity. It is very interesting that the most significant empirical and theoretical investigation of the development of time-consciousness in the child, namely Jean Piaget's,[57] was also prompted by those same problems, and even directly by Einstein himself. Mead and Piaget do not, however, arrive at identical conclusions. Should one consider Mead's theories to be empirically refuted because of these differences, or do deficiencies in Piaget's study become apparent in light of Mead's approach?

In their fundamental approach there are many similarities between the time theories of Mead and Piaget. Both reject the notion of an originality of 'psychological' time; both do not consider the development of the consciousness of time to be endogenous, but instead relate the schematization of time and the acquisition of capacity for action, and locate the beginning of the child's consciousness of time in the sensory-motor phase of its development. With brilliant observations and experiments, Piaget succeeds in explaining numerous phenomena, both from the early phase of merely objective temporality of the infantile organism[58] and from the phase of the constitution of a subjective consciousness of time.

However, for Piaget the constitution of time, like the constitution of the physical object, remains tied exclusively to the development of instrumental action, which is conceived of in separation from intersubjective or social action. In Piaget's studies, and in the investigations based on his work,[59] the social context appears only as a general background, or as an area in which the time-schematizations that have been acquired in instrumental action are applied. The part of Piaget's researches devoted to the temporality of human beings stands completely under the sway of the primary thesis that this temporality is schematized or structured in the same steps as the temporality of physical objects. It is at this point that Piaget's empirical investigations, if one examines them closely, raise the suspicion of a *petitio principii*: he studies only quasi-physical temporal properties of persons, such as, for example, age, for which his thesis certainly holds true. Just as for the problematic of object-constitution, Piaget also believes that the rejection of introspectionist approaches suffices in itself to separate the problem of the constitution of time from the question of the acquisition and use of language or of intersubjectivity. It could be thoroughly demonstrated that this attempted separation must fail. Here is not the place for that demonstration, however, and so let us just compare Piaget's and Mead's approaches in a few crucial points.

Piaget correctly regards the capacity to coordinate two movements having different speeds as the heart of time-consciousness in the sphere of instrumental action. Mead, however, believes that such coordination itself presupposes that the individual is able to put himself into both on-going processes simultaneously, while keeping a firm grasp of their difference from one another as well as from his own self. Piaget considers the coordination of two actions by an individual as being itself the core of time-consciousness in the sphere of interpersonal action. For Mead, though, any such coordination undeniably presupposes a self in an elementary form. Piaget regards the fully formed consciousness of time, which is attained only in adolescence, as the highest form of the flexibility of thought, of operative reversibility. By contrast, for an intersubjectivist understanding of the development of time-consciousness it is crucially important to grasp that the highest form of the relationship of the self to its own temporality consists precisely in an existential acceptance of the irreversibility of its own life and its own limitedness.

Thus, despite Piaget's immense achievement, his theory has, from the standpoint of the theory of intersubjectivity, important deficiencies as regards the structuring of time through instrumental action. As far as the temporality of the self itself is concerned, Piaget's studies are almost completely fruitless. In this situation another theory could suggest itself as an alternative, the theory which made significant contributions to the theory of intersubjectivity and to the founding of all subjectivity in 'temporality'. I am thinking of Heidegger's epoch-making analyses in *Being and Time*. But, in spite of his penetrating analyses of phenomena of temporality, and in spite of the forcefulness with which he places death and the relationship to it in the centre of his analysis of the 'authentic' and 'inauthentic' relationship to one's own temporality, the transformation of this analysis into an empirical theory of the connection between the formation of the self and the experience of time is precluded because Heidegger has an individualistic conception of the action-situation.

This conception separates the individual's strivings from intersubjectively recognized values and the objectifications, the physical products of human activity. It is through the reference to death that he seeks to show the individual's ultimate and radical isolation. Within the framework of Heidegger's thought, the willingness to accept this isolation would, in a way, be the equivalent of the formation of the self. This individualistic concept of the human being's situation is the basis of his concept of history, which does not make superindividual plexuses of collective praxis really thinkable, but rather appears merely as the embeddedness of the individual human life in a fate. Access to historicality is to be had from individual temporality; the identification of subjectivity and temporality effaces the specific features of temporality at the different levels of organismic development and gives support to Heidegger's anonymous concept of history; the thesis of the 'self-reference of time', with which Heidegger's investigation of temporality concludes, is paradoxical for me, since intersubjectivity must make a forced appearance in the exposition because it was not, as in Mead's work, made implicit in the concept of subjectivity from the outset.

An intersubjectivist theory of the constitution of time-consciousness would have to prove its explanatory power by making comprehensible in a coherent manner such frequently observed phenomena of the development of the child's consciousness of time as the dominance of expressions referring to the future over those referring to the past. Finally, it would also have to demonstrate empirically the social genesis of the individual's relationship to death and to conceive of a communal mastering of the fear of death – through the individual's embeddedness in a meaningful communal life and the communicative embedding of death itself in that life.[60] This would be a part, and perhaps the most difficult part, of the scientific treatment of the phenomena of the consciousness of time and of temporal perspectives which become apparent so quickly in the comparison of cultures, social strata, and the sexes. Mead's approach to an intersubjectivist theory of the constitution of time could offer guidance in making the structure of the processes of formation of these differentiated forms analyseable.

9

Scientific Progress and Social Progress

Mead's writings on the constitution of the physical object and of temporality are not, indeed are not even primarily, studies in developmental psychology. They are rather part and parcel of an attempt to show how the fundamental categories of the natural-scientific schematization of the world are constituted. In both of the aforementioned areas this is readily apparent, since Mead developed these theories only in the final phase of his work. However, the large fragments of theory contained in 'The Definition of the Psychical' and the demonstration of the essentially self-reflective character of 'mind' with a theory of communication founded on inherent human characteristics are no less intrinsically connected with the analysis of the constitution of natural science's categories. Mead's critique of psychophysical parallelism was based on the objection that it was made possible only by a naive, objectivist concept of the 'objective world'.[1] Mead's proof of the social character of the mind was aimed at preserving the possibility of universally valid propositions by means of a theory of the constitution of the categories, without having to take recourse in the explanations of transcendental philosophy. Although the emphasis on these two lines of argument – that of developmental psychology and the theory of socialization, and, on the other hand, that of the critique of science and the analysis of the constitution of categories – shifted in the different phases of the development of Mead's thought, they nevertheless remained linked to one another, and their connection highlights one of the profoundest themes of Mead's work. Only by breaking through science's false objectivist understanding of itself can one preserve the possibility of rational ethical and aesthetic values.

It is perhaps the most striking characterization which one can make of the thinking of the Western world since the Renaissance, that it has separated these two essential aspects of the world, has indeed made them incommensurable. Science informs us with increasing exactness of the ultimate elements of stuff or energy out of which the universe is made, and how they change. The world that rewards or defeats us, that entices or repels us, our remunerations and frustrations, our delights and distresses, what is finally significant and worthy of our effort, the beauty, the glory, and the dream, cannot be formulated in the language of exact science, nor have we found any common vernacular in which we can speak of the world of physical things and the values which after all they subtend.

This break between the definition of the things that constitute the means and the ends and values which they embody is not confined to the description of physical instruments and their uses, for it bisects the field of the social sciences as well. It has made economics the dismal science. It has mechanized and anatomized psychology. It has made ethics utilitarian, and aesthetics an affair of esoteric formulae.[2]

If, however, it is Mead's intent to establish the possibility of a rationality of ends and values comparable with scientific rationality, then it would be a grave misunderstanding of him to regard his concept of science as scientistic. This misunderstanding can occur if Mead's remarks about scientific cognition being the highest form of knowledge, and especially his assertions that scientific progress is the quintessence of historical progress in general, are taken as expressions of an uncritical idealization of science. Examination of Mead's theory of science is, therefore, a necessary precondition for a correct understanding of his concept of history.

The textual basis for the following discussion of Mead's concept of science consists primarily of two works written in the final phase of his intellectual development, which offer a broad and systematic presentation of his ideas on this subject. The one is the article 'Scientific Method and Individual Thinker', in which Mead, in a broad historical discourse on the character of ancient, medieval and modern science and theories of science, advances the thesis that individual innovation plays an indispensable role in scientific progress. The other text is a fragmentary manuscript from Mead's literary archive,[3] which for no comprehensible reason has been dismembered in *The Philosophy of the Act*. In this manuscript Mead investigates the constitution of science in a pregiven life-world, 'the world that is there'. To these can be added a short review by Mead of the Gifford Lectures delivered by the British mathematician Hobson, as it is a clear and succinct presentation of the themes of Mead's thought.

Even a brief sketch of Mead's arguments shows that his view of science is astonishingly modern. Mead rejects an independent epistemology that claims to play a normative role vis-à-vis science and calls for reflection on the scientific procedure itself. The theory of science cannot prejudge the procedure of science, but instead must take it seriously; the theory of science must be research on research, investigation of investigation. But this also means that erroneous conceptions of science, such as Mead sees at work chiefly in empiricist positivism and phenomenalism, must be repudiated. A theory of science in the sense of an enquiry into enquiry must conceive of such an investigation in its pragmatic character, as 'cooperative social activity',[4] and not merely as a complex of propositions about states of affairs. According to Mead, science, like all consciousness, must be referred to the occurrence of problems encountered in action. However, these problems occur in a world which has hitherto been accepted without question, but which, owing to the inhibition of the intended action, ceases to be self-evidently that which we have believed it to be and requires reconstruction by us. Following the solution of the action-problem, the horizon of what is simply taken for granted closes about us once again, only to split asunder unexpectedly in another place. In this way scientific knowledge, like all new insights, is absorbed into the implicit cultural agreement about the world. The world itself has changed; what was false in the previous image of the world has now become merely something subjective; the new interpretation tells us how things 'really' are.

Now, where does the modernity of this conception of science lie, and how does Mead pursue it in detail? In his opposition to empiricist positivism, Mead makes use of arguments which also apply to logical positivism. Hence, his position resembles in important respects that which resulted from the laborious, self-critical overcoming of the theory of science proposed by logical positivism and Karl Popper's falsificationism, which had been dominant for decades. There are clearly similarities between Mead's and Thomas Kuhn's approaches,[5] even though the differences, too, are significant. The most general criticism Mead makes of positivism is that it suppresses the subject, or the activity of the subject.[6] This suppression of the subject is expressed by the appearance in the positivist theories of the relation between facts and scientific laws as one of frictionless subsumption of the former under the latter. In point of actuality, Mead objects, this is true only when the scientific law suitable for explaining the facts in question has already been found; it does not hold good for the phase of scientific research or reflection in which this explanation is only being sought. In its acute form the question is whether or not the context in which the new theory originates, or the context in which the new facts are discovered, are to be viewed as a mere externality in comparison with the theory's internal consistency.

> Now the attitude of the positivist toward this fact is that induced by its relation to the law which is *subsequently* discovered. It has then fallen into place in a series, and his doctrine is that all laws are but uniformities of such events. He treats the fact when it is an exception to law as an instance of the new law and assumes that the exception to the old law and the instance of the new are identical. And this is a great mistake – the mistake made also by the neo-realist when he assumes that the object of knowledge is the same within and without the mind, that nothing happens to what is to be known when it by chance strays into the realm of conscious cognition.[7]

Thus the fundamental mistake of the positivist theory of science is, in Mead's eyes, that it regards all events as instances of laws, and that means it conceives of all surprising facts, those which run counter to expectations, as instances of scientific laws which have not yet been ascertained. What this way of thinking does is to eliminate the *constitutive* role of subjectivity. For if it were correct, then all theories would be equally subjective attempts to fit ourselves to an unchanging objective world. This, however, would make definitive the dualist separation of subject and world. By contrast, Mead conceives of objectivity as a collectively accepted interpretation of the world that proves itself in praxis, and of subjectivity as an interpretation of the world deviating from the former. Within this framework, the solution of action-problems is dependent on individual innovation, and the failure to solve these problems condemns the individual's proposal to the status of mere subjectivity, isolated from the social collective.

But the foregoing only delineates in some detail the controversy between the positivist and the pragmatist theories of science. The battle has yet to be engaged and decided.

In Mead's view the pivotal point of the positivist theory is the notion of immediately given sensory data. In logical positivism this idea was, it is true, transformed into the programme of neutral languages of observation, free of theory, but in its essence it was retained. This essence is that the separation of the context of discovery from the context of justification presupposes a separation of observation and interpretation, and of interpretation and comprehensive theory. Such a separation can only exist if facts themselves are given independently of interpretation. Mead undertakes not only to prove that a clear demarcation of fact from interpretation is impossible, but also to demonstrate that the ostensibly immediate sensory data have the character of a construct.

> It would be impossible to separate in the earlier experiences certain facts and certain attitudes of mind entertained by men with reference to these facts. Certain objects have replaced other objects. It is only after the process of analysis, which arose out of the conflicting observations, has broken up the old object that what was a part of the object, . . . can become a mere idea. Earlier it was an object . . . For science at least it is quite impossible to distinguish between what in an object must be fact and what may be idea. The distinction when it is made is dependent upon the form of the problem and is functional to its solution, not metaphysical. So little can a consistent line of cleavage between facts and ideas be indicated, that we can never tell where in our world of observation the problem of science will arise, or what will be regarded as structure of reality or what erroneous ideas.[8]

Because the positivist theory of science passes over the importance of the context or matrix in which the supposedly immediately given facts originated, it is forced to conceive of the world as built up out of these facts. If, however, the facts prove to be not data, not givens, but instead action-problems, then it has been shown that science and the theory of science do in fact begin, not with a world constructed of elements, but with the 'world that is there', an integral life-world of unquestioned validities, values, and forms.

The 'world that is there' is the central concept of the theory of science developed by Mead in the final phase of his work. He returns to this world again and again, to demonstrate that the scientific method is 'but an elaborate form of reflection',[9] 'nothing but the rigorous and detailed development of our everyday intelligence'.[10] Mead disputes the claim of science to be the exact copy of a reality lying beyond the complex of practical interrelations in which humans cope with and in the world. He also disputes this claim, as has been shown,[11] above all for the developments of natural science in the 20th century, of which it has so often been thoughtlessly maintained that they lie essentially beyond the reach of everyday intelligence. For Mead, the possibility that an object can be experienced, or be intuitional, is not identical with the question of its constitution in human activity.[12]

> The whole tendency of the natural sciences, as exhibited especially in physics and chemistry, is to replace the objects of immediate experience by hypothetical objects which lie beyond the range of possible experience. As I have pointed out above, an experimental science must bring any theory to the test of an experience which is immediate, which lies within the 'now'. It is, in my opinion, a legitimate doctrine . . . that it must be possible to regard the hypothetical subexperiential objects as the statements of the methods and formulas for the control of objects in the world of actual experience, in other words, that so-called objects which lie beyond the range of possible experience are in reality complex procedures in the control of actual experience.[13]

Thus, for Mead, the conceptual objects of science do not replicate an ultimate reality which causally determines the subjective phenomena of our perceptual world. Rather, they are inevitably referred to the world of our actions and immediate experiences. This is true in three ways. First, the problem which requires a scientific solution itself makes its appearance in the world of our immediate experiences: it is linked to the observation of 'anomalies' – Kuhn's term – which may indeed presuppose the most complicated apparatuses, but in their use these apparatuses are always dependent on the perceptions of the observer who is reading the meters. Second, the testing of an hypothesis must rely on immediate experiences, which, third, cannot be dispensed with even by those theories which claim to effect a general reconstruction of perceptions themselves. Even the most general theory of matter presupposes the functioning of apparatuses in a world of immediate perceptions. Therefore, for Mead, too, as for the empiricists, experience is the final touchstone of any theory.

It is especially important to recognize that in the operation of the experimental technique, that which serves as the ultimate touchstone of observation and working hypothesis is not of the nature of abstract law or postulate, either of physical nature or of so-called mind, or a subsistent world of universals. On the contrary the ultimate touchstone of reality is a piece of experience found in an unanalyzed world . . . Thus we can never retreat behind immediate experience to analyzed elements that constitute the ultimate reality of all immediate experience, for whatever breath of reality these elements possess has been breathed into them by some unanalyzed experience.[14]

In contrast to the empiricists, though, Mead's concept of immediate experience is not individualistic. It has already been mentioned that Mead rejects the notion of perception devoid of interpretation; that is, all perception is culturally formed, and as conscious perception, identified as such, it is self-reflective. Mead integrates not only his theory of the psychical and of the act into his theory of science, but also his theory of intersubjectivity. The unproblematic world is the world of unshaken *social* validities; the action-problem is thus a problem that occurs for an individual, but precisely for that reason it has the effect of calling into question the social validities. In the action-problem the individual's experience collides with the socially recognized interpretation of the world, which is also deposited in the prejudgmental structure of his own thinking.

There is only one way of locating this world of observation and experiment, and that is by its position within the field of conduct, reflective conduct, within which it appears. The problem inevitably appears in the experience of some individual, for it is the nature of that which is problematic to be, in so far as it is problematic, at variance with the world which is common to us all; and of that which in any way, however slight, has not its place in the public world, the individual who hears, sees, or feels it can only say that he has heard, seen, and felt it. A question, actual or implied, as to any happening carries it back at once to the experience of the individual who reports it, and its actuality is reduced to his experience. And the individual in any experience which is in any sense exceptional finds himself formulating what is exceptional as his own, while the setting and surroundings are there as the world of all.[15]

Now, if the individual wants to cling to his individual perception or observation in the face of the community's 'world', then he must put the observation in a form which can claim to be valid for the community. That means the individual observation itself must be presented as a new hypothesis about the 'world'. Thus, Mead does not only maintain the sociality of science, which he grounds in the *per se* social character of thought and in the relation of science to the communicative community in which science takes place;[16] he also sees scientific progress as a dialectic of particularity and universality, of individuality and sociality. This seems to me to be an important point, one which can be counterposed to a position which, in its efforts to defend the social character of science, asserts that science is virtually uninterruptedly intersubjective. Using this argument, which in my opinion is unjustified, Dietrich Böhler criticizes Thomas Kuhn's book *The Structure of Scientific Revolutions*.[17] In his attack on Kuhn, Böhler cites Peirce, who saw escape from the danger of a subjectivist and operationalist attenuation of pragmatism only in the reality of universals, a position that to me appears to be the result of Peirce's lack of a properly elaborated notion of universalization through communication. By contrast, Mead's notion of universal meaning, based on his theory of intersubjectivity and language, permits complete recognition of individual creativity, without forcing one to draw from that creativity individualistic or irrationalistic implications.[18]

This is not to say that Mead in fact developed the possibilities of a theory of scientific progress that is informed by sociology and social psychology. However, before we turn our attention to the limits of his approach, let us briefly consider its relationship with those positions which likewise express opposition to an objectivist understanding of science. These are all those theories which employ the concept of the life-world or everyday life. These theories range from Husserl's phenomenology and its further development in the areas of psychology and Philosophical Anthropology by Merleau-Ponty and in sociology under the impetus from Schutz's writings, to Whitehead's critiques and Piaget's genetic epistemology, and on to the various theoretical efforts of a critical Marxism, whether in Critical Theory, or in the so-called Lukács school, or in the realm where phenomenology and Marxism came into contact. Since the Marxist works are mostly of a programmatic character, or merely draw implications for social theory from analyses of the constitution of scientific categories elaborated by non-Marxists, and since the difference between Mead and Whitehead has already been indicated in the discussion of the different responses to the theory of relativity,[19] what remains of interest here is chiefly Mead's relationship to phenomenology and to Piaget.

Such a comparison is best begun by examining Mead's own thoughts on the status of 'the world that is there'. For he refuses to accept that this world is 'primary' in any sense going beyond the actually occurring situation of the action-problem. He rejects the metaphor of 'origin' or of 'foundation', and instead defends that of 'environment'. The world which is taken for granted environs the hypothetical constructions of science regardless of the extent of the domain of objects which science investigates.

> It may seem a misnomer to speak of the world within which lie the observation and experiment as surrounding such hypothetical constructions as the electrical theory of matter, or the galactic form of the universe, since these hypothetical constructions so far transcend, in the subatomic world or in the indefinite stretches of the heavens, all the world of objects which includes our observations and experiments. We seem rather to be islanded in a very minute region occupied by perceptual objects that are in their constitution vague, indeterminate, and incurably contingent, surrounded from within and from without by a universe, which science presents, that is occupied by objects that approximate exactness of definition and necessity in their forms and changes.[20]

But this is

> an apparently incongruous situation, for the acceptance of the clear-cut, sharply defined, and necessary world is dependent upon the findings in the island of vague, indeterminate, and contingent data, the field of observation and experiment.[21]

Only from the standpoint of science, however, does 'the world that is there' appear as the possible object of hypotheses and analyses. For the one who is acting in this world – and even the scientist acts in it, outside the limits of the field which he regards as problematical – it is self-evidently just what it seems to be. But this does not mean that this world is 'primary'. For the successful hypotheses, the ones that have proved themselves, of all previous prescientific and scientific knowledge, go into making up this world. *Prereflective experience is, for Mead, not presymbolic.*[22] It is very important not to lose sight of this distinction. In Mead's view, prereflective experience consists in the investment of the world of my activity with meanings that are intersubjectively accepted, that are not regarded as problematical. However, these meanings, which are accepted as self-evident, themselves have a symbolic form.

Mead would agree with Piaget's criticism[23] that the phenomenological concept of the life-world is apragmatic in character. They go separate ways, however, in their interpretation of the intersubjectivity of scientific method. In Piaget's understanding of science the inherent intersubjectivity of logic and of the reproducibility of the scientific experiment, which is independent of the subject, are grounds for considering the criteria of the scientific method to be normative for all thinking. On Mead's view of this matter, though, the intersubjectivity of science is embedded in a concept of the universalization of intersubjectivity in all spheres.[24] Consequently, in Piaget's self-interpretation, which deviates partly from his research practice, the function of philosophy shrinks to the 'coordination of values', whereas in Mead's thought philosophy has the function of integrating all scientific knowledge into a total outlook providing orientation in everyday life.

> It becomes, then, the office of philosohy to present an unfractured universe, qualitied as well as quantitied, together with all its meanings, and overcome the bifurcation of nature that arose from the methods of scientific measurement and philosophic dogma . . . it is the office of philosophy to envisage a universe in which both the methods of experimental science and science's own interpretations, as well as those of everyday experience, are at home.[25]

Nevertheless, Mead is closer to Piaget than to phenomenology. For he defines the function of philosophy, as well as that of the sciences, pragmatically, and thereby passes beyond phenomenology's contemplative notion of theory.[26] The concept of 'the world that is there' does not aspire to an absolute beginning, as does phenomenology's life-world; rather, it is the very refutation of the possibility of an absolute beginning.[27] The distinction Husserl draws between the 'natural' and the 'theoretical attitude' appears also in Mead's work in the distinction between 'the world that is there' and the action-problem; for Mead, though, both are phases of the act, and not fundamentally different attitudes to the world as a whole.[28]

Mead's *'world that is there'* is an intersubjective and practical conception *of the life-world,* and is not – as in the case of Husserl – conceived from the point of view of the subject constituting the world in solitary contemplation.

Yet, even such an intersubjective, practical concept is only the precondition in the domain of philosophical concepts for integrating the theory of science and the sociology of science. How far does Mead himself go toward concretizing his theory here? This question calls attention to the limits of Mead's approach. In my opinion, there are four principal problem areas in which it is inadequate. The first of these has to do with the difference between the situation of the individual actor and the group acting in everyday life and the situation of the relatively autonomous social subsystem which is science. Mead does not recognize the fact that the autonomy of science is the social precondition of the felt need for an analysis of the 'constitution' of science. For had science not developed beyond the level of systematized everyday techniques, then its appearance of self-sufficiency and independence from everyday activity could not have originated at all. But the dangers arising from science's self-sufficiency also offer opportunities for the development of science. Whereas the individual actor is under pressure from his situation to make a decision and has to engage in actions which go beyond the range of the expectations which he is certain will be fulfilled, science can postpone problems or make them solvable through experimental action. Pointing out science's foundation in everyday praxis becomes empirically false, if the separation of science from everyday life is not taken into consideration. And awareness of the relation of science and everyday life remains ineffectual in practical terms as long as no programme of democratic and public direction of science and of its maximum de-professionalization is established that allows for the inherent functional presuppositions of scientific progress.

The second area consists of taking into account the social character of science. Mead lays bare the general social context in which science is carried on as well as the 'society in the scientist',[29] but not the intermediary agencies to be found in the community of scientists, in which a sociology of science finds its object of study. The third area is the problem of the diffusion of the individual innovations. Mead assumes an unconstrained diffusion of convincing new hypotheses. In comparison, Thomas Kuhn's model of the recognition of new paradigms occurring in part through the conversion of scientists to acceptance of it, and in part through the replacement of older by younger generations of scientists is much more differentiated. Fourth, Mead gives hardly any consideration to the material interests which influence the direction of scientific research, or to the conditions of reception which have an effect on how scientific knowledge is applied and exploited.[30]

By calling attention to these shortcomings I am not, of course, requiring of Mead, in an unhistorical manner and from a standpoint external to his work, that he offer solutions to scientific problems which he did not set himself. To do so would run counter to my entire interpretative undertaking. The reason for stressing the limits of Mead's approach with respect to the sociology of science lies, rather, in the fact that only the relative de-concretization of the social phenomenon 'science' makes possible the grounding of Mead's concept of history. Since Mead grounds his concept of historical progress in his theory of scientific progress, deficiencies in his conception of science must necessarily lead to deficiencies of his conception of history. Let us examine this matter more closely.

Like science, history is for Mead a progressive process that can never be completely planned and is essentially unpredictable, since it is the result of intentional action and not of causal determination. But it is progress nonetheless. He stresses very strongly that science must respond to problems that occur in different instances – whether these problems are social and practical in nature, or arise in the course of science's internal development – yet he also claims for scientific knowledge a progress that is more than the mere accumulation of factual detail.

> On the other hand, every acceptable hypothesis which supersedes another must take up into itself not only the so-called facts which the earlier hypothesis accounted for, but it must also account for the superseded hypothesis itself and, as a discarded hypothesis, make it a part of its universe.[31]

If, however, as Mead claims, the structure of scientific progress is also, at least potentially, the structure of the historical progress of society, then the latter cannot consist just in fragmentary-reforms and attempts to remedy abuses or deleterious states of affairs occurring here and there in a society. Rather, it can only consist in an increasing control of social conditions in their entirety. Only then does a society which is consciously planning its development conform to Mead's idea of human society as the strategy of 'adaptation' taken under the direction of human beings themselves, which thereby supersedes the natural ways of adaptation.

Here an odd discrepancy appears in Mead's theory. If historical progress consists specifically in increasing the degree to which history can be planned, then the assertion that history is essentially not susceptible to planning loses some of its plausibility.[32] From the standpoint of the philosophy of history Mead overcomes this discrepancy by recognizing that scientific progress does not provide us with an ever more complete image of the thoroughly determined character of all processes, but rather improves the means which are at the disposal of our actions and rationally enlightens us about ends which are legitimated only by tradition, and by so doing presents us with alternatives for action:

> In a word, science is enabling us to restate our ends by freeing us from slavery to the means and to traditional formulations of our ends.[33]

The expansion of our possibilities for action also permits us, then, to reconstruct our goals in ever new ways.[34] Mead has formulated a non-objectivist, non-evolutionist concept of historical progress. There is no fixed future which is given once and for all; rather, in a present, in the framework of the present conditions, our action projects a future: when a society is not planned, but instead plans itself, then it satisfies Mead's requirement. The openness and non-fixity of the future, which is necessary for a society's self-determination, can be joined with the idea of consciously-aimed-at historical progress only if the historical end itself is conceived of, not as a final state, but as the opening up of a maximum of future possibilities. Human mastery of nature and human freedom from dominance, a society in which all systemically important decisions are made publically and democratically: this is the concept of historical progress that can be rationally legitimated.[35]

Mead himself links his critique of any and every teleological philosophy of history and his emphasis on the exemplary character of scientific progress with immediately political lines of argument again and again.[36] For he declares the setting of any revolutionary end to be teleological and dogmatic, since such a goal-setting does not content itself with a limited attempt to remedy an individual problem. This is a problematic argument. On the one hand, it overlooks the fact that by no means does scientific progress occur simply as a process of accumulating factual information or as a continuous process of advancement through falsification of hypotheses, but that it proceeds, rather, according to a pattern of alternation between 'revolutionary' and 'normal' phases.[37] To be sure, Mead, like Kuhn, takes it as a given that all observation and perception is permeated by interpretation and theory, but he does not develop a concept of the scientific paradigm, in the sense of a basic model within the progressive process which remains stable through a period of time. Although any such reasoning is extremely questionable, it is nevertheless clear that from the viewpoint of the theory of science, the historical necessity of revolutions cannot at all be excluded. Mead's argument with regard to this question is, in the bad sense, abstract in the manner of the philosophy of history, since the limitation of historical progress to reforms cannot itself be elevated to a principle, but should be shown by concrete sociological and economic analyses of the capitalist state's openness to reform in a particular society and epoch. The fact that Mead does not even try to do this indicates deep-seated deficiencies in the sociological concretization of his approach, which in turn point back to aspects of his fundamental concept of social action that he failed to elaborate.[38] However, within the framework of Mead's work the most important immanent problematic seems to me to result from his untenable claim to dogmatize a certain form of politics and history. It is the problematic of the relationship between universal validity and practical suitability in a determinate situation, one which Mead never settled. It is the problematic that could already be observed in Mead's ethics and in his reflections on the question of the possibility of objective historical knowledge, and which holds true generally for the theories of truth and science. Although Mead does have an 'ideal' concept of truth of cognition and correctness of behaviour,[39] in political controversies and those having to do with social theory he adopts the arguments of a relativistic pragmatism. This is a conflict in Mead's work that cannot be overlooked.

It is a conflict that results from the failure of his striving to reconcile in a rational way his contemporary society and the ideal society to which the determinations of intrinsic human characteristics are necessarily directed. The contradiction is repeated when Mead, who denies the possibility of revolutionary social changes, and who asserts the impossibility of anticipating the historical future, is led by practical interest in reform and theoretical interest in the formulation of a universally valid theory to outline utopian countertypes to the existing society. Whereas revolutionary 'scientific socialism' believed it had to prohibit the construction of utopias because of the necessity of concentrating attention on the conditions of the present, the pragmatist reformer became a utopian!

In his writings on education, Mead repeatedly alludes to utopian ideals of a synthesis of work, art, and play, and takes up this theme again in his last years in his only essay on aesthetics, 'The Nature of Aesthetic Experience'. What he describes in that article is well-known in Germany as *Entfremdung*, 'alienation': the separation of the actor from the product of his activity, and consequently, the separation of the motive for action and the end of an action, as the determination of the actor by another. What art and aesthetic experience embody for Mead is the countertype to this alienation: an activity that is satisfying in its very execution, a cooperation that can be clearly seen as such by all participating in it. What art as an ideal anticipates, says Mead, must become the programme for social changes.

> Under the most favourable conditions, one cannot say under normal conditions, a man's work would be in itself interesting, and apart from the immediate interest in the operation, the sense of the whole that he is completing would grow with the advancing production, and give him aesthetic delight.[40]

However, Mead goes on, when the character of the activity makes immediate joy in its execution impossible, then it is the work's involvement in a group's achievement of an end it has determined for itself which can guarantee that the activity is satisfying in itself.

> . . . if out of the drudgery that men put through together there arises a social end in which they are interested, achieving this end will have its delight, and in so far as this end can involve the tasks themselves, the dignity and delight of the social realization will suffuse the tasks.[41]

Mead states explicitly that he has in mind not a return to an idyllic society of handicraft production, but a 'socializing of industry'[42] – whatever this might mean to him. If this is not realized, he says, then the buried human potential will become, not the leaven of social change, but only the material for a culture industry that offers commercial satisfaction of fantasy through the cinema, and of thirst for knowledge through the newspaper. Here Mead is on the track of phenomena which were just beginning to become apparent in his time. Today's reader might find him more contemporary in his discussion of this topic than in his unreservedly positive valuation of the technical results of scientific progress. For we are now faced with the question of what must be done in order to halt developments which can rob science and technology of their liberating power, and ultimately make them appear to many as accessories to domination and to the destruction of nature and the individual personality. This question reminds us that the concept of practical intersubjectivity, which its originator did not apply systematically to the study of highly organized socio-technical relationships, can and must be developed further than Mead himself managed to do.

Notes

CHAPTER 1

[1] My attention was first directed to Mead by Werner Loch's article on him, in which Loch discusses role-taking and self-realization. The first fruit of the endeavour to utilize Mead's ideas in the context of sociolinguistic problems is offered by Hans Joas and Anton Leist, 'Performative Tiefenstruktur und interaktionistischer Rollenbegriff. Ein Ansatz zu einer soziolinguistichen Pragmatik', *Münchner Papiere zur Linguistik* I (1971), pp. 31–54.

[2] See my book on role theory first published in 1973, third edition 1978.

[3] See W. Dilthey, *Der Aufbau der geschichtlichen Welt in den Geisteswissenschaften* (Frankfurt 1970), p. 303ff.

[4] C. W. Mills, *Sociology and Pragmatism, The Higher Learning in America* (New York 1966), especially p. 71.

[5] Here I am opposing the exaggerated claims of a critique of ideology that purports to predict, as it were, future ideological and theoretical developments, or understands them as the mere expression of social relations, and not as attempts to solve problems.

[6] See G. C. Homans, 'Social Behavior as Exchange', *American Journal of Sociology* 63 (1958), pp. 597–606, for a short version of his widely known ideas which have been influential for the more abstract behaviourist sociology. The single passage in which Mead refers to himself as a social behaviourist was inserted into *Mind, Self, and Society* by Morris.

[7] See C. Morris on Peirce and Mead in, 'Peirce, Mead, and Pragmatism', *Philosophical Review* 47 (1938), pp. 109–127.

[8] I. Scheffler, *Four Pragmatists* (London 1974).

[9] For an account of this school by one of its members, see: Manford Kuhn 'Major Trends in Symbolic Interaction Theory in the Past Twenty-Five Years', in: J. E. Manis and B. N. Meltzer, *Symbolic Interaction* (Boston 1973), pp. 57–76; for a critique of it, see B. N. Meltzer and J. Petras, 'The Chicago and Iowa Schools of Symbolic Interaction, in: J. G. Manis and B. N. Meltzer, *Symbolic Interaction* (Boston 1973), pp. 43–57. C. McPhail and C. Rexroat have tried to play off Mead's 'behaviourism' against the methodology of symbolic interactionism, which is misleading; see, 'Mead Vs. Blumer: The Divergent Methodological Perspectives of Social Behaviorism and Symbolic Interactionism', *American Sociological Review* 44 (1979), pp. 449–467.

[10] See the important volume edited by J. Israel and H. Tajfel, *The Context of Social Psychology: A Critical Assessment* (London 1972).

[11] H. Blumer, 'Social Psychology', in: E. P. Schmidt (ed.), *Man and Society* (New York 1938), pp. 144–198.

[12] A good critique of Blumer can be found in the book by Irving Zeitlin, *Rethinking Sociology* (Englewood Cliffs 1973). In my article 'G. H. Mead', in: D. Käsler (ed.), *Klassiker des soziologischen Deukens*, Vol. I, (Munich 1978), p. 35ff., I, too, critically examine the differences between Mead and Blumer. The more recent studies, such as those of Anselm Strauss, show how clearly and productively important representatives of symbolic interactionism are themselves coming to this realization.

[13] See Maurice Natanson, *The Social Dynamics of G. H. Mead* (Washington 1956).

[14] See the following passage in Schutz's essay 'On Multiple Realities' *Collected Papers*, Vol. I (The Hague 1964), p. 217, n. 10: 'It is doubtless Mead's merit to have seen the relations between act, self, memory, time, and reality. The position of the present paper is of course not reconcilable with Mead's theory of the social origin of the self and with his (modified) behaviourism which induces him to interpret all the before mentioned phenomena in terms of stimulus-response. There is much more truth in the famous Chapter X of James's "Principles of Psychology" . . .'

[15] M. Natanson, *The Social Dynamics of G. H. Mead* (Washington 1956), p. 3.

[16] Morris remarked on this in his review of Natanson's book.

[17] On the other hand, there have been repeated attempts, in the fields of both philosophy and sociology, to prove that Schütz's treatment of the problematic of intersubjectivity was inadequate. From the American discussion of this topic, see, for example, the article by R. S. Perinbanayagam, 'The Significance of Others in the Thought of A. Schutz, G. H. Mead and C. H. Cooley', *Sociological Quarterly* 16 (1975), pp. 500–21, or that of Walker Percy, 'Symbol, Consciousness and Intersubjectivity', *Journal of Philosophy* 55 (1958), pp. 631–41. Percy extends the phenomenological concept of intentionality, which refers to the relationship of the cognitive subject to the object, to the triadic relation of a consciousness of something *for us*. See also my critique of Schutz and of Dreitzel's role theory, which was influenced by Schutz, in my book on role theory, *Die gegenwärtige Lage der soziologischen Rollentheorie*, p. 63ff.

[18] This expression has gained currency in the Federal Republic of Germany because of the widely read article by Thomas P. Wilson, 'Conceptions of Interaction and Forms of Sociological Explanation', *American Sociological Review* 35 (1970), pp. 697–710. As an example of the effacing of differences between Mead and Schütz, see Helmut Wagner's article, 'Signs, Symbols, and Interaction Theory', *Sociological Focus* 7 (1973/74), pp. 101–11. In his interpretation of Mead's theories, Richard Ekins attaches great importance to these differences. See Ekins, *G. H. Mead: Contributions to a Philosophy of Sociological Knowledge*. Thesis (University of London 1978).

[19] P. E. Pfuetze, *Self, Society, and Existence. Human Nature and Dialogue in the Thought of G. H. Mead and Martin Buber* (New York 1961).

[20] C. T. Gillin, 'Freedom and the Limits of Social Behaviourism', *Sociology* 9 (1975), pp. 29–47.

[21] K. Raiser, *Identität und Sozialität. George Herbert Meads Theorie der Interaktion und ihre Bedeutung für die theologische Anthropologie* (Munich 1971), p. 18.

[22] See Reck's overview of Mead's life's work and Lee's interpretation of Mead's theory of the 'past'.

[23] See the article by Richard Burke, 'G. H. Mead and the Problem of Metaphysics', *Philosophy and Phenomenological Research* 23 (1962/63), pp. 81–8.

[24] Miller, *Self, Language, and the World* (Austin, Texas 1973).

[25] See the reviews by G. A. Cook, in, *Transactions of the Ch. S. Peirce Society* 10 (1974), pp. 253–60, M. K. Tillman in, *Man and World* 7 (1974), pp. 293–300 and R. Donovan in, *International Philosophical Quarterly* 14 (1974), pp. 131–3.

[26] See G. A. Cook's dissertation, *The Self as Moral Agent* (Yale 1965/66) and articles.

[27] See the essays by E. Faris, 'The Social Psychology of G. H. Mead', *American Journal of Sociology* 43 (1937/38), pp. 391–403 and C. J. Bittner, 'G. H. Mead's Social Concept of the Self', *Sociology and Social Research* 16 (1931), pp. 6–22.

[28] In addition to the works by Tibbetts and Rosenthal, I should like to call attention above all to the almost completely unnoticed dissertation by Tom Clifton Keen, *Mead's Social Theory of Meaning and Experience* (Columbus, Ohio 1968), who, as a solitary pioneer, brilliantly undertook to confront Mead's work with the approaches of analytic philosophy. Miller's book contains some ideas taken from Keen's dissertation, but the latter work is by no means exhausted.

[29] A biography of this kind is being written by Harold Orbach, of the University of Kansas.

[30] For the German reception of Dewey, see the book by Fritz Bohnsack, *Erziehung zur Demokratie. John Dewey's Pädagogik und ihre Bedeutung für die Reform unserer Schule* (Ravensburg 1976).

[31] See my reply to J. Berger 'Intersubjektive Sinnkonstitution und Sozialstruktur', *Zeitschrift für Soziologie* 8 (1979), pp. 198–201.

CHAPTER 2

[1] This information I have obtained from a hitherto unused source: the eulogy of Mead's father published in the *Oberlin Review* 8 (1880/81), pp. 212–214.

[2] The sources for my remarks about Mead's youth were, in addition to scattered autobiographical retrospects (see especially the fragment in the Chicago collection of Mead's papers, Box IX, Folder 19) and the early articles in the *Oberlin Review*, chiefly the opinions expressed by Mead in public discussions, which are recorded clearly in the *Oberlin Review*.

[3] This correspondence has been used as a source of information in a coherent fashion by only one author: Neil Coughlan, in his book, *Young John Dewey. An Essay in American Intellectual History* (Chicago 1975), on Dewey's early life. However, his commentary prevents to a great degree any serious reconstruction of the course of Mead's education.

[4] Mead's letter to Henry Castle, 16 March, 1884.

[5] Mead's letter to Henry Castle, 7 March, 1884.

[6] See several of Mead's letters to Henry Castle.

[7] Henry Castle's letter to his sister, 9 October, 1887.

[8] It seems to be impossible to find that text, which probably is rather short since it had to be written in one day. (Mead's letter to Henry Castle, 19 June, 1888.)

[9] See the fragment mentioned in Note 2. There Mead writes: 'My contact with James was not academic. Through the concatenation of events I took no courses of his, but I spent a summer with his family at Chicoroa, in the White Mountains. He made no such overwhelming impression upon me as did Royce – as a philosophic intellect. I failed at the time to realize his far greater importance as an intellectual power in the American community. What I did realize was his unique personality.'

[10] In addition to the autobiographical sketch, see Mead's eulogies to Royce (No. 72) and to A. W. Moore (No. 94).

[11] Mead's letter to Henry Castle, 6 May, 1887: 'What a contrast there is between the mental philosophers of 100 years ago and the busy student of idiots and the insane, the hunter after nerves and nerve ganglions, the discusser of methods of pedagogics . . . [The] scientific spirit of modern psychology . . . saves the class of philosophers as a whole from wasting themselves upon meaningless formulae.'

[12] In a letter to his parents from Leipzig, dated 3 February, 1889, Henry Castle gives a report on Mead [*Letters* (London 1902), p. 579]: 'George thinks he must make a specialty of this branch, because in America, where poor, bated, unhappy Christianity, trembling for its life, claps the gag into the the mouth of Free Thought, and says "Hush, hush, not a word, or nobody will believe in me any more", he thinks it would be hard for him to get a chance to utter any ultimate philosophical opinions savouring of independence. In Physiological Psychology, on the other hand, he has a harmless territory in which he can work quietly without drawing down upon himself the anathema and excommunication of all-potent Evangelicism.'

[13] Henry Castle told his parents of Mead's efforts quickly to improve his knowledge of German (3 February, 1889).

[14] This information I received from the Archives of the Karl Marx University of Leipzig in a communication written on 9 January, 1979, after having tried futilely for years to obtain it.

[15] In a communication of 2 April, 1975, the director of the Archives of the Humboldt University in Berlin (German Democratic Republic) informed me that Mead was registered in the Philosophical Faculty of the University of Berlin from 2 April, 1889, to 24 October, 1891, and enrolled in the following lecture courses: *Summer Semester 1889*: Ebbinghaus, Experimental Psychology; Paulsen, History of More Recent Modern Philsophy, with Consideration of the Modern Development of Culture in its Entirety; Paulsen, Psychology and Anthropology; Paulsen, Philosophical Exercises Based on Schopenhauer's *The World as Will and Idea*; Waldeyer, General Anatomy. *Winter Semester 1889/1890*: Ebbinghaus, Psychology with Consideration of Experimental and Physiological Psychology. *Summer Semester 1890*: Dilthey, Ethics, Presented in its Principles and Particular Explications; Pfleiderer, Philosophy of Religion. *Winter Semester 1890/1891*: Munk, Physiology; Paulsen, Pedagogics. *Summer Semester 1891*: Dilthey, History of Philosophy; Paulsen, Philosophical Exercises Based on Kant's *Critique of Pure Reason*; Paulsen, Anthropology and Psychology; Schmoller, General or Theoretical Political Economy.

[16] In her review of Miller's book in *Man and World* 7 (1974), Mary Katherine Tillman makes the astonishing conjecture that Mead's theories had something to do with the Dilthey–Ebbinghaus controversy, even though the documentary evidence for this connection was unknown to her. In my opinion, though, her

interpretation suffers from an identification of Dilthey's and Husserl's views.

[17] Mead's letter to Henry Castle, 20 October, 1891.

[18] As a source of information on this point, the published correspondence of Dilthey and Yorck von Wartenburg is also of importance. See, there, p. 90ff.

[19] Mead's letter to Henry Castle, 24 October, 1891.

[20] Other, unrealized plans which Mead formed under the impression made on him by his stay in Germany were translations of Windelband's history of philosophy and of a history of Germanic mythology, which I have been able to identify as that of Eugen Mogk (letter of 12 January, 1892).

[21] See Mead's letter to Henry Castle, 21 October, 1890: 'We must get into politics of course – city politics above all things because there we can begin to work at once in whatever city we settle because city politics need men more than any other branch – and chiefly because according to my opinion the immediate application of the principles of corporate life – of socialism in America, must start from the city.'

[22] With regard to this information, see Irvin Shaw's history of the University of Michigan and the article by George Dykhuizen, 'John Dewey and the University of Michigan', *Journal of the History of Ideas* 23 (1962), pp. 513–44.

[23] Undated letter from Mead in Ann Arbor to Henry Castle.

[24] In the secondary literature on Mead, it is often maintained that Mead had contact with Cooley, who also had a post at the University of Michigan. I was unable to find any evidence for such contact.

[25] For an account of the relevant background, see Lewis Feuer's article, 'John Dewey and the Back to the People Movement in American Thought', *Journal of the History of Ideas* 20 (1959), pp. 545–68. In Coughlan's book, *Young John Dewey*, the revolutionary syndicalists are made to appear simple crackpots.

[26] The text is in Chicago, Box X, Folder 1. Unfortunately, the title page is missing. I suspect that this text was intended to be a sermon for the Student Christian Association.

[27] Ibid., p. 38–9.

[28] Dewey's letter of recommendation for Mead has been preserved: Chicago, University President's Papers 1889–1925, Box 39, Folder 6.

[29] See Jane Addams's book, *Twenty Years at Hull House* (New York 1910). See Mead's review of another book of Jane Addams (No. 31) and his essay on Settlements (No. 37).

[30] On Mead as a speaker at meetings in support of women's suffrage, see *The Chicago Tribune*, 9 January, 1912 (this reference from Mary Jo Deegan, in: *Society for the Study of Symbolic Interaction, Notes I* (1975), No. 2, p. 8. There are many passages on the reform of the juvenile penal code in Mead's writings, especially in the article on the psychology of punitive justice (No. 57). From the afterword of the editors of the journal *Survey* to the controversy between W. H. Allen and Mead over policies regarding universities (see No. 64 and 65), one can gather that Mead wrote a work of some length on the reform of the juvenile penal code and the punishment of juvenile offenders. However, my research has so far failed to unearth any bibliographical information about this work.

[31] Cf. papers in Chicago, Mead papers, Box IX, Folder 22.

[32] See the book (No. 55).

[33] See papers in Chicago, University President's Papers 1889–1925, Box 39.

[34] See titles (Nos. 54 and 65).

[35] See the essay 'The Psychology of Social Consciousness Implied in Instruction' (No. 49): 'I have sought to indicate that the process of schooling in its barest form cannot be successfully studied by a scientific psychology unless that psychology is social, i.e. unless it recognizes that the processes of acquiring knowledge, of giving attention, of evaluating in emotional terms must be studied in their relation to selves in a social consciousness. So far as education is concerned, the child does not become social by learning. He must be social in order to learn' in: J. W. Petras (ed.), *G. H. Mead: Essays on his Social Philosophy* (New York 1968), p. 41.

[36] See passages on the Liberty Loan in his letters.

[37] See No. 67. A letter of 1 March, 1917, shows that Mead first submitted this text to the City Club for publication, and then, after its rejection by that organization, allowed it to be published by the chauvinist 'National Security League'.

[38] See 'Germany's Crisis – Its Effect on Labor' (No. 68, Part II).

[39] See the important writings of W. A. Williams, *The Contours of American History* (New York 1973) and *The Shaping of American Diplomacy* (Chicago 1956), on the destruction of this myth.

[40] See H.-U. Wehler's article, 'Sprungbrett nach Ostasien. Die amerikanische Hawaii-Politik bis zur Annexion von 1898', *Jahrbuch für Amerikastudien* 10 (1965), pp. 153–81, and William's writings (ibid.). Also Mead's letter of 2 February, 1892.

[41] See at this point especially the articles in Williams, *The Shaping of American Diplomacy*.

[42] Mead's letter of 16 July, 1914.

[43] See Mead (No. 76).

[44] Wolfgang Abendroth, *Sozialgeschichte der europäischen Arbeiterbewegung* (Frankfurt 1965), p. 89.

[45] Mead's letter to his son Henry (3 March, 1918) and to Cynthia Tufts (21 August, 1919).

[46] Cf. his remarks on a strike of railway workers in a letter of 26 August, 1919.

[47] Passages on Dewey in Mead's letters and the article 'The Genesis of the Self and Social Control' (No. 84).

[48] This expression was coined by the famous liberal Supreme Court Justice, Oliver Wendell Holmes, who was associated with the pragmatists. I found it in Margaret Boveri, *Der Verrat im 20. Jahrhundert*, Vol. 4 (Reinbek 1960), p. 14. Her description of the atmosphere in the United States at the end of the First World War (and after the October Revolution) is worth quoting: 'In retrospect the period described here appears to be a dress rehearsal for what was to happen after the out-break of the Cold War. As early as 1917, with America's entry into the war, the persecution of those with dissenting views had begun. Whoever spoke out against the war, or against the draft, was arrested. After the end of the war the pacifists became uninteresting. But now it was the turn of the revolutionaries. A total of 70 'sedition bills' were placed before Congress. It took only minutes for juries to find persons who had criticized the United States guilty. The "foreign born" were deported by the hundreds.'

[49] See 'National-Mindedness and International-Mindedness' (No. 89), p. 403ff. and p. 407.

[50] T. V. Smith, 'The Social Philosophy of G. H. Mead', *American Journal of Sociology* 37 (1931), p. 384.

[51] David Miller has in his possession papers that show unequivocally that the reason for Mead's desire to leave Chicago and for his profound resignation lay in the policies of the new President of the University of Chicago, Hutchins, and in particular in the appointment of the Neo-Thomist, Mortimer Adler, to a professorship there. In contrast, Mead's foster son, John U. Nef, says in his autobiography that the reason was a 'rationalization of the university', which is clearly false. His book, an interesting source of information, is entitled *Search for Meaning. The Autobiography of a Nonconformist* (Washington, DC, 1973). Hutchins and Adler became important figures for the conservative emigrants from the Third Reich, for whom the University of Chicago became a gathering place – very much in contrast to the traditions of that university's first decades. Cf. the book by Radkau, *Die deutsche Emigration in den USA. Ihr Einfluss auf die amerikanische Europapolitik 1933–43* (Düsseldorf 1971), especially pp. 216–17, where a characterization of Mortimer Adler appears by Thomas Mann and others, who ascribe to him a 'spiritual fascism'.

[52] Randolph Bourne, 'Twilight of Idols', in: *Untimely Papers* (New York 1919), pp. 114–39.

[53] Ibid., p. 132.

[54] Mead's review of Le Bon (No. 16), p. 412.

[65] Ibid., p. 409.

[56] Popper, *The Poverty of Historicism* (London 1960).

[57] Karl–Otto Apel in the introduction to his *Transformation der Philosophie*, Vol. 1 (Frankfurt 1973), p. 14.

[58] Mead (No. 66).

CHAPTER 3

[1] See Mead's review of C. Lloyd Morgan (No. 9).

[2] The passage runs as follows: 'If the Pragmatic doctrine is a logical generalization of scientific method, it cannot merge the problem that engages thought with a larger problem which denies validity to the conditions that are the necessary tests of the solution which thought is seeking' (Mead, 'A Pragmatic Theory of Truth', in: A. Reck (ed.), *G. H. Mead: Selected Writings* (Indianapolis 1964), p. 334.)

[3] As the worst example of the 'Marxist' (i.e. Stalinist) analysis of pragmatism, see the book by Wells, *Der Pragmatismus, eine Philosophie des Imperialismus* (Berlin (DDR) 1957).

[4] 'Philosophy of the Act', p. 97–98.

[5] Peirce, *Collected Papers* (Harvard 1932), paragraph 5.412.

[6] See 'A Pragmatic Theory of Truth', pp. 328–29; 'The Philosophies of Royce, James, and Dewey in Their American Setting' (No. 93), p. 386; 'The Definition of the Psychical' (No. 20).

[7] Only twice in No. 93.

[8] See Mead papers, Chicago, Box X, Folder 26.

[9] Lincourt conjectured that this was so in his dissertation *Precursors in American Philosophy of G. H. Mead's Theory of Emergent Selfhood* (Buffalo, New York 1972); see Chapter 5 of the present work for a more detailed substantiation of this assertion.

[10] Karl–Otto Apel, *Charles Sanders Peirce, From Pragmatism to Pragmaticism* (Amherst, Massachusetts 1981), p. 59.

[11] Cf. C. W. Mills, *Sociology and Pragmatism, The Higher Learning in America (New York 1966), p. 155.* It is also striking that Mead (*e.g., Movements of Thought* (No. 98), p. 351–52 and elsewhere) refers to behaviourist psychology as a source of pragmatism and not as an application of it.

[12] Cf. Jane M. Dewey, 'Biography of John Dewey', in: P. A. Schilpp (ed.), *The Philosophy of John Dewey* (New York 1951), pp. 1–45, particularly p. 26.

[13] Scheler, *Erkenntnis und Arbeit* (Frankfurt 1977); Horkheimer, *Zur Kritik der instrumentellen Vernunft* (Frankfurt 1974).

[14] See Apel, *Charles Sanders Peirce*; Habermas, 'Zu Nietzsches Erkenntnis-Theorie', in: *Kultur und Kritik* (Frankfurt 1973), pp. 239–267; Heidegger had also attacked such a way of thinking in *Sein und Zeit* (Tübingen 1977), p. 101.

[15] See Mead's article on Royce, James, Dewey (No. 93), p. 388ff. and his arguments with Bergson (Nos. 98 and 32).

[16] Mead (No. 16).

[17] Because of their general relevance today, I would like to quote the beautiful and profound sentences in which Adorno criticizes Bergson (*Negative Dialectics* (London 1973), p. 8–9):

> A matter of urgency to the concept would be what it fails to cover, what its abstractionist mechanism eliminates, what is not already a case of the concept.
>
> Bergson and Husserl, carriers of philosophical modernism, both have innervated this idea but withdrawn from it to traditional metaphysics. Bergson, in a tour de force, created another type of cognition for non-conceptuality's sake. The dialectical salt was washed away in an undifferentiated tide of life; solidified reality was disposed of as subaltern, not comprehended along with its sub-alternity. The hater of the rigid general concept established a cult of irrational immediacy, of sovereign freedom in the midst of unfreedom. He drafted his two cognitive modes in as dualistic an opposition as that of the Cartesian and Kantian doctrines he fought had ever been; the causal-mechanical mode, as pragmastic knowledge, was no more affected by the intuitive one than the bourgeois establishment was by the relaxed unself-consciousness of those who owe their privileges to that establishment.
>
> The celebrated intuitions themselves seem rather abstract in Bergson's philosophy; they scarcely go beyond the phenomenal time consciousness which even Kant had underlying chronological-physical time – spatial time, according to Bergson's insight. Although it takes an effort to develop, the intuitive mode of mental conduct does continue to exist in fact as an archaic rudiment of mimetic reactions. What preceded its past holds a promise beyond the ossified present. Intuitions succeed only desultorily, however. Every cognition including Bergson's own needs the rationality he scorns, and needs it precisely at the moment of concretion. Absolutized duration, pure becoming, the pure act – these would recoil into the same timelessness which Bergson chides in metaphysics since Plato and Aristotle. He did not mind that the thing he groped for, if it is not to remain a mirage, is visible solely with the equipment of cognition, by reflection

upon its own means, and that it grows arbitrary in a procedure unrelated, from the start, to that of cognition.

18 Cf. texts by Riedel, Johach, Habermas, *Erkenntnis und Interesse* (Frankfurt 1968).

19 In my opinion, Riedel's interpretation of Dilthey's thought does not stress this point sufficiently.

20 Cf. Dilthey, *Der Aufbau der geschichtlichen Welt in den Geisteswissenschaften* (Frankfurt 1970); on the relationship between Dilthey and Husserl see their correspondence edited by Biemel, 'Briefwechsel Dilthey–Husserl', *Man and World I* (1968), pp. 428–46.

21 Karl–Otto Apel, *Charles Sanders Peirce*, p. 110.

22 I have great difficulty with the distinction between a psychological and a hermeneutic phase in the development of Dilthey's thought on which Gadamer and Habermas base their interpretations. It is my opinion that in this distinction several dimensions overlap one another: the merely empathic hermeneutics versus a hermeneutics directed to the understanding of meaning, and a relativist versus normative method of understanding. In addition, this distinction suggests that hermeneutics itself does not require more than a linguistic grounding, whereas it must also be grounded in philosophical anthropology. Helmuth Plessner saw this, and used it to justify his hermeneutics of non-linguistic expression. Habermas's *Erkenntnis und Interesse* opposes Peirce and Dilthey far too much on the basis of the distinction between instrumental and communicative action, which results in the slightly unjust treatment of both of them. See also R. Bernstein's critique of Habermas's interpretation of Peirce in his introduction to the German edition of *Praxis and Action* (Frankfurt 1975).

23 Husserl, *Philosophie als strenge Wissenschaft* (Frankfurt 1965).

24 Cf. Goldmann and Tugendhat.

25 On Gehlen's early philosophical writings, see Böhler 'Arnold Gehlen: Die Haudlung', in: Josef Speck (ed.), *Grundprobleme der grossen Philosophen, Philosophie der Gegenwart II* (Göttingen 1973); on his mature philosophical anthropology, see my article 'Intersubjektivität bei Mead und Gehlen', *Archiv für Rechts – und Sozialphilosophie* 65 (1979), pp. 105–21.

26 For a critique of Plessner from the standpoint of the theory of intersubjectivity, see Habermas's letter to Plessner, in: *Kultur und Kritik*, pp. 232–5; see also the chapter on Plessner in Axel Honneth and Hans Joas, *Soziales Handeln und menschliche Natur* (Frankfurt 1980), p. 72ff.

27 I leave out of consideration the peculiar twist that Karl–Otto Apel gives to transcendental philosophy by making the motives for going beyond it, such as corporeality and intersubjectivity, building blocks of a new 'transformed' transcendental philosophy.

28 As for French sociology, I recommend the article by Stone and Farberman on the difference and similarity between Durkheim and Mead, 'On the Edge of Rapprochement: Was Durkheim Moving Toward the Perspective of Symbolic Interaction', in: Stone and Farberman (eds), *Social Psychology through Symbolic Interaction* (Waltham, Massachusetts 1970), pp. 100–112.

29 On Lukács, see my introduction to Agnes Heller, *Das Alltagsleben*; for a critique of an instrumentalist limitation implicit in Weber's concept of action, see

Karl–Siegbert Rehberg, 'Rationales Handeln als großbürgerliches Aktions-modell. Thesen zu einigen handlungstheoretischen Implikationen der 'Soziolog-ischen Grundbegriffe' Max Webers', in: *Kölner Zeitschrift für Soziologie und Sozialpsychologie* 31 (1979), pp. 199–236.

[30] For an especially vivid account of this relationship, see Dewey's essay on Renan, 'Renan's Loss of Faith in Science', in: *The Early Works* 4 (Carbondale, Illinois 1971), pp. 11–18.

[31] Charles Morris was the first to call for a study of this material by a historian of philosophy.

[32] See Mead's lecture 'Rationalism and Empiricism', a copy of which is among his unpublished papers in Chicago.

[33] Cf. Josiah Royce, *The Spirit of Modern Philosophy* (New York 1983).

[34] Mead's course on Hume (Box VII, Folder 7–12).

[35] *Movements of Thought* (No. 98), p. 67. I do not consider here Mead's extremely problematical concept of Romanticism and his assignment of post-Kantian idealism to Romanticism. Many of the simplifications in this book are un-doubtedly due to the fact that the lectures on which it is based were given as an elementary introduction for undergraduate students.

[36] *Movements of Thought* (No. 98), pp. 85–110.

[37] Ibid., p. 90.

[38] Ibid., p. 101ff. [my emphasis H.J.].

[39] Ibid., pp. 91–92.

[40] It is indeed no accident that Habermas, in his short but impressively concise interpretation of Fichte in *Erkenntnis und Interesse* (see p. 52), adduces Fichte as the forerunner of the second, non-Kantian moment in the concept of synthesis through social work.

[41] See Lukács's essay on Moses Hess, 'Moses Hess und die Probleme der idealist-ischen Dialektik', in: Lukács, *Werke* Vol. 2 (Neuwied 1965), pp. 643–86.

[42] Mead, 'The Objective Reality of Perspectives' (No. 86), p. 161 (in: *The Philosophy of the Present* (No. 95)).

[43] See Apel on Peirce.

[44] For qualifications of this assessment see chapter 2.

[45] See *Movements of Thought*, p. 472, where he posits a connection between German idealism and the early development of physiological psychology.

[46] Ibid., p. 417.

[47] This is particularly true of American sociologists, from some of whom I encountered an aggressive rejection of any connection between German idealism and Mead.

[48] See Sidney Hook's review of 'Movements of Thought' in *The Nation* 143 (1936), pp. 220–21.

[49] Cf. Dewey's assessment of Hegel in an autobiographical retrospect, quoted in R. Bernstein's *Praxis und Handeln*, p. 33.

[50] Kurt Lasswitz, 'Die moderne Energetik in ihrer Bedeutung für die Erkennt-niskritik', *Philosophische Monatshefte* 29 (1893). See Mead's texts Nos. 7 and 8.

[51] Mead (No. 7), p. 173.

[52] See the early text (No. 6), 'The Problem of Psychological Measurement'.

[53] Schleiermacher, *Monologe*.

[54] Mead's review of Class (No. 13), p. 789.

[55] Ibid., p. 790.

[56] Ibid., p. 791.

[57] Mead on D'Arcy (No. 19), pp. 94–95.

[58] Ibid., p. 92.

[59] Ibid., p. 96.

[60] Mead, 'Suggestions Toward a Theory of the Philosophical Disciplines' (No. 17), p. 2.

[61] See, for example, Piaget's book on the psychology of intelligence, *Psychologie der Intelligenz* (Munich 1974).

[62] Mead, 'Suggestions', p. 13.

[63] Ibid., p. 12.

CHAPTER 4

[1] 'The Definition of the Psychical' (No. 20).

[2] About half of it has been reprinted in the collection of Mead's articles edited by Reck, *G. H. Mead: Selected Writings*.

[3] Cf. James R. Angell's expression of gratitude to Mead in the article on reaction time, 'Reaction-Time: A Study in Attention and Habit', *Psychological Review* 3 (1896), pp. 245–58; on the significance of this article see Harrison, 'Functionalism and Its Historical Significance', *Genetic Psychology Monographs* 68 (1963), pp. 387–423.

[4] Dewey's letter to James, published in Ralph Berton Perry, *The Thought and Character of William James*, 2 Vols (Boston 1936).

[5] Dewey, 'The Reflex Arc Concept in Psychology', in: *The Early Works* 5 (Carbondale, Illinois 1972), pp. 96–109.

[6] Mead, 'What Social Objects Must Psychology Presuppose?' (No. 51), p. 175.

[7] G. A. Cook, 'The Development of G. H. Mead's Social Psychology', *Transactions of the Ch. S. Peirce Society* 8 (1972), pp. 167–86; 'G. H. Mead's Alleged Behaviorism', *Journal of the History of the Behavioral Sciences* 13 (1977), pp. 207–16; 'Whitehead's Influence on the Thought of G. H. Mead', *Transactions of the Ch. S. Peirce Society* 15 (1979), pp. 107–31.

[8] Mead (No. 51), pp. 174–5.

[9] Harrison gives a good overview of this school in 'Functionalism and Its Historical Significance'.

[10] This anticipatory character is recognized by C. F. Graumann, *Handbuch der Psychologie*. In my opinion, Shibutani's interpretation does not do justice to this topic.

[11] On Piaget, Gehlen, Merleau-Ponty cf. the bibliography; Viktor von Weizsäcker, *Der Gestaltkreis* (Frankfurt 1973). For comparisons of these approaches: Voort on Piaget and Mead, de Mey on Piaget and Gehlen, Zaner on Piaget and Merleau-Ponty, Tibbetts and Rosenthal on Mead and Merleau-Ponty, and Joas on Mead and Gehlen.

[12] Cf. Wartenberg, *Logischer Sozialismus, Die Transformation der Kantschen Transzendentalphilosophie durch Ch. S. Peirce* (Frankfurt 1971), p. 62: 'Wundt's discovery that "the function of our thinking-organ lies in its regulation of motor reactions" was called by Peirce "the substance of pragmatism in the dress of physiology"' (*Collected Papers*, 8.201, n. 3).

[13] On this problem, see chapter 9.

[14] Mead, 'Definition of the Psychical', p. 3.

[15] Ibid., pp. 3–4.

[16] I select this work of Husserl, as it is almost contemporaneous with Mead's endeavours. Husserl's *Die Krisis der europäischen Wissenschaften und die transzendentale Phänomenologie* (The Hague 1976) is, of course, much more thoroughgoing.

[17] Husserl and Mead did not influence one another. To my knowledge Husserl does not mention Mead anywhere; Mead mentions Husserl only once, in a letter of 15 September 1926, and then only to identify Moritz Geiger. For the present work the appreciation and critique of phenomenology have an important role. It is a matter of importance for me to ascertain the relation of these two currents of thought, beginning with their ideas on science and psychology, and not to limit the comparison only to the question of the social formation of the self.

[18] Husserl's counter-objection would have been the accusation of 'naturalism'.

[19] See especially Wundt, *Grundriß der Psychologie* (Leipzig 1922). A recent interesting discussion of Wundt is to be found in Theodore Mischel's article, 'Wundt and the Conceptual Foundations of Psychology', *Philosophy and phenomenological research* 31 (1970), pp. 1–26.

[20] Husserl, *Krisis*, p. 235, gives quite a similar criticism of Wundt.

[21] Mead, 'Definition of the Psychical', p. 26.

[22] Ibid., p. 20.

[23] Mead used an English translation of Oswald Külpe, *Grundriß der Psychologie*.

[24] Mead, 'Definition of the Psychical', p. 8.

[25] Ibid.

[26] See chapter 9.

[27] Münsterberg, *Grundzüge der Psychologie* (Leipzig 1900).

[28] Mead, 'Definition', p. 9.

[29] See Bradley 'Association and Thought', *Mind* 12 (1887), pp. 354–81 and on Bradley: Hamlyn, 'Bradley, Ward, and Stout', in: Benjamin Wolman (ed.), *Historical Roots of Contemporary Psychology* (New York 1968), pp. 298–320.

[30] On this thesis cf. Gadamer's interpretation of Dilthey in *Wahrheit und Methode* (Tübingen 1975) and Merleau-Ponty, *Phenomenology of Perception* (London 1962).

[31] Mead, 'Definition', p. 13.

[32] Stout, *A Manual of Psychology* (New York 1899).

[33] Mead, 'Definition', p. 14.

[34] Ibid.

[35] Ibid., p. 17.

[36] Cf., for example, the opening of his *Psychology*. James later changed his position regarding dualism and presented his change of mind in a famous essay, to which Mead referred again and again: 'Does "Consciousness" Exist?' There he undertakes to overcome dualism with a concept of pure experience and to conceive of subject and object as mere functions in this process of pure experience. On the failure of this attempt because James did not develop a concept of the symbol and of internalized sociality, see the important article by Cronk, 'James and the Problem of Intersubjectivity: An Interpretative Critique, in: W. R. Corti (ed.), *The Philosophy of William James* (Hamburg 1976), pp. 221–44.

[37] The expression 'two different linguistic systems' alludes to the form that the

problem assumed within the framework of analytical philosophy. (Cf. the famous controversy between Feigl and Meehl.)

[38] Mead, 'Definition', p. 19.

[39] Ibid., p. 35.

[40] Ibid., pp. 19–20.

[41] Ibid., pp. 21–22.

[42] Ibid., p. 22.

[43] This argument is made also in *Mind, Self, and Society*, sections 5 and 6 of Part I.

[44] See chapter 9.

[45] Mead, 'Definition', p. 23.

[46] Ibid.

[47] Ibid., p. 27.

[48] Ibid., pp. 27–28. In this connection I call the reader's attention to Gehlen's interpretation – made from the standpoint of a critique of culture – of the 'stream of consciousness' as a luxuriating of unburdened functions.

[49] See Baldwin, *Mental Development in the Child and the Race* (New York 1895), chapter 11; his article in the *Psychological Review* 10, 1903.

[50] I do not discuss here Mead's later critical examination of Baldwin's theories, especially of his concept of imitation. On these points, see chapter 5 of the present work.

[51] Mead, 'Definition', p. 32.

[52] Ibid., p. 34.

[53] Ibid., pp. 34–35.

[54] I return to this point repeatedly in the following chapters.

[55] For a critique of the pragmatist concept of consciousness which makes use of this argument, see A. Gehlen, *Der Mensch* (Frankfurt 1971), p. 144; L. Goldmann, *Lukács und Heidegger* (Darmstadt 1975), p. 90ff. Mead's solution to this problem is also a refutation of these critiques.

[56] A critique doing justice to the scientific accomplishment of Holzkamp and his school and pursuing the topics outlined is still lacking.

[57] See Hans-Christian Harten's book, *Der vernünftige Organismus – oder gesell-schaftliche Evolution der Vernunft. Zur Gesellschaftstheorie des genetischen Struktur-alismus von Piaget* (Frankfurt 1977).

[58] Husserl, *Krisis*, § 73ff.

[59] Beside Theodore Mischel's writings cf. Norman Malcolm's critique of Skinner, 'Behaviorism as a Philosophy of Psychology', in: T. W. Wann, *Behaviorism and Phenomenology* (Chicago 1964), pp. 141–55.

[60] In discussions of my interpretation and assessment of Mead's 'Definition of the Psychical', it became clear that the German reader of my work wanted to know how the 'psychical', as defined by Mead, and Freud's concept of the unconscious, are related to one another. What is striking in this regard is that the everyday use of the term 'psychical' obviously now suggests a close association with Freud's 'unconscious'. In opposition to such an association, one must keep in mind that Mead was defining what is conscious in a way that does not hypostasize it to 'consciousness'. Further, it is at least a critical result that Freud's 'Unconscious', too, may not be declared to be a domain in its own right, and as potentially conscious must be embedded in a theory of action in a manner analogous to the definition of the psychical given by Mead. It would be possible to effect an

integration of Mead and Freud only if the theory of the social formation of the self, which will be presented in the next chapter, were systematically referred back to a failure of the self in operations of integration and presentification. How that might be done is, however, still very unclear to me. (Cf. E. Tugendhat's brief, but illuminating remarks on Freud in *Selbstbewusstsein und Selbstbestimmung. Sprachanalytische Interpretationen* (Frankfurt 1979), p. 140ff.)

CHAPTER 5

[1] In the German version of this book I employed the expression 'symbolically mediated interaction' (*symbolvermittelte Interaktion*), coined by Habermas, rather than 'symbolic interaction', which was introduced by Blumer, since it seemed to me to eliminate any suggestion of theatrical metaphor. Mead himself used neither.

[2] See E. Faris's review of 'Mind, Self, and Society', *American Journal of Sociology* 41 (1936), pp. 909–13.

[3] Comparison of the student notes for these lectures from different years shows that Mead repeatedly changed the way he organized them.

[4] See the works of Blumer and Habermas. It must become clear in the course of my exposition that the thesis of the historical novelty of Mead's theory does not rest on the fact that he proposed simply some conception of intersubjectivity, but rather one that is tenable in light of anthropological knowledge.

[5] Mead, 'Social Psychology as Counterpart to Physiological Psychology' (No. 47).

[6] See Mead's review of Draghiscesco's books (No. 24), p. 403. Since I did not have access to the works of this forgotten author, I refer the reader to the account of his theories in Pitirim Sorokin, *Soziologische Theorien im 19. und 20. Jahrhundert* (Munich 1931), pp. 141–5.

[7] Mead, Ibid., p. 404.

[8] William McDougall, *An Introduction to Social Psychology* (London 1908). On this book, see Mead (No. 38).

[9] Ibid., p. 386. On this assessment of the psychology of instincts, see also the two articles by Ellsworth Faris, Mead's student: 'Current Trends in Social Psychology' and 'Are Instincts Data or Hypotheses?', both in E. Faris, *The Nature of Human Nature* (New York 1937), pp. 155–66 and 61–72. The second of these articles represents a breakthrough in motivation theory, inasmuch as it rejects the psychology of instincts with the argument of the reconstructive character of the concept of instinct, which comes from hypotheses to explain actual behaviour and cannot legitimately be used as an originarily given datum.

[10] Mead, 'The Relations of Psychology and Philology' (No. 23), p. 380.

[11] Wundt, *Völkerpsychologie*, Vol. 1 (Leipzig 1911), p. 255.

[12] Mead, 'Philology', p. 382.

[13] Ibid., p. 383.

[14] Edward Alsworth Ross, *Social Psychology* (New York 1909)]. This book and the one by McDougall previously mentioned were the very first textbooks of social psychology.

[15] See Mead, 'Social Psychology as Counterpart to Physiological Psychology' (No. 47), p. 406. For a comparison of Royce and Mead see D. L. Miller's thorough essay, 'Josiah Royce and G. H. Mead on the Nature of the Self', *Transactions of the Ch. S. Peirce Society* 11 (1975), No. 2, pp. 67–89.

[16] Mead, 'Counterpart', p. 406.

[17] Ibid., pp. 406–7.

[18] Charles Darwin, 'The Expression of the Emotion in Man and Animals', (1872). See also 'Mind, Self, and Society'.

[19] Mead, 'Social Consciousness and the Consciousness of Meaning' (No. 48), pp. 398-9.

[20] Mead, 'A Theory of Emotions' (No. 10); Dewey, 'The Theory of Emotions', in: *The Early Works* 4 (Carbondale, Illinois 1971) particularly p. 167, n. 14.

[21] Mead, 'Mind, Self, and Society', p. 21, n. 12.

[22] Mead, 'Emotions', p. 164.

[23] Mead, 'Social Consciousness', p. 401.

[24] Ibid.

[25] Ibid., p. 403.

[26] Ibid., p. 405.

[27] Mead, 'What Social Objects Must Psychology Presuppose?' (No. 51), p. 180.

[28] See chapter 7.

[29] Mead, 'The Mechanism of Social Consciousness' (No. 54), p. 403.

[30] Ibid., p. 404.

[31] In various writings, Ulrich Oevermann has stressed repeatedly the counterfactual assumption of competence in interaction on the part of the child as the very condition of the development of this competence.

[32] Mead, 'The Mechanism of Social Consciousness', p. 405.

[33] Ibid.

[34] Mead, 'The Social Self' (No. 58), p. 376.

[35] Ibid.

[36] Ibid., p. 377.

[37] Ibid., pp. 377–8.

[38] Mead (No. 80).

[39] I assume that this was due to Mead's extreme loyalty to Dewey.

[40] This makes necessary a study of the methodological developments of American sociology between the two world wars.

[41] Mead, 'Mind, Self, and Society', p. 7.

[42] Ibid., pp. 7–8 (my emphasis).

[43] Ibid., p. 139, n. 2.

[44] Cf. Schurig. Mead advanced his arguments, by the way, prior to the discovery of 'bees' language'. That this discovery does not disprove his ideas is shown by L. von Bertalanffy, 'Symbolismus und Anthropogenese', in: B. Reusch (ed.), *Handgebrauch und Verständigung bei Affen und Frühmenschen* (Bern/Stuttgart 1968), pp. 131–48.

[45] Mead, 'Mind, Self, and Society', p. 244.

[46] Mead, 'Objective Reality', p. 169 (in *The Philosophy of the Present*).

[47] Mead, 'Mind, Self, and Society', p. 6, n. 6.

[48] I have these expressions from Tom Clifton Keen's dissertation, *Mead's Social Theory*.

[49] On this point there is a wealth of philosophical literature. An early and good paper, which makes direct reference to Mead, is W. B. Gallie, 'Solipistic and Social Theories of Meaning', *Proceedings of the Aristotelian Society*, New Series, 38 (1937/38), pp. 61–84.

[50] Cf. Habermas's critique of C. Morris in *Zur Logik der Sozialwissenschaften* (Tübingen 1967); and Apel's frequent rejections of misunderstandings of Peirce. Apparently ineradicable misinterpretations of Mead make this mistake.

[51] As a documentation of this that is beyond suspicion, see Schurig's excellent book, *Die Entstehung des Bewusstseins* (Frankfurt 1976).

[52] Cf. Konrad Lorenz and Paul Leyhausen, 'Theoretical Considerations in Criticism of the Concept of the "Displacement Movement"', in: *Motivation of Human and Animal Behavior. An Ethological View* (New York 1973), pp. 59–69. See also Habermas's lecture on Philosophical Anthropology (1966/67) and my book on role theory.

[53] See W. van de Voort's dissertation, *Interaktion und Kognition. Die Bedeutung der Sozialen Interaktion für die Entwicklung der kognitiven Strukturen nach Jean Piaget* (Frankfurt 1977).

[54] Such an investigation must consider all senses, and not accord an erroneous primacy to the development of linguistic abilities.

[55] See the articles by M. Miller 'Sprachliche Sozialisation', in: K. Hurrelmann and D. Ulich (eds), Handbuch der Sozialisationsforachung (Weinheim 1980) and R. A. Clark, 'The Transition from Action to Gesture', in: A. Lock (ed.), *Action, Gesture and Symbol. The Emergence of Language* (London 1978), pp. 231–57.

[56] On this topic see M. Miller, ibid.

[57] In response to this recurrent assertion, it must be pointed out that since Yerkes's famous studies of chimpanzees the small capacity of these animals for imitating *sounds* has been proven. Cf. I. Schwidetzky's introduction to the volume she edited *Über die Evolution der Sprache* (Frankfurt 1973) and M. Yerkes and B. W. Learned, *Chimpanzee Intelligence and Its Vocal Expression* (Baltimore 1925).

[58] See the works by Berg, Keller, van de Voort.

[59] See chapter 7 and 8.

[60] The following exposition draws upon my article on Mead, 'G. H. Mead', in: D. Käsler (ed.), *Klassiker der soziologischen Denkens*, Vol. 2 (Munich 1978), pp. 7–39. I should like to take advantage of this opportunity to add to the mention of Mead's first use of the concept of role a remark about its alleged implications as a theatrical metaphor, which has generated much fuss in German role theory. Mead explicitly rejected such implications: 'It is this perfecting of the self by the gesture which mediates the social activities that gives rise to the process of taking the role of the other. The latter phrase is a little unfortunate because it suggests an actor's attitude which is actually more sophisticated than that which is involved in our own experience. To this degree it does not correctly describe that which I have in mind.' ('Mind, Self, and Society', p. 161.)

[61] Cf. passages in Mead's article 'National-Mindedness and International-Mindedness' (No. 89). In this connection let me point out that we still lack a thorough analysis of the relation of Mead and Freud. Such a study would have to examine the concept of the psychical, the moments of Mead's and Freud's personality models, and the structure of the commerce of these moments with one another. Further, this investigation would have to include Mead's study of Freud and his difficulties with the concept of the 'unconscious', as well as the reception of Freud by the important American psychiatrist Harry Stack Sullivan, which was coloured by Meadian pragmatism. It was hitherto unknown that in 1914 Mead was working on a review of Freud's work, which I have not been able to locate

bibliographically – assuming that it was published (see the letters of 12 July, 1914, and 16 July, 1914). In Mead's draft of a review of William Alanson White, *Thoughts of a Psychiatrist on the War and After*, there occurs a sentence which points forward to future research: 'What our Freudian psychology still lacks is an adequate study of the growth of the self.' (Austin collection.)

CHAPTER 6

[1] See the article on D'Arcy (No. 19).

[2] The most important pieces are Nos. 92, 36, 81, 58 and part IV 'Value and the Act' of the 'Philosophy of the Act'.

[3] 'Elementary Ethics' (Chicago, Box VII, Folders 3 and 4). The 'Fragments on Ethics' printed in the appendix to *Mind, Self, and Society* are passages selected from this manuscript.

[4] J. Dewey and J. Tufts, *Ethics* (New York 1913).

[5] This is Moran's opinion.

[6] 'Elementary Ethics', p. 181.

[7] Cf. Dewey and Tufts, *Ethics*, pp. 237–8.: 'Their common error, as we shall attempt to show in the sequel, lies in trying to split a voluntary act which is single and entire into two unrelated parts, the one termed "inner", the other, "outer"; the one called "motive", the other, "end". A voluntary act is always a disposition, or habit of the agent *passing into a overt act*, which, so far as it can, produces certain consequences. A "mere" motive which does not do anything, which makes nothing different, is not a genuine motive at all, and hence is not a voluntary act. On the other hand, consequences which are not intended, which are not personally wanted and chosen and striven for are no part of a voluntary act. *Neither the inner apart from the outer, nor the outer apart from the inner has any voluntary or moral quality at all. The former is mere passing sentimentality or reverie; the latter is mere accident or luck.*'

[8] 'Mind, Self, and Society', pp. 384–5.

[9] 'Elementary Ethics', p. 135.

[10] 'Mind, Self, and Society', p. 382.

[11] Attempts at rehabilitation have been made by Richard Bernstein and recently especially by James Gouinlock; a mediatory position was taken by S. Cavell and A. Sesonske; in my opinion the best secondary literature on Mead's ethics is to be found in 'Mead and Recent Moral Philosophy', chapter V, pp. 156–197 of G. A. Cook's dissertation *The Self as Moral Agent*, Diss. (Yale 1965/6.)

[12] J. L. Austin, *How To Do Things with Words* (Cambridge, Massachusetts 1962).

[13] H. Lenk, 'Kann die sprachanalytische Moralphilosophie neutral sein?, in: H. Albert and E. Topitsch (eds), *Werturteilsstreit* (Darmstadt 1971), pp. 533–52.

[14] Mead (No. 81).

[15] Ibid., p. 86 (in Petras (ed.) *G. H. Mead*).

[16] Ibid., p. 87.

[17] Ibid., p. 88.

[18] Ibid., p. 96.

[19] I do not bring into consideration the reservations expressed by C. Wright Mills and Karl–Otto Apel regarding the transferral of the concept of experiment to historical relationships, as they are of no consequence for the ideas with which I am concerned here.

[20] 'Mind, Self, and Society', p. 388.

[21] In his earlier writings on the theory of communicative competence and universal pragmatics.

[22] Mead's action-related concept of emotion is sufficient in itself to preclude construing valuation as a subjective emotion. (Cf. chapter 5 of the present work.)

[23] See chapter 7.

[24] See chapter 9.

[25] Mead, 'The Philosophical Basis of Ethics' (No. 36), p. 85 (Reck (ed.)).

[26] This criticism is applicable to Alfred Schutz's phenomenological theory of action.

[27] Mead, 'Philosophical Basis', p. 86.

[28] Blumer points out that Mead's model of the phases of an action must be modified by his central notion of discursive self-control in action. Cf. his reply to Jonathan Turner, 'Parsons as a Symbolic Interactionist', *Sociological Inquiry* 44 (1974), pp. 283–94; ibid., 45 (1975), pp. 59–62.

[29] 'Mind, Self, and Society', pp. 319–20.

[30] Mead, 'The Social Self' (No. 58), p. 378.

[31] Cf., for example, 'The Psychology of Punitive Justice' (No. 75), p. 220 (Reck (ed.)): 'The escape from selfishness is not by the Kantian road of an emotional response to the abstract universal, but by the recognition of the genuinely social character of human nature.'

[32] Cf. the writings of J. H. Broyer, who gives special attention to this point.

[33] See L. Kohlberg, 'Stage and Sequence: The Cognitive–Developmental Approach to Socialization', in: D. A. Goslin (ed.), *Handbook of Socialization Theory and Research*, (Chicago 1969), pp. 347–480; the central importance of the theory of the development of the moral consciousness is made clear in a letter of 10 September, 1925, in which Mead says of this theory that it is his 'Phenomenology of Mind': 'Now I take the function of philosophy to be the attempted harmonizing of this larger self and its implied larger community, with the immediate community in which the individuals find themselves members . . . What I want to bring out is the inevitableness of this in the development of the personality. In a sense it is an attempt to do from my own standpoint what Hegel undertook in his Pheno-menology. I hope it won't be as inscrutable.'

[34] 'Mind, Self, and Society', p. 379.

[35] D. L. Miller recognizes this in his book *G. H. Mead. Self, Language, and the World* (Austin, Texas 1973), p. 247.

[36] Ibid., p. 327.

[37] Mead in his essay on Cooley (quoted from the reprint in a Cooley edition, p. XXXVII).

[38] This expression is taken from Albrecht Wellmer.

[39] Mead, 'Philanthropy from the Point of View of Ethics' (No. 92), pp. 404–5. (Reck (ed.)). On this article cf. T. V. Smith's interesting discussion, 'G. H. Mead and the Philosophy of Philanthropy', *Social Services Review* 6 (1932), pp. 37–54.

[40] 'Mead, Self, and Society', p. 168.

[41] Mead, 'Philanthropy', p. 406.

[42] Mead, 'Natural Rights and the Theory of the Political Institution' (No. 60).

[43] Ibid.

[44] Ibid., p. 152.

[45] Mead, 'Punitive Justice' (No. 75).

[46] Cf. Nos. 89 and 62.

[47] Cf. Habermas's penetrating observations on the notion of a 'class-compromise' in *Legitimation Crisis (Legitimationsprobleme im Spätkapitalismus* (Frankfurt 1973)), p. 112: 'Even if a "class-compromise" came about in advanced capitalism under conditions of a balance of power, the justifiability of the compromise would remain questionable as long as it excluded the possibility of discursively testing whether it was in fact a matter, on both sides, of particular interests that did not permit of a rational will and were thus accessible only to compromise.'
Cf. also Habermas's question (ibid., p. 113): 'how would the members of a social system, at a given stage in the development of productive forces, have collectively and bindingly interpreted their needs (and which norms would they have accepted as justified) if they could and would have decided on organization of social intercourse through discursive will-formation, with adequate knowledge of the limiting conditions and functional imperatives of their society?'

[48] 'Mind, Self, and Society', p. 308.

[49] See my article, on Mead in Käsler (ed.), *Klassiker des soziologischen Denkens'*, p. 31.

[50] Chasin's critique of Mead as a utopian is completely mistaken; it is ironical that Schwendinger/Schwendinger make the diametrically opposed criticism that Mead's reformism was completely lacking in utopian vision. Both positions fail to develop Mead's internal contradiction in this point.

[51] Peirce, *Collected Papers*, (Harvard 1932), paragraphs 5.133 and 5.135.

[52] See C. W. Mills, *Sociology and Pragmatism*, p. 444, p. 456.

[53] See *Leon Trotsky, John Dewey, and George Novack, Their Morals and Ours. Marxist vs. Liberal Views on Morality* (New York 1973). See also Isaac Deutscher, *Trotsky*, Vol. 3 (Oxford 1970). The expression 'a failed Stalin' comes from Willy Huhn.

[54] Trotsky, ibid., p. 48.

[55] Coined by Karl-Otto Apel.

[56] Dewey, 'Means and Ends', in: Leon Trotsky et al., *Their Morals and Ours*, p. 72.

[57] Ibid.

CHAPTER 7

[1] Mead, 'Concerning Animal Perception' (No. 29).

[2] This is pointed out by Pfuetze; Royce's article is to be found in the *Philosophical Review* 3 (1894) and 4 (1895).

[3] Mead, 'Philosophy of the Act', p. 149.

[4] Ibid., pp. 3–4.

[5] Although this model was put together in this form by Mead's editors, it appears to correspond to Mead's intentions.

[6] Mead, 'Philosophy of the Act', p. 267.

[7] I leave aside here animal play and curiosity behaviour.

[8] For example, in Mead, 'Concerning Animal Perception', p. 389.

[9] Tibbetts cites numerous confirmations of this thesis in experimental psychology.

[10] See *Movements of Thought*, p. 88; however, as the transcript of his lectures on social psychology, contained in the Austin collection of his unpublished papers shows, Mead explicitly stated that he did not believe contact perceptions were more frequent than distance perceptions – quite the contrary!

234   G. H. Mead

[11] Mead, 'Philosophy of the Act', p. 24.
[12] Mead, 'Concerning Animal Perception', p. 388.
[13] Ibid., p. 390.
[14] In his view of the object there is a similarity with Heidegger's concept of 'equipment' (Zeug); see (*Sein und Zeit* (Tübingen 1777)), p. 97.
[15] Keen, *Mead's Social Theory*, p. 151.
[16] Mead, 'Philosophy of the Act', p. 143.
[17] Cf. M. Merleau-Ponty, *Phenomenology of Perception* (*Phänomenologie der Wahrnehmung* (Berlin 1966)), p. 315: 'Even on the most sensitive parts of our tactile surface, pressure without movement produces a scarcely identifiable phenomenon.'
[18] In *The Philosophy of the Act*, p. 427, Mead refers to Theodor Lipps as a proponent of this view.
[19] My interpretation is based to a large extent on the fragment 'The Physical Thing', in the appendix to *The Philosophy of the Present*, and the section 'The Mechanism of Role-Taking in the Appearance of the Physical Object', *The Philosophy of the Act*, pp. 426–32.
[20] Mead, 'Philosophy of the Act', pp. 109–10.
[21] Ibid., p. 310.
[22] Mead, *Philosophy of the Present*, p. 127.
[23] See chapter 8.
[24] Mead, *Philosophy of the Present*, p. 128.
[25] Mead, 'Mind, Self, and Society', pp. 377–8.
[26] In my article on Mead 'Klassiker des soziologischen Denkens', in Käsler (ed.), p. 26.
[27] Published passages having a bearing on this analysis can be found in *The Philosophy of the Act*, p. 120, p. 431. The most important text is the manuscript in the Austin collection which begins with the words: 'The human individual has as part of his self the physical organism . . .' (Now included in the Chicago Papers under the title 'Self and Teleological Behavior'.)
[28] Ibid., p. 5.
[29] Mead, 'Philosophy of the Act', p. 266.
[30] Mead, 'The Human Individual . . .', p. 20.
[31] This expression was introduced by Paul Schilder, *Das Körperschema*, (Berlin 1923).
[32] Mead, 'The Human Individual . . .'
[33] See the works of Wygotski and Leontjew.
[34] See Hans Joas, 'Intersubjektivität bei Mead and Gehlen'.
[35] This is the title of one of Piaget's books.
[36] See H.-C. Harten, M. Keller and W. van de Voort.
[37] J. Piaget, *The Child's Construction of Reality* (London 1955), p. 4.
[38] Ibid.
[39] Ibid., p. 93.
[40] J. Smedslund, 'Les origines sociales de la décentration', in: F. Bresson and M. de Montmollin (eds), *Psychologie et épistémologie génétiques. Thèmes Piagétiens* (Paris 1966), pp. 159–67.
[41] See the works listed for W. Doise and A. Perret-Clermont in the bibliography for the present work.

[42] See A. Perret-Clermont, 'Une approche psychosociologique du développement cognitif', in: *Archives de Psychologie* 44 (1976), No. 171, p. 142.

[43] Principally in his dissertation, for which the article, 'Die Bedeutung von Vorformen', in Leist (ed.), *Ansätze* (Kronberg 1975) is a preliminary stage.

[44] Jürgen Habermas, *Notizen zur Entwicklung der Interaktionskompetenz* (1974), now published in Habermas, *Vorstudien und Ergänzungen zur Theorie des kommunikativen Handelns* (Frankfurt 1984), pp. 187–225.

[45] René Spitz, *The First Year of Life* (New York 1965).

[46] Silvia M. Bell, 'The Development of the Concept of Object as Related to Infant-Mother Attachment', *Child Development* 41 (1970), pp. 291–311.

[47] See Helene Borke.

[48] See the review essay by G. Steiner, 'Jean Piaget: Versuch einer Wirkungs-und Problemgeschichte', in: *Hommage à Jean Piaget zum achtzigsten Geburtstag* (Stuttgart 1976), pp. 49–114.

[49] See L. Kohlberg, *Stage and Sequence*, and R. Selman, 'Taking another's perspective'; Monika Keller, *Kognitive Entwicklung und soziale Kompetenz. Zur Entstelung der Rollenübernahme in der Familie und ihrer Bedentung für den Schulerfolg* (Stuttgart 1976), pp. 65–6.

[50] L. Kohlberg, ibid., p. 229.

[51] Ibid., p. 84.

[52] On Blumer see my remarks in Käsler (ed.), *Klassiker des soziologischen Denkens*, p. 35ff.

[53] Cf. Richard Bernstein's thesis, in opposition to Habermas (in the introduction to the German edition of *Praxis and Action*, p. 26), that there is no such thing as a truly monological use of language, and Schurig's insistence on a 'socialization of the instrument or the manipulated object' among human beings (Schurig, *Die Entstehung des Bewusstseins*, p. 26).

[54] In my earlier writings on Mead I strongly stressed that Mead's concept of action is oriented too much to the model of adaptive commerce with nature and too little to the objectification of human activity in its products and the material production of new objects. I stand by this assessment and continue to consider this deficiency in Mead's concept of action an important one with negative implications for his theory of society. On the other hand, I can no longer see that it has detrimental consequences for the psychology of perception. Arthur Murphy's critique of Mead rests on a silly misunderstanding; from Murphy's standpoint of common-sense realism, any theory of object-constitution is a subjectivism.

CHAPTER 8

[1] I should explain why the 'fragments from Mead's literary estate', which were published by Miller (Nos. 100 and 101), play such a small role in my interpretation. As I was able to establish beyond all doubt, these texts are not at all the fragments of Mead's own writings which Miller claims they are. Rather, they are a compilation of student notes arranged by Miller, which were intentionally excluded from *The Philosophy of the Act*. These 'fragments' are editorially a very questionable matter.

[2] Mead, *Philosophy of the Present*, p. 1.

[3] Ibid., p. 14.

236   G. H. Mead

[4] See chapter 2.

[5] On this complex of themes, see also the interpretation of Hegel in *Movements of Thought*.

[6] See Hermann Weyl (quoted from Kröner, *Philosophie*).

[7] Mead, *Philosophy of the Present*, p. 28.

[8] See D. L. Miller's article on James, 'William James and the Specious Present', in: W. R. Corti (ed.), *The Philosophy of William James* (Hamburg 1976), pp. 51–79.

[9] Cf. above all Mead, 'Passage, Process, and Permanence', in: *Philosophy of the Act*.

[10] See M. Capek's excellent article on this topic, 'The Myth of Frozen Passage: The Status of Becoming in the Physical World', in: *Boston Studies in the Philosophy of Science* 2 (1965), pp. 441–63.

[11] Mead, *Philosophy of the Present*, p. 32.

[12] On Mead's reception of Whitehead's ideas, see the editor's remarks in the introduction to *The Philosophy of the Act* (p. xliv, n. 55) and also Cook's article, 'Whitehead's Influence on the Thought of G. H. Mead'. Contrary to an opinion which is widespread in Mead scholarship, Mead was by no means in complete agreement with the relevant book by Dewey, *Experience and Nature* (London 1929). As one of several proofs, see the transcript of his course on Dewey (Chicago, Box VII, Folder 1).

[13] Mead, *Philosophy of the Present*, p. 43.

[14] J. v. Uexküll, G. Kriszat, *Streifzüge durch die Umwelten von Tieren und Menschen/Bedeutungslehre* (Hamburg 1976).

[15] Mead, *Philosophy of the Present*, p. 43.

[16] Ibid., pp. 20–21.

[17] Ibid., p. 33.

[18] Ibid., pp. 27–28.

[19] C. Lloyd Morgan, *Emergent Evolution* (London 1923); Samuel Alexander, *Space, Time, and Deity* (London 1920). For a critique of the emergentists, see Piaget, *Biology and knowledge* (Edinburgh 1972). In Germany, the work of Gehlen's teacher, Hans Driesch, is similar to this current of thought.

[20] Mead, *Philosophy of the Present*, p. 33.

[21] Ibid., p. 12.

[22] Here I am thinking of Jacques Monod, on the one hand, and of the ecological movement, on the other.

[23] Mead, *Philosophy of the Present*, p. 15.

[24] Ibid., pp. 25–26.

[25] This corresponds to the meaning of the concept of the 'passive synthesis' of time in the works of Husserl and Merleau-Ponty.

[26] Mead, *Philosophy of the Present*, p. 18.

[27] Ibid., pp. 30–31.

[28] In a happy formulation, M. Natanson said that Mead was not a historical relativist, but a temporal relationist (in 'G. H. Mead's Metaphysics of Time', *Journal of Philosophy* 50 (1953), pp. 770–82).

[29] Mead, *Philosophy of the Present*, p. 31.

[30] Ibid.

[31] Mead, 'Theory of the Past' (Reck (ed.)), p. 353.

[32] Mead, *Philosophy of the Present*, p. 49.

[33] Ibid., p. 86.

[34] Ibid., p. 63.

[35] Ibid., p. 47.

[36] See C. A. van Peursen, *Wirklichkeit als Ereignis. Eine deiktische Ontologie* (Freiburg/Munich 1973).

[37] Cf. the article 'Social Psychology as Counterpart to Physiological Psychology' (No. 47), discussed in chapter 5.

[38] Mead, *Philosophy of the Present*, p. 48.

[39] Mead, 'The Objective Reality of Perspectives' (in: *Philosophy of the Present*), p. 172.

[40] See the transcript by G. E. M. Shelbury (Chicago, Box VIII, Folder 5), p. 44.

[41] See Mead, 'Suggestions' (No. 17), p. 2 and chapter 3 of this book.

[42] Oddly, a passage on just this point is missing in a fragment included in *The Philosophy of the Act*.

[43] Piaget, *Biology and Knowledge*.

[44] Mead, *Philosophy of the Present*, p. 62.

[45] On this point see the article by Peter Keiler, who draws strongly on the arguments of Jessor, 'The Problem of Reductionism in Psychology', *Psychological Review* 65 (1958), pp. 170–78. See also Mead, 'Philosophy of the Act', pp. 224–5.

[46] Mead, *Philosophy of the Present*, pp. 80–1.

[47] This manuscript is part of a coherent portion of Mead's literary estate, which was divided by Mead's editors. The quotation is to be found in the appendix to *Mind, Self, and Society*, pp. 350–1.

[48] Mead, 'Theory of the Past', p. 349.

[49] Merleau-Ponty, *Phenomenology of Perception*; Piaget.

[50] Mead, *Philosophy of the Present*, pp. 87–8.

[51] Ibid., p. 76.

[52] See chapter 5.

[53] See chapter 7.

[54] Mead, 'Genesis of the Self' (in: *Philosophy of the Present*), p. 190: 'If we reduce the world to a fictitious instantaneous present, all objects fall to pieces. There is no reason to be found except in an equally fictitious mind, why any lines should be drawn about any group of physical particles constituting them objects . . . When we take this passage of nature seriously, we see that the object of perception is the existent future of the act.'

[55] Mead, 'Philosophy of the Act', pp. 236–7.

[56] Ibid., p. 266.

[57] See the preface to his book on time and his book *Genetic Epistemology*.

[58] Investigated more thoroughly by Piaget in *The Child's Construction of Reality*.

[59] Such as those of Paul Fraisse.

[60] Agnes Heller, *Das Alltagsleben* (Frankfurt 1978), pp. 301–9; and William Smoot, 'The Social Context of Death Anxiety', *Philosophy Today* 21 (1977), pp. 84–9.

CHAPTER 9

[1] See this book, pp. 108–9.

[2] Mead, 'The Nature of Aesthetic Experience' (No. 85), pp. 382–3.

[3] This includes Manuscripts II, III, IV, XXX F and other parts.

⁴ Charles Morris, 'G. H. Mead: A Pragmatist's Philosophy of Science', in: B. B. Wolman (ed.), *Scientific Psychology* (New York 1965).

⁵ Thomas Kuhn, *The Structure of Scientific Revolutions* (Chicago 1970).

⁶ I leave out of consideration here Mead's important observations on the status of subjectivity in ancient philosophy, in which it appears only as scepticism or anarchy, and in German idealism, to which Mead ascribed the merit of mediating objectivity by way of subjectivity, but which he criticized because of its separation of speculation from science, declared to be essentially limited.

⁷ Mead, 'Scientific Method and Individual Thinker' (No. 73), pp. 190–1 (in Reck (ed.)). This passage and many others in which Mead expresses opposition to neo-realism also show how wrong it was of Morris and other editors to give titles to fragments from his unpublished writings in which Mead is made into a 'realist'.

⁸ Ibid., pp. 193–4.

⁹ Mead, 'Mind, Self, and Society', p. 352.

¹⁰ Mead's review of Hobson (No. 82).

¹¹ See chapter 8.

¹² This distinction is made by Apel in his introduction to the German translation of Peirce's works (Vol. I, p. 55). This is also an important problem for Marxism's understanding of itself as a science. See, for the present, my reply to Johannes Berger and his counter-answer, 'Intersubjektive Sinnkonstitution und Sozialstruktur', in: *Zeitschrift für Soziologie* 8 (1979), pp. 198–201.

¹³ Mead, 'Philosophy of the Act', pp. 291–2.

¹⁴ Ibid., p. 32.

¹⁵ Ibid., pp. 33–4.

¹⁶ Ibid., pp. 398–9: 'While science is a social undertaking both because of the social nature of the scientist's mind and because of the social character of the scientist's universe of discourse within which investigation takes place, the conception of a determined social and moral order has no place in the technique and method of research science.'

¹⁷ Böhler, 'Paradigmawechsel in der analytischen Wissenschaftstheorie?'; *Zeitschrift für allgemeine Wissenschaftstheorie* 3 (1972), pp. 219–42. The criticism of Thomas Kuhn because of putative irrationalism is in my opinion without foundation.

¹⁸ See D. L. Miller, 'William James and the Specious Present' and chapter 5 of this book.

¹⁹ See chapter 8; Jonathan Bennett's article on Whitehead and Husserl is excellent: 'Husserl's "Crisis" and Whitehead's Process Philosophy', *The Personalist* 56 (1975), pp. 289–300.

²⁰ Mead, 'Philosophy of the Act', p. 49.

²¹ Ibid., p. 57.

²² See also T. C. Keen, *Mead's Social Theory*, pp. 179–80.

²³ See Piaget, *Weisheit und Illusionen*, p. 114 (*Sagesse et Illusions de la Philosophie*). The articles by Sandra Rosenthal revolve around this problematic.

²⁴ For a critique of Piaget in this regard, see the important book by H.-C. Harten, *Der vernünftige Organismus*.

²⁵ Mead, 'Philosophy of the Act', p. 516.

²⁶ Scheler's critical examination of pragmatism accepts the pragmatic character of science, but emphatically rejects such a character for philosophy. For the opposite

position, see Herbert Marcuse, 'On Science and Phenomenology', *Boston Studies in the Philosophy of Science* 2 (1965), pp. 279–91, and Habermas's remarks on Husserl in his lecture, 'Erkenntnis und Interesse', published in: *Technik und Wissenschaft als Ideologie* (Frankfurt 1968).

[27] In my opinion, the view, which is widespread among sociologists, that Husserl also took this path in *Die Krisis der europäischen Wissenschaften*, is convincingly refuted by Gadamer in his work 'Die phänomenologische Bewegung', *Philosophische Rundschau* (1963), pp. 1–45.

[28] On this point Peter Gross is very clear.

[29] The expression is from Walter Bühl, *Einführung in die Wissenschaftssoziologie* (München 1974).

[30] The lectures on 'Movements of Thought' are an exception, cf. p. 168.

[31] Mead, 'Philosophy of the Act', p. 39.

[32] See the important essay by Gernot Böhme et al., 'Die Finalisierung der Wissenschaft', *Zeitschrift für Soziologie* 2 (1973), pp. 128–44.

[33] Mead, 'Philosophy of the Act', p. 474.

[34] Mead, 'Scientific Method and Individual Thinker', p. 209.

[35] See also chapter 6.

[36] See also chapter 2.

[37] See Kuhn, *The Structure of Scientific Revolutions*.

[38] Symbolic interactionism is not simply the authentic sociological concretization of Mead's approach. For a critique of the deficiencies of Mead's concept of action, see my article in Käsler (ed.), *Klassiker*, where, in connection with this question, I also discuss Mead's relation to the economic theory of value. There is now additional material for the study of this relation, thanks to the recent discovery (by Harold Orbach) of Mead's review of Simmel's *The Philosophy of Money (Philosophie des Geldes)* (No. 18). I do not undertake such a study in the present work, as its proper place seems to me to be in a general clarification of the relationship between pragmatism and historical materialism.

[39] Although this is denied most of the time with regard to both Dewey and Mead, there is for Mead, in particular, sufficient evidence to the contrary; for example, *Movements of Thought*, p. 30, p. 276.

[40] Mead, 'The Nature of Aesthetic Experience' (No. 85), p. 388.

[41] Ibid., p. 389.

[42] Ibid.

Bibliography

1. LIST OF WORKS

The following bibliography of the published writings of George Herbert Mead is the most comprehensive to date. It lists numerous works not contained in the usual Mead bibliography, found in the appendix to *Mind, Self, and Society*. Recent years have seen a steady rediscovery of Mead's works. Moreover, my own bibliographical inquiries have led to many additional discoveries. But simply because of these successes I would not want to claim comprehensiveness; rather, I would be grateful for further endeavours and for information about other works. Since this bibliography was first published in Volume 2 of Dirk Käsler (ed.) *Klassiker des soziologischen Denkens* (Munich 1978), p. 417ff. a new find has come to light, which appears here as No. 18.

1.1. Works in Chronological Order

1 'The Relation of Art to Morality', *Oberlin Review* 9 (1881), pp. 63/64.
2 'Charles Lamb', *Oberlin Review* 10 (1882–83), pp. 15/16.
3 'De Quincey', *Oberlin Review* 10 (1882–83), pp. 50–2.
4 'John Locke', *Oberlin Review* 10 (1882–83), pp. 217–9.
5 'Republican Persecution (Letter to the Editor)', *The Nation* 39 (1884), pp. 519–20.
6 'The Problem of Psychological Measurement' (Abstract of a paper read to the second annual meeting of the American Psychological Association, 1893). *Proceedings of the American Psychological Association* (New York 1894), pp. 22/23.
7 'Herr Lasswitz on Energy and Epistemology', *Psychological Review* 1 (1894), pp. 172–5.
8 'Review of K. Lasswitz, Die moderne Energetik in ihrer Bedeutung für die Erkenntniskritik', *Psychological Review* 1 (1894), pp. 210–3.
9 'Review of C. L. Morgan, An Introduction to Comparative Psychology', *Psychological Review* 2 (1895), pp. 399–402.

240

10 'A Theory of Emotions from the Physiological Standpoint' (Abstract of a paper read to the third annual meeting of the American Psychological Association, 1894), *Psychological Review* 2 (1895), pp. 162–4.

11 'The Relation of Play to Education', *University of Chicago Record* 1 (1896), pp. 140–5.

12 'Some Aspects of Greek Philosophy', *University of Chicago Record* 1 (1896), p. 42.

13 'Review of G. Class, Untersuchungen zur Phänomenologie und Ontologie des menschlichen Geistes', *American Journal of Theology* 1 (1897), pp. 789–92.

14 'The Child and His Environment', *Transactions of the Illinois Society for Child Study* 3 (1898), pp. 1–11.

15 'The Working Hypothesis in Social Reform', *American Journal of Sociology* 5 (1899), pp. 367–71.

16 'Review of G. Le Bon, The Psychology of Socialism', *American Journal of Sociology* 5 (1899), pp. 404–12.

17 'Suggestions Towards a Theory of the Philosophical Disciplines', *Philosophical Review* 9 (1900), pp. 1–17.

18 'Review of G. Simmel, Philosophie des Geldes', *Journal of Political Economy* 9 (1900–1), pp. 616–9.

19 'A New Criticism of Hegelianism: Is It Valid? (Review of C. F. D'Arcy, Idealism and Theology)', *American Journal of Theology* 5 (1901), pp. 87–96.

20 'The Definition of the Psychical', *Decennial Publications of the University of Chicago*, First Series, Vol. III (Chicago 1903), pp. 77–112.

21 'The Basis for a Parents' Association', *Elementary School Teacher* 4 (1903–4), pp. 337–46.

22 'Image or Sensation', *Journal of Philosophy* 1 (1904), pp. 604–7.

23 'The Relations of Psychology and Philology', *Psychological Bulletin* 1 (1904), pp. 375–91.

24 'Review of D. Draghiscesco, Du rôle de l'individu dans le déterminisme social, and D. Draghiscesco, Le problème du déterminisme, déterminisme biologique et déterminisme social', *Psychological Bulletin* 2 (1905), pp. 399–405.

25 'Review of Paul Jacoby, Etudes sur la sélection chez l'homme', *Psychological Bulletin* 2 (1905), pp. 407–12.

26 'Science in the High School', *School Review* 14 (1906), pp. 237–49.

27 'The Imagination in Wundt's Treatment of Myth and Religion', *Psychological Bulletin* 3 (1906), pp. 393–9.

28 'The Teaching of Science in College', *Science* 24 (1906), pp. 390–7.

29 'Concerning Animal Perception', *Psychological Review* 14 (1907), pp. 383–90.

30 'The School System of Chicago: Editorial Note', *School Review* 15 (1907), pp. 160–5.

31 'Review of Jane Addams, The Newer Ideals of Peace', *American Journal of Sociology* 13 (1907), pp. 121–8.

32 'Review of Henri Bergson, L'Evolution créatrice', *Psychological Bulletin* 4 (1907), pp. 379–84.

33 'The Relation of Imitation to the Theory of Animal Perception' (Abstract of a paper read to the fifteenth annual meeting of the American Psychological Association, 1906), *Psychological Bulletin* 4 (1907), pp. 210/211.

34 'The Educational Situation in the Chicago Public Schools', *City Club Bulletin* 1 (1907–8), pp. 131–8.

35 'Educational Aspects of Trade Schools', *Union Labor Advocate* 8 (1908), pp. 19/20.

36 'The Philosophical Basis of Ethics', *International Journal of Ethics* 18 (1908), pp. 311–23.

37 'The Social Settlement, Its Basis and Function', *University of Chicago Record* 12 (1907–8), pp. 108–10.

38 'Review of W. McDougall, An Introduction to Social Psychology', *Psychological Bulletin* 5 (1908), pp. 385–91.

39 'Review of P. Gaultier, L'Idéal moderne', *Psychological Bulletin* 5 (1908), pp. 403–4.

40 'Policy Statement of the "Elementary School Teacher", Editorial Note', *Elementary School Teacher* 8 (1907–8), pp. 281–4.

41 'Industrial Education and Trade Schools, Editorial Note', *Elementary School Teacher* 8 (1907–8), pp. 402–6.

42 'Resolution on Industrial Education, Editorial Note', *Elementary School Teacher* 9 (1908–9), pp. 156–7.

43 'Industrial Training, Editorial Note', *Elementary School Teacher* 9 (1908–9), pp. 212–4.

44 'Industrial Education, the Working-Man, and the School', *Elementary School Teacher* 9 (1908–9), pp. 369–83.

45 'Moral Training in the Schools, Editorial Note', *Elementary School Teacher* 9 (1908–9), pp. 327–8.

46 'The Problem of History in the Elementary School', Editorial Note, *Elementary School Teacher* 9 (1908–9), pp. 433–4.

47 'Social Psychology as Counterpart to Physiological Psychology', *Psychological Bulletin* 6 (1909), pp. 401–8.

48 'Social Consciousness and the Consciousness of Meaning', *Psychological Bulletin* 7 (1910), pp. 397–405).

49 'The Psychology of Social Consciousness Implied in Instruction', *Science* 31 (1910), pp. 688–93.

50 'What Social Objects does Psychology Presuppose' (Abstract of a paper read to the eighteenth annual meeting of the American Psychological Association, 1909), *Psychological Bulletin* 7 (1910), pp. 52–3.

51 'What Social Objects Must Psychology Presuppose?', *Journal of Philosophy* 7 (1910), pp. 174–80.

52 'Review of B. M. Anderson jr., Social Value, A Study in Economic Theory', *Psychological Bulletin* 8 (1911), pp. 432–6.

53 'Review of W. Fite, Individualism: Four lectures on the Significance of Consciousness for Social Relations', *Psychological Bulletin* 8 (1911), pp. 323-8.

54 'The Mechanism of Social Consciousness', *Journal of Philosophy* 9 (1912), pp. 401–6.

55 'A Report on Vocational Training in Chicago and in other Cities', by a committee of the City Club, George H. Mead, Chairman (Chicago 1912).

56 'Exhibit of the City Club Committee on Public Education', *City Club Bulletin* 5 (1912), p. 9.

57 'Remarks on Labor Night Concerning Participation of Representatives of Labor in the City Club', *City Club Bulletin* 5 (1912), pp. 214–5.

58 'The Social Self', *Journal of Philosophy* 10 (1913), pp. 374–80.

59 'A Heckling School Board and an Educational Stateswoman', *Survey* 31 (1914), pp. 443–4.

60 'Natural Rights and the Theory of the Political Institution', *Journal of Philosophy* 12 (1915), pp. 141–55.

61 'Constitutional and Political Guarantees' (Lecture to the American Philosophical Association), *Philosophical Review* 24 (1915), p. 193f; Summary by W. F. Dodd.

62 'The Psychological Bases of Internationalism', *Survey* 33 (1915), pp. 604–7.

63 'The Larger Educational Bearings of Vocational Guidance', in: Meyer Bloomfield (ed.), *Readings in Vocational Guidance* (Boston 1915), pp. 43–55.

64 'Madison: The passage of the University of Wisconsin through the state political agitation of 1914; the survey by William H. Allen and his staff and the legislative fight of 1915, with the indications these offer of the place the state university holds in the community, *Survey* 35 (1915), pp. 349–51, pp. 354–61.

65 'Smashing the Looking-Glass: A Rejoinder', *Survey* 35 (1915), p. 607, p. 610 (Answer to criticism of No. 64).

66 'Professor Hoxie and the Community', *University of Chicago Magazine* 9 (1916–7), pp. 114–7.

67 'The Conscientious Objector'. (*National Security League, Patriotism through Education Series*. Pamphlet No. 33) New York 1918.

68 'Germany's Crisis – Its Effect on Labor', *Chicago Herald* 1917.

69 'America's Ideals and the War', *Chicago Herald* 1917.

70 'Democracy's Issues in the World War', *Chicago Herald* 1917.

71 'War Issues to U.S. Forced by Kaiser', *Chicago Herald* 1917.

72 'Josiah Royce – A Personal Impression', *International Journal of Ethics* 27 (1917), pp. 168–70.

73 'Scientific Method and Individual Thinker', in: John Dewey et al.

(eds), *Creative Intelligence: Essays in the Pragmatic Attitude* (New York 1917), pp. 176–227.

74 'Review of E. Abbott and S. P. Breckinridge, Truancy and Non-Attendance in the Chicago Schools', *Survey* 38 (1917), pp. 369–70.

75 'The Psychology of Punitive Justice', *American Journal of Sociology* 23 (1918), pp. 577–602.

76 'Review of Th. Veblen, The Nature of Peace and the Terms of Its Perpetuation', *Journal of Political Economy* 26 (1918), pp. 752–62.

77 'Review of A Translation of Wundt's "Folk Psychology"', *American Journal of Theology* 23 (1919), pp. 533–36.

78 'Retiring President's Address', *City Club Bulletin* 13 (1920), pp. 94–5, pp. 97–9.

79 'Articles: "Idea", "Ideal", "Individualism", "Infinity", "Law of Nature" and "Natural Law" in: Shailer Mathews and Gerald Birney Smith (eds), *A Dictionary of Religion and Ethics* (New York 1921).

80 'A Behavioristic Account of the Significant Symbol', *Journal of Philosophy* 19 (1922), pp. 157–63.

81 'Scientific Method and the Moral Sciences', *International Journal of Ethics* 33 (1923), pp. 229–47.

82 'Review of E. W. Hobson, The Domain of Natural Science', *Journal of Religion* 4 (1924), pp. 324–7.

83 'Ella Adams Moore', *Bulletin of the Vocational Supervision League*, 1924.

84 'The Genesis of the Self and Social Control', *International Journal of Ethics* 35 (1925), pp. 251–77.

85 'The Nature of Aesthetic Experience, *International Journal of Ethics* 36 (1926), pp. 382–92.

86 'The Objective Reality of Perspectives', in: Edgar S. Brightman (ed.), *Proceedings of the Sixth International Congress of Philosophy* (New York 1926), pp. 75–85.

87 'A Pragmatic Theory of Truth, "Studies in the Nature of Truth"' *University of California Publications in Philosophy* 11 (1929), pp. 65–88.

88 'Bishop Berkeley and his Message', *Journal of Philosophy* 26 (1929), pp. 421–430.

89 'National-Mindedness and International-Mindedness', *International Journal of Ethics* 39 (1929), pp. 385–407.

90 'The Nature of the Past', in: John Coss (ed.), *Essays in Honor of John Dewey* (New York 1929), pp. 235–42.

91 'Cooley's Contribution to American Social Thought', *American Journal of Sociology* 35 (1930), pp. 693–706.

92 'Philanthropy from the Point of View of Ethics', in: E. Faris, F. Laune and A. J. Todd (eds), *Intelligent Philanthropy* (Chicago 1930), pp. 133–48.

93 'The Philosophies of Royce, James, and Dewey in Their American Setting', *International Journal of Ethics* 40 (1930), pp. 211–31.

94 'Dr. A. W. Moore's Philosophy', *University of Chicago Record*, New Series, 17 (1931), pp. 47–9.
95 *The Philosophy of the Present*. Edited by Arthur E. Murphy. La Salle (Illinois) 1932. (This volume contains the following essays in its appendix: Empirical Realism, pp. 93–118; The Physical Thing, pp. 119–39; Scientific Objects and Experience, pp. 140–60; and nos 84 and 86 of this bibliography).
96 *Mind, Self, and Society*, Edited by Charles W. Morris (Chicago 1934).
97 *The Philosophy of John Dewey*, International Journal of Ethics 46 (1936), pp. 64–81.
98 *Movements of Thought in the Nineteenth Century*, Edited by Merritt H. Moore (Chicago 1936).
99 *The Philosophy of the Act*, Edited by Charles W. Morris et al. (Chicago 1938).
100 Relative Space-Time and Simultaneity, *Review of Metaphysics* 17 (1963–4), pp. 514–35.
101 Metaphysics, *Review of Metaphysics* 17 (1963–4), pp. 536–56.
102 'Mead on the Child and the School', edited by Darnell Rucker, *School and Society* 44 (1968), pp. 148–52.

1.2. Volumes of Collected Works

Anselm Strauss (ed.), *G. H. Mead on Social Psychology* (Chicago 1964).
Andrew Reck (ed.), *G. H. Mead: Selected Writings* (Indianapolis 1964).
John W. Petras (ed.), *G. H. Mead: Essays on his Social Philosophy* (New York 1968).
Since many works of Mead are difficult to obtain from their original place of publication, I indicate in the following the contents of these collected volumes:
Strauss contains essays Nos. 86 and 91 as well as excerpts from all four books of Mead. (95, 96, 98, 99).
Reck Nr. 17, 28, 29, 36, 47, 49, 51, 54, 58, 60, 73, 75, 80, 81, 84, 85, 86, 87, 89, 90, 92, 93 as well as excerpts from Nos. 15 and 20.
Petras contains Nos. 11, 15, 21, 35, 36, 40, 44, 45, 56, 62, 75, 81, 92, 93.

2. SELECT BIBLIOGRAPHY OF SECONDARY LITERATURE ON MEAD

Barry, Robert M., 'A Man and a City: G. H. Mead in Chicago', in: Michael Novak (ed.), *American Philosophy and the Future* (New York 1968), pp. 173–92.
Baumann, Bedrich, G. H. Mead and Luigi Pirandello, Some Parallels between the Theoretical and Artistic Presentations of the Social Role Concept, *Social Research* 34 (1967), pp. 563–607.

Berg, Lars-Erik, 'Människans Födelse, En socialpsykologisk diskussion kring G. H. Mead och J. Piaget' (Göteborg 1976) (English summary, pp. 169–78).

Betz, Joseph, 'G. H. Mead on human rights', *Transactions of the Ch. S. Peirce Society* 10 (1974), pp. 199–223.

Bittner, Carl J., 'G. H. Mead's Social Concept of the Self', *Sociology and Social Research* 16 (1931), pp. 6–22.

Blumer, Herbert, 'Sociological Implications of the Thought of G. H. Mead', *American Journal of Sociology* 71 (1966), pp. 535–44.

Brewster, John M., 'A Behavioristic Account of the Logical Function of Universals', *Journal of Philosophy* 33 (1936), pp. 505–14 and pp. 533–47.

Brotherston, Bruce W., 'The Genius of Pragmatic Empiricism', *Journal of Philosophy* 40 (1943), pp. 14–21 and pp. 29–39.

Broyer, John Albin, *The Ethical Theory of G. H. Mead*. Diss. 1967 (University of Southern Illinois).

Broyer, John Albin, 'Mead's Ethical Theory', in: W. R. Corti (ed.), *The Philosophy of G. H. Mead* (Winterthur 1973), pp. 171–92.

Burker, Richard, 'G. H. Mead and the Problem of Metaphysics', *Philosophy and Phenomenological Research* 23 (1962–3), pp. 81–8.

Chang, Yen-Ling, 'The Problem of Emergence: Mead and Whitehead', *Kinesis* 2 (1970), pp. 69–80.

Chasin, Gerald, 'G. H. Mead: Social Psychologist of the Moral Society', *Berkeley Journal of Sociology* 9 (1964), pp. 95–117.

Cook, Gary Allan, *The self as moral agent*. Diss. 1965–6 (Yale).

Cook, Gary Allan, 'The development of G. H. Mead's Social Psychology', *Transactions of the Ch. S. Peirce Society* 8 (1972), pp. 167–86.

Cook, Gary Allan, 'Review of D. L. Miller', *Transactions of the Ch. S. Peirce Society* 10 (1974), pp. 253–60.

Cook, Gary Allan, 'G. H. Mead's Alleged Behaviorism', *Journal of the History of the Behavioral Sciences* 13 (1977), pp. 307–16.

Cook, Gary Allan, 'Whitehead's Influence on the Thought of G. H. Mead', *Transactions of the Ch. S. Peirce Society* 15 (1979), pp. 107–31.

Corti, Walter Robert (ed.), *The Philosophy of G. H. Mead* (Winterthur 1973).

Cronk, George Francis, *G. H. Mead on Time and Action*. Diss. 1972 (University of Southern Illinios).

Cronk, George Francis, 'Symbolic Interactionism: A "Left-Meadian" Interpretation', *Social Theory and Practice* 2 (1973), pp. 313–33.

Coser, Lewis, 'G. H. Mead', in: Coser, *Masters of Sociological Thought* (New York 1971), pp. 333–55.

Desmonde, William, 'G. H. Mead and Freud: American Social Psychology and Psychoanalysis', *Psychoanalysis* 4/5, 1955–6, pp. 31–50.

Doan, Frank M., 'Remarks on G. H. Mead's Conception of Simultaneity', *Journal of Philosophy* 55 (1958), pp. 203–9.

Donovan, Richard, 'Review of D. L. Miller', *International Philosophical Quarterly* 14 (1974), pp. 131–3.

Eames, Elizabeth R., 'Mead's Concept of Time', in: W. R. Corti (ed.), *The Philosophy of G. H. Mead* (Winterthur 1973), pp. 59–81.

Ekins, Richard, *G. H. Mead: Contributions to a Philosophy of Sociological Knowledge*. Diss. 1978 (University of London).

Faris, Ellsworth, 'Review of "Mind, Self, and Society"', *American Journal of Sociology* 41 (1936), pp. 909–13.

Faris, Ellsworth, 'The Social Psychology of G. H. Mead', *American Journal of Sociology* 43 (1937–8), pp. 391–403.

Fen, Sing-Nan, 'Present and Re-Presentation: A Discussion of Mead's Philosophy of the Present', *Philosophical Review* 60 (1951), pp. 545–50.

Fisher, Berenice M. and Strauss, Anselm L., 'G. H. Mead and the Chicago Tradition of Sociology', *Symbolic Interaction* 2 (1979), pp. 9–25.

Fleck, Leonard, 'G. H. Mead on Knowledge and Action', *Proceedings of the American Catholic Philosophical Association* 17 (1973), pp. 76–86.

Gillin, Charles T., 'Freedom and the Limits of Social Behaviorism', *Sociology* 9 (1975), pp. 29–47.

Harris, Donalf F., *A Categorical Approach to G. H. Mead's Concept of the Self*. Diss. 1972 (Columbia University).

Hinkle, Gisela J., '"Forms" and "Types" in the Study of Human Behavior: An Examination of the Generalizing Concepts of Mead and Schutz', *Kansas Journal of Sociology* 8 (1972), pp. 111–22.

Hook, Sidney, 'Review of "Movements of Thoughts"', *The Nation*, 143 (1936), pp. 220–1.

Joas, Hans, 'G. H. Mead', in: Dirk Käsler (ed.), *Klassiker des soziologischen Denkens* 2 (Munich 1978), pp. 7–39.

Joas, Hans, 'Intersubjektivität bei Mead und Gehlen', *Archiv für Rechts- und Sozialphilosophie* 65 (1979), pp. 105–21.

Jones, Martin Monroe, *The Categorial Concept of Emergence in the Philosophy of G. H. Mead*. Diss. 1970 (Tulane University).

Kang, Wook, *G. H. Mead's Conception of Rationality: A Study in Philosophical Anthropology*. Diss. 1970 (Columbia University).

Keen, Tom Clifton, *Mead's Social Theory of Meaning and Experience*. Diss. 1968 (Columbus, Ohio).

Kellner, Hansfried, 'Introduction to G. H. Mead', *Philosophie der Sozialität* (Frankfurt 1969), pp. 9–35.

Lee, Grace Chin, *G. H. Mead, Philosopher of the Social Individual* (New York 1945).

Lee, Harold N., 'Mead's Doctrine of the Past', *Tulane Studies in Philosophy* 12 (1963), pp. 52–75.

Lewis, J. David, 'Peirce, Mead, and the Objectivity of Meaning', *Kansas Journal of Sociology* 8 (1972), pp. 111–22.

Lewis, J. David, 'The Classical American Pragmatists as Forerunners to

Symbolic Interactionism', *Sociological Quarterly* 17 (1976), pp. 347–59.

Lincourt, John M., *Precursors in American Philosophy of G. H. Mead's Theory of Emergent Selfhood*. Diss. 1972 (Buffalo, New York).

Loch, Werner, 'Rollenübernahme und Selbstverwirklichung', in: G. Bräuer et al., *Studien zur Anthropologie des Lernens* (Essen 1968), pp. 65–89.

McKinney, John C., 'The Contribution of G. H. Mead to the Sociology of Knowledge', *Social Forces* 34 (1955), pp. 144–9.

McKinney, John C., 'G. H. Mead and the Philosophy of Science', *Philosophy of Science* 22 (1955), pp. 264–71.

McPhail, Clark, and Rexroat, Cynthia, 'Mead Vs. Blumer: The Divergent Methodological Perspectives of Social Behaviorism and Symbolic Interactionism', *American Sociological Review* 44 (1979), pp. 449–67.

Meltzer, Bernard N., 'Mead's Social Psychology', in: Jerome G. Manis, and Bernard N. Meltzer (eds), *Symbolic Interaction* (Boston 1972), pp. 4–22.

Miller, David L., 'The Nature of the Physical Object', *Journal of Philosophy* 44 (1947), pp. 352–9.

Miller, David L., *G. H. Mead. Self, Language, and the World* (Austin, Texas 1973).

Miller, David L., 'Mead's Theory of Universals', in: W. R. Corti (ed.), *The Philosophy of G. H. Mead* (Winterthur 1973), pp. 89–106.

Miller, David L., 'Josiah Royce and G. H. Mead on the Nature of the Self', *Transactions of the Ch. S. Peirce Society* 11 (1975), No. 2, pp. 67–89.

Moran, Jon S., 'Mead on the Self and Moral Situations', *Tulane Studies in Philosophy* 22 (1973), pp. 63–78.

Morris, Charles, 'Peirce, Mead, and Pragmatism', *Philosophical Review* 47 (1938), pp. 109–27.

Morris, Charles, 'G. H. Mead: 'A Pragmatist's Philosophy of Science', in: B. B. Wolman (ed.), *Scientific Psychology* (New York 1965).

Morris, Charles, 'Review of Natanson', *International Journal of Ethics* 67 (1957), pp. 145–6.

Murphy, Arthur E., 'Concerning Mead's *Philosophy of the Act*', *Journal of Philosophy* 36 (1939), pp. 85–103.

Musolino, Giovanna Rosa, 'G. H. Mead: per una "tecnologia" della creatività umana', in: Ada Lamacchia et al., *Per una storia della critica del conoscere* (Bari 1976), pp. 143–63.

Natanson, Maurice, 'The Concept of the Given in Peirce and Mead', *The Modern Schoolman* 32 (1955), pp. 143–57.

Natanson, Maurice, 'G. H. Mead's Metaphysics of Time', *Journal of Philosophy* 50 (1953), pp. 770–82.

Natanson, Maurice, *The Social Dynamics of G. H. Mead* (Washington 1956).

Nieddu, Anna Maria, *G. H. Mead* (Sassari 1978).

Perinbanayagam, Robert S., 'The Significance of Others in the Thought of A. Schütz, G. H. Mead and C. H. Cooley', *Sociological Quarterly* 16 (1975), pp. 500–21.

Petras, John W., 'G. H. Mead's Theory of Self: A Study in the Origin and Convergence of Ideas', *The Canadian Review of Sociology and Anthropology* 10 (1973), pp. 148–59.

Pfuetze, Paul E., *Self, Society, Existence. Human Nature and Dialogue in the Thought of G. H. Mead and Martin Buber* (New York 1961).

Raiser, Konrad, *Identität und Sozialität. George Herbert Meads Theorie der Interaktion und ihre Bedeutung für die theologische Anthropologie* (Munich 1971).

Reck, Andrew, 'The Philosophy of G. H. Mead', *Tulane Studies in Philosophy* 12 (1963), pp. 5–51.

Ropers, Richard, 'Mead, Marx, and Social Psychology', *Catalyst* 7, 1973, pp. 42–61.

Rosenthal, Sandra, 'Peirce, Mead, and the Logic of Concepts', *Transactions of the Ch. S. Peirce Society* 5 (1969), pp. 173–87.

Rosenthal, Sandra, 'Mead, Merleau-Ponty, and the Lived Perceptual World, *Philosophy today* 21 (1977), No. 1, pp. 56–61.

Rosenthal, Sandra, 'Activity and the Structure of Perceptual Experience: Mead and Peirce Revisited', *Southern Journal of Philosophy* 15 (1977), pp. 207–14.

Scheffler, Israel, *Four Pragmatists* (London 1974).

Schellenberg, James A., *Masters of Social Psychology* (Oxford 1978).

Shibutani, Tamotsu, 'G. H. Mead', in: *International Encyclopedia of the Social Sciences* 10, (New York 1968), pp. 83–87.

Smith, Richard Lee, *G. H. Mead and Sociology: The Chicago Years.* Diss. 1977 (University of Illinois at Urbana-Champaign).

Smith, T. V., 'G. H. Mead and the Philosophy of Philanthropy', *Social Services Review* 6 (1932), pp. 37–54.

Smith, T. V., 'The Religious Bearings of a Secular Mind: G. H. Mead', *Journal of Religion* 12 (1932), pp. 200–13.

Smith, T. V., 'The Social Philosophy of G. H. Mead', *American Journal of Sociology* 37 (1931), pp. 368–85.

Stevens, Edward, 'Sociality and Act in G. H. Mead', *Social Research* 34 (1967), pp. 613–31.

Stormer, Gerald D., 'G. H. Mead: A Survey of Recent Critical Literature', *Southern Journal of Philosophy* 12 (1974), pp. 405–15.

Swanson, Guy, 'Mead and Freud: Their Relevance for Social Psychology', *Sociometry* 24 (1961), pp. 319–39.

Tibbetts, Paul, *Perception, Action and Reality in the Writings of G. H. Mead.* Diss. 1973 (Purdue University).

Tibbetts, Paul, 'Mead's Theory of Reality and the Knower-known Transaction', *Dialectica* 27 (1973), pp. 27–41.

Tibbetts, Paul, 'Mead, Phenomenalism and Phenomenology', *Philosophy today* 17 (1973), pp. 328–36.

Tibbetts, Paul, 'Mead's Theory of the Act and Perception: Some Empirical Confirmations', *The Personalist* 55 (1974), pp. 115–38.

Tibbetts, Paul, 'Peirce and Mead on Perceptual Immediacy and Human Action', *Philosophy and Phenomenological Research* 36 (1975), pp. 222–32.

Tillman, Mary Katherine, 'Temporality and Role-Taking in G. H. Mead', *Social Research* 37 (1970), pp. 533–46.

Tillman, Mary Katherine, Review of D. L. Miller, *Man and World* 7 (1974), pp. 293–300.

Tonness, Alfred, 'A Notation on the Problem of the Past – with Especial Reference to G. H. Mead', *Journal of Philosophy* 29 (1932), pp. 599–606.

Troyer, W. L., 'Mead's Social and Functional Theory of Mind', *American Sociological Review* 11 (1946), pp. 198–202.

Victoroff, David, G. H. Mead, *Sociologue et Philosophe*. (Paris 1953).

Wallace, David, 'Reflections on the Education of G. H. Mead', *American Journal of Sociology* 72 (1967), pp. 396–408.

Zeitlin, Irving, 'The Dialectical Philosophy of G. H. Mead', in: *Rethinking Sociology* (Englewood Cliffs 1973), pp. 219–42.

3. GENERAL BIBLIOGRAPHY

Abel, Reuben, 'Pragmatism and the Outlook of Modern Science', *Philosophy and Phenomenological Research* 27 (1966), pp. 45–54.

Angell, James R., and Moore, Addison, 'Reaction-Time: A Study in Attention and Habit', *Psychological Review* 3 (1896), pp. 245–58.

Apel, Karl-Otto, 'Das Leibapriori der Erkenntnis' (eine Betrachtung im Anschluß an Leibnizens Monadenlehre), *Archiv für Philosophie* 12 (1963), pp. 152–72.

Apel, Karl-Otto, *Transformation der Philosophie* 2 volumes (Frankfurt 1973).

Apel, Karl-Otto, *Charles Sanders Peirce, From Pragmatism to Pragmaticism* (Amherst, Massachusetts 1981).

Austin, John L., *How To Do Things with Words* (Cambridge, Massachusetts 1962).

Bell, Silvia M., The development of the concept of object as related to infant-mother attachment, *Child Development* 41 (1970), pp. 291–311.

Bennett, Jonathan, 'Husserl's "Crisis" and Whitehead's Process Philosophy', *The Personalist* 56 (1975), pp. 289–300.

Bergson, Henri, *Materie und Gedächtnis (und andere Schriften)* (Frankfurt 1964).

Bernstein, Richard, *Praxis and Action* (Philadelphia 1971).

Bernstein, Richard, *Einleitung zur deutschen Ausgabe* (Frankfurt 1975), pp. 7–30.

Bernstein, Richard, 'Peirce's Theory of Perception', in: Edward C. Moore, and Richard S. Robin, *Studies in the Philosophy of Ch. S. Peirce*. Second Series (Amherst, Massachusetts 1964), pp. 165–89.

Bernstein, Richard, 'In Defence of American Philosophy', in: John E. Smith (ed.), *Contemporary American Philosophy*. Second Series (London and New York 1970), pp. 293–311.

Bertalanffy, Ludwig von, 'Symbolismus und Anthropogenese', in: Bernhard Rensch (ed.), *Handgebrauch und Verständigung bei Affen und Frühmenschen* (Bern and Stuttgart 1968), pp. 131–48.

Biemel, Walter (ed.) 'Briefwechsel Dilthey', in: Husserl, *Man and World* 1 (1968), pp. 428–46.

Bieri, Peter, *Zeit und Zeiterfahrung* (Frankfurt 1972).

Blumer, Herbert, 'Social Psychology', in: Emerson P. Schmidt (ed.), *Man and Society* (New York 1938), pp. 144–98.

Blumer, Herbert, *Symbolic Interactionism. Perspective and Method* (Englewood Cliffs, New Jersey 1969).

Böhler, Dietrich, 'Arnold Gehlen: Die Handlung', in: Josef Speck (ed.), *Grundprobleme der großen Philosophen. Philosophie der Gegenwart II* (Göttingen 1973), pp. 230–80.

Böhler, Dietrich, 'Paradigmawechsel in der analytischen Wissenschafts-theorie?', *Zeitschrift für allgemeine Wissenschaftstheorie* 3 (1972), pp. 219–42.

Böhler, Dietrich, 'Sprachkritische Rehabilitierung der Philosophischen Anthropologie. Wilhelm Kamlahs Ansatz im Licht rekonstruktiven Philosophierens', in: Jürgen Mittelstraß and Manfred Riedel (eds), *Vernünftiges Denken. Studien zur praktischen Philosophie und Wissenschaftstheorie* (Berlin and New York 1978), pp. 342–73.

Böhme, Gernot et al. 'Die Finalisierung der Wissenschaft', *Zeitschrift für Soziologie* 2 (1973), pp. 128–44.

Bohnsack, Fritz, *Erziehung zur Demokratie, John Deweys Pädagogik und ihre Bedeutung für die Reform unserer Schule* (Ravensburg 1976).

Borke, Helene, 'Interpersonal perception of young children: egocentrism or empathy?', *Developmental Psychology* 5 (1971), pp. 263–9.

Borke, Helene, 'Chandler and Greenspan's *Ersatz Egocentrism*: A Rejoinder', *Developmental Psychology* 7 (1972), pp. 107–109.

Boydston, Jo Ann, *Guide to the Works of John Dewey* (Carbondale, Illinois 1972).

Bradley, F. H., 'Association and Thought', *Mind* 12 (1887), pp. 354–81.

Brodsky, Garry M. et al., 'Perspectives on the History of Pragmatism, A Symposium on Thayer', *Transactions of the Ch. S. Peirce Society* 11 (1975), pp. 229–88.

Capek, Milic, 'The Myth of Frozen Passage: The Status of Becoming in the

Physical World', in: *Boston Studies in the Philosophy of Science* 2 (1965), pp. 441–63.

Carey, James T., *Sociology and Public Affairs. The Chicago School* (London 1975).

Cavell, Stanley, and Sesonske, Alexander, 'Logical Empiricism and Pragmatism in Ethics', *Journal of Philosophy* 48 (1951), pp. 5–17.

Chandler, M. J., and Greenspan, S., 'Ersatz Egocentrism', *Developmental Psychology* 7 (1972), pp. 104–6.

Clark, Roger A., 'The Transition from Action to Gesture', in: Andrew Lock (ed.), *Action, Gesture and Symbol. The Emergence of Language* (London 1978), pp. 231–57.

Cooley, Charles Horton, *Human Nature and the Social Order* (New York 1964).

Coughlan, Neil, *Young John Dewey. An Essay in American Intellectual History* (Chicago 1975).

Count, Earl, *Das Biogramm* (Frankfurt 1971).

Cronk, George Francis, 'James and the Problem of Intersubjectivity: An Interpretative Critique', in: Walter Robert Corti (ed.), *The Philosophy of William James* (Hamburg 1976), pp. 221–44.

Dahmer, Helmut, *Libido und Gesellschaft, Studien über Freud und die Freudsche Linke* (Frankfurt 1973).

Denzin, Norman K., 'The Genesis of Self in Early Childhood', *Sociological Quarterly* 13 (1972), pp. 291–314.

Denzin, Norman K., *Childhood Socialization. Studies in the Development of Language, Social Behavior, and Identity* (San Francisco 1977).

Dewey, John, 'Renan's Loss of Faith in Science', in: *The Early Works* 4 (Carbondale, Illinois 1971), pp. 11–8.

Dewey, John, 'The Theory of Emotion', in: *The Early Works* 4 (Carbondale, Illinois 1971), pp. 152–88.

Dewey, John, 'The Reflex Arc Concept in Psychology', in: *The Early Works* 5 (Carbondale, Illinois 1972), pp. 96–109.

Dewey, John, *Human Nature and Conduct* (New York 1922).

Dewey, John, 'Means and Ends', in: Leon Trotsky et al., *Their Morals and Ours* (New York 1969), pp. 67–73.

Dewey, John, and Tufts, James, *Ethics* (New York 1913).

Dilthey, Wilhelm, 'Beiträge zur Lösung der Frage vom Ursprung unseres Glaubens an die Realität der Außenwelt und seinem Recht', in: *Gesammelte Schriften* Vol. 1 (Leipzig 1924), pp. 90–138.

Dilthey, Wilhelm, 'Ideen über eine beschreibende und zergliedernde Psychologie', in: *Gesammelte Schriften* Vol. 1 (Leipzig 1924), pp. 139–240.

Dilthey, Wilhelm, *Der Aufbau der geschichtlichen Welt in den Geisteswissenschaften* (Frankfurt 1970).

Döbert, Rainer, Habermas, Jürgen and Nunner-Winkler, Gertrud (eds), *Entwicklung des Ichs* (Köln 1977).

Doise, Willem et al., 'Social interaction and the development of cognitive operations', *European Journal of Social Psychology* 5 (1975).

Ebbinghaus, Hermann, 'Über erklärende und beschreibende Psychologie', *Zeitschrift für Psychologie und Physiologie der Sinnesorgane* 9 (1896), pp. 161–205.

Faris, Ellsworth, *The Nature of Human Nature* (New York 1937).

Faris, Robert E. L., *Chicago Sociology 1920–32* (Chicago 1967).

Ferguson, L. R., 'Origins of social development in infancy', *Merrill-Palmer Quarterly* 17 (1971), pp. 119–39.

Fetscher, Iring et al., *Probleme der Ethik, zur Diskussion gestellt* (Freiburg and Munich 1972).

Feuer, Lewis S., 'John Dewey and the Back to the People Movement in American Thought', *Journal of the History of Ideas* 20 (1959), pp. 545–68.

Fichte, Johann Gottlieb, *Die Bestimmung des Menschen* (Stuttgart 1976).

Flach, Werner, 'Die biographische Methode bei Wilhelm Dilthey', *Archiv für Geschichte der Philosophie* 52 (1972), pp. 172–86.

Gadamer, Hans-Georg, *Wahrheit und Methode* (Tübingen 1975).

Gadamer, Hans-Georg, 'Die phänomenologische Bewegung', *Philosophische Rundschau* (1963), pp. 1–45.

Gehlen, Arnold, *Urmensch und Spätkultur* (Frankfurt 1956).

Gehlen, Arnold, *Studien zur Anthropologie und Soziologie* (Neuwied 1963).

Gehlen, Arnold, *Theorie der Willensfreiheit und andere frühe Schriften* (Neuwied 1965).

Gehlen, Arnold, *Anthropologische Forschung* (Reinbek 1967).

Gehlen, Arnold, 'Ein anthropologisches Modell', *The Human Context* 1 (1968), pp. 1–10.

Gehlen, Arnold, *Moral und Hypermoral* (Frankfurt 1956).

Gehlen, Arnold, *Der Mensch* (Frankfurt 1971).

Goldmann, Lucien, *Lukács und Heidegger* (Darmstadt 1975).

Gorman, Bernard S., and Wessman Alden E. (eds), *The Personal Experience of Time* (New York 1977).

Gouinlock, James, Introduction to J. Dewey, *The Moral Writings* (New York and London 1976), pp. XVII–LVI.

Gouinlock, James, 'Dewey's Theory of Moral Deliberation', *Ethics* 88 (1978), pp. 218–28.

Green, H. B., 'Temporal Stages in the Development of the Self', in: J. T. Fraser, and N. Lawrence, *The Study of Time* 11 (Berlin 1975), pp. 1–19.

Gross, Peter, *Reflexion, Spontaneität und Interaktion. Zur Diskussion soziologischer Handlungstheorien* (Stuttgart 1972).

Habermas, Jürgen, *Theorie und Praxis* (Neuwied 1963).

Habermas, Jürgen, *Zur Logik der Sozialwissenschaften* (Tübingen 1967).

Habermas, Jürgen, *Erkenntnis und Interesse* (Frankfurt 1968).

Habermas, Jürgen, *Technik und Wissenschaft als Ideologie* (Frankfurt 1968).

Habermas, Jürgen, *Philosophisch-politische Profile* (Frankfurt 1971).

Habermas, Jürgen, *Kultur und Kritik* (Frankfurt 1973).

Habermas, Jürgen, *Legitimationsprobleme im Spätkapitalismus* (Frankfurt 1973).

Habermas, Jürgen, *Zur Rekonstruktion des Historischen Materialismus* (Frankfurt 1976).

Habermas, Jürgen, and Luhmann, Niklas, *Theorie der Gesellschaft oder Sozialtechnologie* (Frankfurt 1971).

Hamlyn, D. W., 'Bradley, Ward, and Stout', in: Benjamin Wolman (ed.), *Historical Roots of Contemporary Psychology* (New York 1968), pp. 298–320.

Harrison, Ross, 'Functionalism and Its Historical Significance', *Genetic Psychology Monographs* 68 (1963), pp. 387–423.

Harten, Hans-Christian, *Der vernünftige Organismus – oder gesellschaftliche Evolution der Vernunft. Zur Gesellschaftstheorie des genetischen Strukturalismus von Piaget* (Frankfurt 1977).

Hegel, Georg Wilhelm Friedrich, *Phänomenologie des Geistes* (Berlin 1973).

Heidegger, Martin, *Sein und Zeit* (Tübingen 1977).

Heisenberg, Werner, *Physik und Philosophie* (Berlin 1959).

Heller, Agnes, *Das Alltagsleben*. Edited and introduced by Hans Joas (Frankfurt 1978).

Heller, Agnes, 'Jenseits der Pflicht. Das Paradigmatische der Ethik der deutschen Klassik im Oeuvre von Georg Lukács', *Revue internationale de philosophie* 27 (1973), pp. 439–56.

Holzkamp, Klaus, *Sinnliche Erkenntnis. Historischer Ursprung und gesellschaftliche Funktion der Wahrnehmung* (Frankfurt 1973).

Homans, George C., 'Social Behavior as Exchange', in: *American Journal of Sociology* 63 (1958), pp. 597–606.

Honneth, Axel, 'Geschichte und Interaktionsverhältnisse. Zur strukturalistischen Deutung des Historischen Materialismus', in: Urs Jaeggi and Axel Honneth (eds), *Theorien des Historischen Materialismus* (Frankfurt 1977), pp. 405–48.

Horkheimer, Max, *Kritische Theorie*. 2 volumes (Frankfurt 1968).

Horkheimer, Max, *Zur Kritik der instrumentellen Vernunft* (Frankfurt 1974).

Husserl, Edmund, *Philosophie als strenge Wissenschaft* (Frankfurt 1965).

Husserl, Edmund, *Die Idee der Phänomenologie* (The Hague 1950).

Husserl, Edmund, *Cartesianische Meditationen* (The Hague 1973).

Husserl, Edmund, *Die Krisis der europäischen Wissenschaften und die transzendentale Phänomenologie* (The Hague 1976).

Husserl, Edmund, 'Phänomenologie und Anthropologie', *Philosophy and Phenomenological Research* 2 (1941), pp. 1–14.

Israel, Joachim and Tajfel, Henri, *The context of social psychology: A critical assessment* (London 1972).

James, William, *Psychologie* (Leipzig 1909).

James, William, 'Does "Consciousness" Exist?', in: *Essays in Radical Empiricism* (London 1912), pp. 1–38.

Joas, Hans, 'Thesen über Feuerbach und Marx: Intersubjektivität und historischer Materialismus', in: Anton Leist (ed.), *Ansätze zur materialistischen Sprachtheorie* (Kronberg 1975), pp. 46–54.

Joas, Hans, Introduction to A. Heller, *Das Alltagsleben* (Frankfurt 1978), pp. 7–23.

Joas, Hans, *Die gegenwärtige Lage der soziologischen Rollentheorie* (Frankfurt 1978).

Joas, Hans, Commentary on J. Berger 'Intersubjektive Sinnkonstitution und Sozialstruktur', *Zeitschrift für Soziologie* 8 (1979), pp. 198–201.

Joas, Hans, 'Rollen- und Interaktionstheorien in der Sozialisationsforschung', in: Klaus Hurrelmann and Dieter Ulich (eds), *Handbuch der Sozialisationsforschung* (Weinheim 1980), pp. 147–160.

Johach, Helmut, *Handelnder Mensch und objektiver Geist. Zur Theorie der Geistes- und Sozialwissenschaften bei Wilhelm Dilthey* (Meisenheim am Glan 1974).

Kant, Immanuel, *Werke* (Frankfurt 1974).

Keiler, Peter, 'Behaviorismus, Reduktionismus, "Emergenz" – Theorie. Grundlagenprobleme der Verhaltenspsychologie', in: *Kritische Psychologie* 2, Argument-Sonderband 15, pp. 170–87.

Keller, Monika, *Kognitive Entwicklung und soziale Kompetenz. Zur Entstehung der Rollenübernahme in der Familie und ihrer Bedeutung für den Schulerfolg* (Stuttgart 1976).

Kohlberg, Lawrence, *Zur kognitiven Entwicklung des Kindes. Drei Aufsätze* (Frankfurt 1974).

Kuhn, Manford H., 'Major Trends in Symbolic Interaction Theory in the Past Twenty-Five Years', in: Jerome G. Manis and Bernard N. Meltzer, *Symbolic Interaction* (Boston 1973), pp. 57–76.

Kuhn, Thomas, *The Structure of Scientific Revolutions* (Chicago 1970).

Lenk, Hans, 'Kann die sprachanalytische Moralphilosophie neutral sein?', in: Hans Albert and Ernst Topitsch (eds), *Werturteilsstreit* (Darmstadt 1971), pp. 533–52.

Lenneberg, Eric H., *Biological Foundations of Language* (New York 1967).

Leontjew, Alexej N., *Probleme der Entwicklung des Psychischen* (Frankfurt 1973).

Leontjew, Alexej N., 'Das Problem der Tätigkeit in der Psychologie', in: *Sowjetwissenschaft, Gesellschaftswissenschaftliche Beiträge* (1973), pp. 415–35.

Leontjew, Alexej N., 'Tätigkeit und Bewußtsein', in: *Sowjetwissenschaft, Gesellschaftswissenschaftliche Beiträge* (1973), pp. 515–31.

Lichtman, Richard, 'Symbolic Interactionism and Social Reality: Some Marxist Queries', *Berkeley Journal of Sociology* 15 (1970), pp. 75–94.

Lipps, Hans, 'Pragmatismus und Existenzphilosophie', in: Lipps, *Die Wirklichkeit des Menschen* (Frankfurt 1977), pp. 38–54.

Lukács, Georg, *Geschichte und Klassenbewußtsein* (Berlin 1923, Amsterdam 1967).

Lukács, Georg, 'Moses Heß und die Probleme der idealistischen Dialektik', in: *Lukács, Werke* 2 (Neuwied 1965), pp. 643–86.

Lukács, Georg, *Die Zerstörung der Vernunft* (Neuwied and Darmstadt 1973).

Lynch, Frederick, 'Social Theory and the Progressive Era', *Theory and Society* 4 (1977), pp. 159–210.

Malcolm, Norman, 'Behaviorism as a Philosophy of Psychology', in: T. W. Wann, *Behaviorism and Phenomenology* (Chicago 1964), pp. 141–55.

Marck, Siegfried, *Der amerikanische Pragmatismus in seinen Beziehungen zum kritischen Idealismus und zur Existenzphilosophie* (Wilhelmshaven 1950).

Marcuse, Herbert, 'On Science and Phenomenology', *Boston Studies in the Philosophy of Science* 2 (1965), pp. 279–91.

Markus, György, 'Uber die erkenntnistheoretischen Ansichten des jungen Marx', in: Alfred Schmidt (ed.), *Beiträge zur marxistischen Erkenntnistheorie* (Frankfurt 1969), pp. 18–72.

Markus, György, 'Der Begriff des "menschlichen Wesens" in der Philosophie des jungen Marx', in: Andras Hegedüs et al, *Die Neue Linke in Ungarn* 2 (Berlin 1976), pp. 41–89.

Markus, György, 'Die Seele und das Leben. Der "junge" Lukács und das Problem der Kultur', in: Agnes Heller et al., *Die Seele und das Leben. Studien zum frühen Lukács* (Frankfurt 1977), pp. 99–130.

Marx, Karl and Engels, Friedrich, *Werke* (Berlin (DDR)).

Meltzer, Bernard and Petras, John, 'The Chicago and Iowa Schools of Symbolic Interactionism', in: Manis, J. G. and Meltzer, B. N. (eds), *Symbolic Interaction* (Boston 1973), pp. 43–57.

Merleau-Pontry, Maurice, *Phänomenologie der Wahrnehmung* (Berlin 1966).

Merleau-Pontry, Maurice, *Die Struktur des Verhaltens* (Berlin 1976).

Merleau-Pontry, Maurice, *Die Abenteuer der Dialektik* (Frankfurt 1968).

de Mey, M., 'Anthropologie Philosophique et Psychologie Génétique. Une confrontation de l'anthropologie philosophique d'Arnold Gehlen avec la psychologie génétique de Jean Piaget', *Studia philosophica Gandensia* 2 (1964), pp. 41–67.

Miller, David L., 'William James and the Specious Present', in: Walter Robert Corti (ed.), *The philosophy of William James* (Hamburg 1976), pp. 51–79.

Miller, Max, 'Sprachliche Sozialisation', in: Klaus Hurrelmann and Dieter Ulich (eds), *Handbuch der Sozialisationsforschung* (Weinheim 1980), pp. 649–668.

Mills, C. Wright, *Sociology and Pragmatism. The Higher Learning in America* (New York 1966).

Misch, Georg, *Vorbericht des Herausgebers zu W. Dilthey* V/1 (Leipzig 1924), pp. VII-CXVII.

Misch, Georg, Lebensphilosophie und Phänomenologie. Eine Auseinandersetzung mit Heidegger', *Philosophischer Anzeiger* 3 (1929), pp. 267–368, pp. 405–75 and 4 (1930), pp. 182–330.

Mischel, Theodore, 'Wundt and the Conceptual Foundations of Psychology', *Philosophy and phenomenological research* 31 (1970), pp. 1–26.

Mischel, Theodore, 'Psychological Explanations and Their Vicissitudes', *Nebraska Symposium on Motivation* 38 (1975), pp. 133–204.

Morison, Samuel Eliot and Commager, Henry Steele, *The Growth of the American Republic* 2 volumes (New York 1965).

Morris, Charles, *Foundations of the Theory of Signs* (Chicago 1938).

Morris, Charles, *Signs, Language and Behavior* (New York 1955).

Morris, Charles, *Pragmatische Semiotik und Handlungstheorie. Herausgegeben und eingeleitet von Achim Eschbach* (Frankfurt 1977).

Münsterberg, Hugo, *Grundzüge der Psychologie* (Leipzig 1900).

Novack, George, *Pragmatism versus Marxism. An appraisal of John Dewey's philosophy* (New York 1975).

Oevermann, Ulrich, 'Programmatische Überlegungen zu einer Theorie der Bildungsprozesse und zur Strategie der Sozialisationsforschung', in: Klaus Hurrelmann (ed), *Sozialisation und Lebenslauf* (Reinbek 1976), pp. 34–52.

O'Neill, John, *Perception, Expression, and History. The Social Phenomenology of Maurice Merleau-Ponty* (Evanston 1970).

Paris, Rainer, 'Schwierigkeiten einer marxistischen Interaktionstheorie', *Gesellschaft* 7 (1976), pp. 11–44.

Peirce, Charles Sanders, *Collected Papers*, 8 vols., Charles Hartshorne and Paul Weiss, (eds), (Cambridge, Massachusetts 1931–58).

Percy, Walker, 'Symbol, Consciousness and Intersubjectivity', *Journal of Philosophy* 55 (1958), pp. 631–41.

Perret-Clermont, Anne et al., 'Une approche psychosociologique du développement cognitif', in: *Archives de Psychologie* 44 (1976), No. 171, pp. 135–44.

van Peursen, Cornelius Anthonie, *Wirklichkeit als Ereignis. Eine deiktische Ontologie* (Freiburg and Munich 1973).

Piaget, Jean, *The Child's Construction of Reality* (London 1955).

Piaget, Jean, *Biology and Knowledge* (Edinburgh 1972).

Piaget, Jean, *Das moralische Urteil beim Kinde* (Frankfurt 1973).

Piaget, Jean, *Einführung in die genetische Erkenntnistheorie* (Frankfurt 1973).

Piaget, Jean, *Das Erwachen der Intelligenz beim Kinde* (Stuttgart 1974).

Piaget, Jean, *Die Bildung des Zeitbegriffs beim Kinde* (Frankfurt 1974).

Piaget, Jean, *Nachahmung, Spiel und Traum* (Stuttgart 1974).

Piaget, Jean, *Psychologie der Intelligenz* (München 1974).

Piaget, Jean, *Theorien und Methoden der modernen Erziehung* (Frankfurt 1974).

Piaget, Jean, *Weisheit und Illusionen der Philosophie* (Frankfurt 1974).

Piaget, Jean, *Die Psychologie des Kindes* (Frankfurt 1977).

Plessner, Helmut, *Diesseits der Utopie. Ausgewählte Beiträge zur Kultur-Soziologie* (Frankfurt 1974).

Plessner, Helmut, *Philosophische Anthropologie (Lachen und Weinen. Das Lächeln. Anthropologie der Sinne)* (Frankfurt 1970).

Plessner, Helmut, *Die verspätete Nation* (Frankfurt 1974).

Plessner, Helmut, *Die Stufen des Organischen und der Mensch* (Berlin 1975).

Plessner, Helmut, *Die Frage nach der Conditio humana. Aufsätze zur philosophischen Anthropologie* (Frankfurt 1976).

Popper, Karl Raimund, *The Poverty of Historicism* (London 1974).

Radkau, Joachim, *Die deutsche Emigration in den USA. Ihr Einfluß auf die amerikanische Europapolitik 1933–45* (Düsseldorf 1971).

Raphelson, Alfred C., 'The Pre-Chicago Association of the Early Functionalists', *Journal of the History of the Behavioral Sciences* 9 (1973), pp. 115–22.

Richey, H. G., *Die Überwindung der Subjektivität in der empirischen Philosophie Diltheys und Deweys*. Diss. 1935 (Göttingen).

Riedel, Manfred, Introduction to Dilthey, *Aufbau* (Frankfurt 1970), pp. 9–86.

Rosenthal, Sandra, 'Pragmatism, Phenomenology and the World of Appearing Objects', *International Philosophical Quarterly* 17 (1977), pp. 285–91.

Rosenthal, Sandra, 'Pragmatism, Scientific Method, and the Phenomenological Return to Lived Experience', *Philosophy and Phenomenological Research* 38 (1977), pp. 56–65.

Rubinstein, Sergej L., *Sein und Bewußtsein. Die Stellung des Psychischen im allgemeinen Zusammenhang der Erscheinungen in der materiellen Welt*. (Berlin (DDR) 1962).

Rubinstein, Sergej L., *Grundlagen der allgemeinen Psychologie* (Berlin (DDR) 1971).

Rucker, Darnell, *The Chicago Pragmatists* (Minneapolis 1969).

Scheler, Max, *Erkenntnis und Arbeit* (Frankfurt 1977).

Scheler, Max, *Die Stellung des Menschen im Kosmos* (Bern and Munich 1966).

Schneewind, Klaus (ed.), *Wissenschaftstheoretische Grundlagen der Psychologie* (Munich and Basel 1977).

Schurig, Volker, *Die Entstehung des Bewußtseins* (Frankfurt 1976).

Schütz, Alfred, *Der sinnhafte Aufbau der sozialen Welt* (Frankfurt 1974).

Schütz, Alfred, *Collected Papers*. 3 volumes (The Hague 1964/66).

Schwendinger, Herman and Julia, *The Sociologists of the Chair: A Radical Analysis of the Formative Years of North American Sociology (1883–1922)* (New York 1974).

Schwidetzky, Ilse (ed.), *Über die Evolution der Sprache* (Frankfurt 1973).

Selman, R., 'Taking another's perspective. Role-taking development in early childhood', *Child Development* 42 (1971), pp. 1721–34.

Sherohman, James, 'Conceptual and Methodological Issues in the Study of Role-Taking Accuracy', *Symbolic Interaction* 1 (1977), pp. 121–31.

Shibutani, Tamotsu, 'A cybernetic approach to motivation', in: Walter Buckley (ed.), *Modern Systems Research for the Behavioral Scientist* (Chicago 1969), pp. 330–6.

Smedslund, Jan, 'Les origines sociales de la décentration', in: François Bresson and Maurice de Montmollin (eds), *Psychologie et épistémologie génétiques. Thèmes Piagétiens* (Paris 1966), pp. 159–67.

Smoot, William, 'The Social Context of Death Anxiety', *Philosophy today* 21 (1977), pp. 84–9.

Spitz, René, *The First Year of Life. A Psychoanalytic Study of Normal and Deviant Development of Object Relations* (New York 1965).

Stäuble, Irmingard, 'Politischer Ursprung und politische Funktionen der pragmatistischen Sozialpsychologie, in: Helmut Nolte and Irmingard Stäuble, *Zur Kritik der Sozialpsychologie* (Munich 1972), pp. 7–65.

Steiner, Gerhard, 'Jean Piaget: Versuch einer Wirkungs- und Problemgeschichte', in: *Hommage à Jean Piaget zum achtzigsten Geburtstag* (Stuttgart 1976), pp. 49–114.

Stone, Gregory and Farberman, Harvey, 'On the Edge of Rapprochement: Was Durkheim Moving Toward the Perspective of Symbolic Interaction', in: Stone and Farberman (eds), *Social Psychology through Symbolic Interaction* (Waltham, Massachusetts 1970), pp. 100–12.

Stout, G. F., *A Manual of Psychology* (New York 1899).

Thayer, Horace S., *Meaning and Action. A Study of American Pragmatism* (Indianapolis 1973).

Trotsky, Leon, Dewey, John and Novack, George, *Their Morals and Ours. Marxist versus Liberal Views on Morality* (New York 1973).

Tugendhat, Ernst, *Selbstbewußtsein und Selbstbestimmung. Sprachanalytische Interpretationen* (Frankfurt 1979).

Uexküll, Jakob von and Kriszat, Georg, *Streifzüge durch die Umwelten von Tieren und Menschen/Bedeutungslehre* (Hamburg 1956).

Van de Voort, Werner, 'Die Bedeutung von Vorformen des kommunikativen Handelns für die Entwicklung der vorsprachlichen Intelligenz beim Kinde', in: A. Leist (ed.), *Ansätze zur materialistischen Sprachtheorie* (Kronberg 1975), pp. 206–33.

Van de Voort, Werner, *Interaktion und Kognition. Die Bedeutung der sozialen Interaktion für die Entwicklung der kognitiven Strukturen nach Jean Piaget.* Diss. 1977 (Frankfurt).

Wagner, Helmut, 'Signs, Symbols, and Interaction Theory', *Sociological Focus* 7 (1973/74), pp. 101–11.

Waller, Manfred, *Soziales Lernen und Interaktionskompetenz. Die Ausbildung von Verhaltenserwartungen und die Konstruktion von Regeln interpersonalen Verhaltens beim Kinde* (Stuttgart 1978).

Wartenberg, Gerd, *Logischer Sozialismus. Die Transformation der Kantschen*

Transzendentalphilosophie durch Ch. S. Peirce (Frankfurt 1971).

Wehler, Hans-Ulrich, 'Sprungbrett nach Ostasien. Die amerikanische Hawaipolitik bis zur Annexion von 1898', *Jahrbuch für Amerikastudien* 10 (1965), pp. 153–81.

Wellmer, Albrecht, 'Kommunikation und Emanzipation. Überlegungen zur "sprachanalytischen Wende" der kritischen Theorie', in: Urs Jaeggi and Axel Honneth (eds), *Theorien des Historischen Materialismus* (Frankfurt 1977), pp. 465–500.

Wells, Harry K., *Der Pragmatismus, eine Philosophie des Imperialismus* (Berlin (DDR) 1957).

Wetzel, Manfred, *Erkenntnistheorie. Die Gegenstandsbeziehung und Tätigkeit des erkennenden Subjekts als Gegenstand der Erkenntnistheorie* (Munich 1978).

Whitehead, Alfred North, *Science and the Modern World. Lowell Lectures 1925* (New York 1953).

Williams, William Appleman, *The Tragedy of American Diplomacy* (1962).

Williams, William Appleman, *The Contours of American History* (New York 1956).

Williams, William Appleman, (ed.), *The Shaping of American Diplomacy* (Chicago 1956).

Wilson, Thomas P., 'Conceptions of Interaction and Forms of Sociological Explanation', *American Sociological Review* 35 (1970), pp. 697–710.

Winter, Gibson, *Grundlegung einer Ethik der Gesellschaft* (Munich 1970).

Wittgenstein, Ludwig, *Tractatus logico-philosophicus* (Frankfurt 1969).

Wittgenstein, Ludwig, *Philosophische Untersuchungen* (Frankfurt 1967).

Wundt, Wilhelm, *Grundriß der Psychologie* (1922).

Wundt, Wilhelm, *Völkerpsychologie* (Leipzig 1911).

Wygotski, Lew S., *Denken und Sprechen* (Frankfurt 1974).

Zaner, Richard M., 'Piaget and Merleau-Ponty: A Study in Convergence', *Review of Existential Psychology and Psychiatry* 6 (1966), pp. 7–23.

4. APPENDIX TO THE BIBLIOGRAPHY

The following publications of and about George Herbert Mead have been published since completion of the German-language manuscript of this book in 1979 and seem to be especially worth mentioning.

4.1. Works of G. H. Mead

David L. Miller (ed.), *The Individual and the Social Self. Unpublished Work of George Herbert Mead* (Chicago 1982).

Hans Joas (ed.), *George Herbert Mead. Gesammelte Aufsätze.* Two volumes (Frankfurt 1980–83).

John Burger, Chicago, has discovered two publications by Mead:

George Herbert Mead, 'The Adjustment of Our Industry to Surplus and Unskilled Labor', in: *Proceedings of the National Conference of Charities and Corrections* 34 (1909), pp. 222–225.

George Herbert Mead, 'Social Work, Standards of Living and the War', in: *Proceedings of the National Conference of Social Work* 45 (1918), pp. 637–644.

4.2. *Secondary Literature on Mead*

Batiuk, Mary Ellen and Sacks, Howard L., 'G. H. Mead and Karl Marx: Exploring Consciousness and Community', in: *Symbolic Interaction* 4 (1981), pp. 207–223.

Bergmann, Werner, 'Zeit, Handlung und Sozialität bei G. H. Mead', in: *Zeitschrift für Soziologie* 10 (1981), pp. 351–363.

Bhattacharya, Nikhil, 'Psychology and Rationality: The Structure of Mead's Problem', in: *The Philosophical Forum* 10 (1978), pp. 112–138.

Blumer, Herbert, 'G. H. Mead', in: Rhea, Buford (ed.), *The Future of the Sociological Classics* (London 1981), pp. 136–169.

Bolton, Charles D., 'Some Consequences of the Meadian Self', in: *Symbolic Interaction* 4 (1981), pp. 245–259.

Campbell, James, 'G. H. Mead on Intelligent Social Reconstruction', in: *Symbolic Interaction* 4 (1981), pp. 191–205.

Campbell, James, *Pragmatism and Reform: Social Reconstruction in the Thought of John Dewey and G. H. Mead*. Diss. 1979 (SUNY at Stony Brook).

Cottrell, Leonard S. Jnr., 'G. H. Mead. The Legacy of Social Behaviorism', in: Robert K. Merton and Matilda White Riley (eds), *Sociological Tradition from Generation to Generation* (Norwood, N.J. 1980), pp. 45–65.

Deegan, Mary Jo and Burger, John S., 'G. H. Mead and Social Reform: His Work and Writings', in: *Journal of the History of the Behavioral Sciences* 14 (1978), pp. 362–373.

Elliot, Rodney D. and Meltzer, Bernard N., 'Symbolic Interactionism and Psychoanalysis: Some Convergences, Divergences, and Complementarities', in: *Symbolic Interaction* 4 (1981), pp. 225–244.

Fisher, Berenice M. and Strauss, Anselm L., 'G. H. Mead and the Chicago Tradition of Sociology', in: *Symbolic Interaction* 2 (1979), No. 1, pp. 9–26 (Part One) and No. 2, pp. 9–20 (Part Two).

Franks, David D. and Seeburger, Francis F., 'The Person Behind the Word: Mead's Theory of Universals and A Shift of Focus in Symbolic Interactionism', in: *Symbolic Interaction* 3 (1980), pp. 41–58.

Goff, Tom W., *Marx and Mead. Contributions to a sociology of knowledge* (London 1980).

Habermas, Jürgen, 'Der Paradigmawechsel bei Mead und Durkheim: Von

262   G. H. Mead

der Zwecktätigkeit zum kommunikativen Handeln', in: J.H., *Theorie des kommunikativen Handelns*. Vol. 2 (Frankfurt 1981), pp. 7–169.

Joas, Hans, 'G. H. Mead and the "Division of Labor": Macro-sociological Implications of Mead's Social Psychology', in: *Symbolic Interaction* 4 (1981), pp. 177–190.

Johnson, G. David and Shifflet, Peggy A., 'G. H. Who? A Critique of the Objectivist Reading of Mead', in: *Symbolic Interaction* 4 (1981), pp. 177–190.

Lewis, G. David and Smith, Richard L., *American Sociology and Pragmatism. Mead, Chicago Sociology, and Symbolic Interaction* (Chicago 1980). (Cf. the excellent review symposium on this book with contributions by H. Blumer, E. Rochberg-Halton, J. Campbell and the rejoinder by Lewis and Smith in: *Symbolic Interaction* 6 (1983), pp. 123–174.)

Lewis, J. David, 'A Social Behaviorist Interpretation of the Meadian "I"', in: *American Journal of Sociology* 85 (1979), pp. 261–287.

Lewis, J. David, 'G. H. Mead's Contact Theory of Reality: The Manipulatory Phase of the Act in the Constitution of Mundane, Scientific, Aesthetic, and Evaluative Objects', in: *Symbolic Interaction* 4 (1981), pp. 129–142.

Miller, David L., 'The Meaning of Role-Taking', in: *Symbolic Interaction*, pp. 167–176.

Renger, Paul, 'G. H. Mead's Contribution to the Philosophy of American Education', in: *Educational Theory* 30 (1980), pp. 115–133.

Rock, Paul, *The Making of Symbolic Interactionism* (London 1979).

Tugendhat, *Selbstbewußtsein und Selbstbestimmung. Sprachanalytische Interpretationen* (Frankfurt 1979), pp. 245–292.

Turner, Jonathan H., 'Returning to "Social Physics": Illustrations from the Work of G. H. Mead', in: *Current Perspectives in Social Theory* 2 (1981), pp. 187–208.

Wood, Mark and Wardwell, Mark L., 'G. H. Mead's Social Behaviorism vs. The Astructural Bias of Symbolic Interactionism', in: *Symbolic Interaction* 6 (1983), pp. 85–96.

Index